It's Monday

— *Only in* —

Your Mind

You Are Not *Your Thoughts*

Michael Cupo

BALBOA
PRESS

A DIVISION OF HAY HOUSE

Library of Congress Control Number: 2012916968

Balboa Press books may be ordered through booksellers or by contacting:

Balboa Press
A Division of Hay House
1663 Liberty Drive
Bloomington, IN 47403
www.balboapress.com
1-(877) 407-4847

ISBN: 978-1-4525-5854-7 (sc)
ISBN: 978-1-4525-5855-4 (e)

Because of the dynamic nature of the Internet, any web addresses or links contained in this book may have changed since publication and may no longer be valid. The views expressed in this work are solely those of the author and do not necessarily reflect the views of the publisher, and the publisher hereby disclaims any responsibility for them.

The author of this book does not dispense medical advice or prescribe the use of any technique as a form of treatment for physical, emotional, or medical problems without the advice of a physician, either directly or indirectly. The intent of the author is only to offer information of a general nature to help you in your quest for emotional and spiritual well-being. In the event you use any of the information in this book for yourself, which is your constitutional right, the author and the publisher assume no responsibility for your actions.

Any people depicted in stock imagery provided by Thinkstock are models, and such images are being used for illustrative purposes only.
Certain stock imagery © Thinkstock.

Printed in the United States of America

Balboa Press rev. date: 10/05/2012

Our greatest relief is to accept things the way they are.
Our greatest misgiving is wanting them to be in some other way.

About the Book

Although in 1987 I stopped using certain substances as a solution to cope with life, many of my inner conflicts persisted because I didn't understand the true nature of my malady. I had no knowledge whatsoever, as to why I constantly reached outside myself for a solution, and why these solutions were developed to begin with. I found this reaching was caused by the need to fulfill a self-created, inner sense of lack; a lack I didn't even know existed. In this book I explain what caused this, and why anything has to be reached for in the first place. I also describe a path that has led me to discovering my own inner truth; truth that has led to my freedom from this lack. I've learned as human beings we are really in conflict with ourselves, and we don't understand where these conflicts originate from. I discovered it is our own mind, which has been conditioned to constantly think about our self that makes us look for our answers out there somewhere. This is the root cause of our conflicts. It's a mind that is leading us around like we're a puppet on a string. I have found through self investigation a practical gateway to freedom that anyone can learn.

There is a website www.mondayinyourmind.com for It's Monday Only in Your Mind: You Are Not Your Thoughts, along with a short You-tube video, explaining the core content of my book. There is also a Facebook page link on the website with the same name as my book. I implore you to take a serious look at this. What I have come to understand about the way most of us view life is truly mind-boggling. My aspiration for writing this is not that you believe anything that I've written, but that through self investigation you find your own truth, so you can cut the strings that hold you in bondage, and allow the necessary energy for you to awaken to your higher self. This bondage is a dilemma we all face.

One day if you ever want to understand your life and know why there is conflict within, you will need to learn how to let go. Let go of what? Your ego, (the I Self). My book describes a step by step process on how to do this. This is not a magical solution, but one of practicality. If you ever want to be *truly* free of these conflicts, you will have to realize that you are going to have to let go of the limited world that has been devised in your head. Hopefully it will not be when you are on your deathbed. Think about it, learn to let go now while there is still time to really enjoy life, or let go when there is no time left. That is up to you. Well, not really because right now you don't have that choice. Please take this seriously. Really look within to see what you are holding onto and why. Find out what it is that's not allowing you to live your life to the fullest, the way it was intended.

Contents

Introduction

Did you ever wonder what goes through the mind of someone who acts like a jerk; totally self-absorbed in their behavior. Did you ever see someone scream at a stranger in public? Or did you ever see a drunk or an addict passed out in a doorway? And more importantly, were you ever that screaming jerk or that over intoxicated person? Did you ever do something completely crazy without understanding why you did it?

I've been there — big time — and I've stopped being there.

In this book, I share my journey of change and discovery.

I describe in detail about all these behaviors, as I spent years living unconsciously — suffering, and causing others to suffer. I also describe the less subtle behaviors that hold us in the same bondage as these behaviors described above.

But I've written about even more than controlling my reckless behavior and addictions. The best part of this book is about living from a new place, a beautiful and peaceful place. It's about going somewhere I never expected to be. No, I didn't leave home; didn't leave my wife, my job or my family. I left my ego.

I never intended to write a book, but the more I talked to people about the changes in my life, the more interested they became. Many say that my account "made sense" to them, they just "never thought about it in this way." So I sensed a need to share what I've discovered.

It is not my purpose to save or change anyone. This book has been written to be used as a pointer, to assist in your life journey. I share my experience so I might touch someone out there who feels as frustrated and confused about life as I did.

Admittedly, this is simply an expression of my own experience, strength, and hope. This book does not claim to have all the answers. I understand that people reading this may be facing challenges that require professional help well beyond the scope of this book.

My prayer is for you to read my story, and then to look within yourself to discover your own path. As you read, please do not feel judged as to whether you're living right or living wrong. Rather, based on my own insights, I hope to cast a light on why we behave and react to life the way we do. I will explain how certain influences cause us to develop habitual behavior patterns that I call Conditioned Mind Patterns. These patterns are the cause, of which dictates our reactions and behavior. I use capital letters when I write about Conditioned Mind Patterns because I feel they have become so engrained in our private and collective lives that they've assumed an unwarranted prominence.

I will describe how I understand Conditioned Mind Patterns are formed, how they influence what we think, say, do, and feel. I reveal how they control our lives, but can be changed — if you *truly* want to change them.

We do not react randomly to life circumstances; we behave as we have been conditioned. Every day we come upon situations that bring us to a spiritual fork in the road. When this occurs we have a choice that either puts us in harmony, or out of harmony, with life. Many of us are not aware we have this choice. We think there is only one way to go: the default way we have been conditioned to go. We take this route again and again. This is just what we do until something happens which allows us to become aware of another way.

We're deeply habituated by what we know, and can't seem to let go of our familiar ways. We may see there is another way, but we still go where our conditioning leads us. Then one day we stop and, for whatever reason, we actually take the other way. We learn that it offers greater benefits, and we never want to go the old way again. We will go the familiar way again because that is the nature of a Conditioned Mind. But a new awareness has entered our being, which starts us upon a new road; a road that will lead us to love ourselves and in the process love all beings.

This awareness can be called a spiritual awakening, but I am not a certified religious trainer, clergyman or psychologist. I don't profess to be an expert on any of this. I share strictly about my experience. I am only a person coming to understand his own mind, life, my inner being, and I share my discoveries. I have embarked on a journey to investigate why I've acted without regard for consequences; why, when I had everything a person thought he could want, I wasn't happy. I've been led to an answer that has allowed me to view things differently and to become truly happy, joyous, and free.

Learning to live this new way will not happen without our cooperation. The old way will try to draw us back in because that is what's familiar. But when we start the discovery about our Conditioned Mind Patterns and how to quiet them, we cease to use those old fixes as solutions. As our minds become quieter through a steady practice of meditation, we become more aware of these Conditioned Mind Patterns. As we become more aware of our conditioning, we then have a choice to not be controlled by them. We can then begin to live in cooperation and harmony with life. This harmony is what allows us to bring joy, peace, and happiness into our life and thus into the lives of others.

Once these changes begin to occur our behavior will change. We have a new choice of responding to life from a place of love. We will probably have this choice for the first time in our life. By learning to quiet our mind through the discipline of meditation, what we are really learning is to open our heart. The more our heart is opened, the less our life is controlled by our Conditioned Thinking and the more we become guided by love.

In the first part of this book, I describe my own life and how I now understand it, from infancy to right now. The second part of this book is a re-interpretation of the Twelve Steps originated by the founders of Alcoholics Anonymous (AA). As I qualify, this is not an attempt to change the original Twelve Steps. Rather, I've imbued them with the vocabulary of this book, which emphasizes that we're addicted to our egos before anything else. I've benefited from AA, and drawn parallels from its teachings to my own experience. But I've also had to find out a lot through my own self investigation.

By sharing my life candidly and proposing a step-by-step model of transformation, I aspire to help others understand themselves and find strength. But please do not take my word for anything that has been written here; investigate this for yourself. I do not know all there is to know about the mind, but I do understand my own mind enough to want to help others avoid the pitfalls I have endured. Suffering does not have to get to the point of desperation before you seek relief. Through your own self-investigation (finding your own answers) you can find your true nature, and find peace. Then you will become a benefit to all beings, with love being the default setting of your mind.

CHAPTER 1

The Conditioned Mind Patterns

This is my understanding of how a mind starts its existence in this world, pure, innocent, and free and becomes conditioned, cluttered, and full of noise. The mind's attachment to the I Self, or ego, causes most of — if not all — of our problems. The real addictions in our society are not to substances, (drugs, alcohol, food, etc.) or to things, (gambling, pornography, sex, money, success, etc.), but to an "I-based sense of self," or I Self, that commands our exclusive allegiance. We react to the promptings of this I Self and base important life choices upon it. Throughout this book our ego is referenced as the I Self.

Conditioned Mind Patterns are formed as we unconsciously adopt the biases of society, and allow personal biases and compulsions to control our behavior. When the I Self starts building defense mechanisms as a way to deal with our fears and discontentment's, a Conditioned Mind Pattern is formed. We use this as a way of coping with life, to remove any unpleasantness. Think about it: From the time we are infants, we cry and someone puts a bottle in our mouth to quiet us. We fuss and we're put in a swing or held until the fussing stops. The development of a Conditioned Mind Pattern has started; even at this age we understand how outside things bring us inner peace. This is also one of the main

1

reasons why it's so hard to quiet our mind, since the conditioning goes back to when we were infants.

The longer a Conditioned Mind Pattern is engrained in our psyche, the more noise (which is how energy manifests) is generated in our head. So I came to understand that if I ever wanted to be free of my I Self I was going to have to learn how to stop all the noise that was constantly going on in my head. I learned this through the discipline of meditation. Learning how to meditate so the mind can become quiet takes practice, and it is a practice that needs to be cultivated if our transformation of energy is to progress from a self-centered perspective to quietness, and from quietness to love.

When infants are uncomfortable and discontented, they cry. Then, either someone will give them physical comfort or they will find relief through something else — a toy or child's TV show or some substance, such as a bottle or snack. A diversion has to be created so attention can be diverted from the discontentment. What would happen if no one responded to the crying? The crying would stop and the infant would just develop some other form of coping. Maybe they would tap their feet, bite their nails, pull their hair or, as they grow older, start cutting themselves — but they will develop a form of conditioning to cope with the discontentment. So the discontentment will be dealt with in one form or another.

Conditioning and Its Discontents

Our conditioning is created through our misunderstanding of what to do when our mind becomes discontented. It is not the discontentment itself that causes our conditioning. We don't know how to quiet the discontentment. That's what leads us to become conditioned. And so begins the development of our Mind Patterns; we look outside ourselves to fix an inner discontentment whatever that cause of the discontentment is. This pattern continues throughout our life or until we become aware of it and learn to stop it.

The conditioning just gets reinforced as we grow older, for example, when our parents try to give us all the things that they didn't have growing up. Or they give into our whining, just to keep us quiet so they can keep doing whatever it is that they are doing. This is through no fault of theirs; they're just doing what *they* were conditioned to do. And so the cycle repeats. This is the beginning; the beginning of the formations of Mind Patterns.

These Mind Patterns are just conditioning us to use things external to us, as our solution, to make us feel better on the inside. The more these Mind Patterns are repeated, the deeper they get engrained into our psyches (subconscious) and the more they become our mind's default setting.

As we become more and more conditioned with thinking that things on the outside will make us feel better on the inside, we live more from our I Self. As we live more from our I Self we slowly lose touch with what is really going on in our life (the truth). The more our mind becomes conditioned, the less control we have over it, the less choice we have, and the less truth we see. We think we are in control, but are we? The reality is we are being controlled as if we are a puppet on a string and our Conditioned Mind Patterns is the puppeteer.

Since we are strictly looking towards what is outside of us and everything that matters to us is based on that view, we try to present an outer picture that everyone will like, at least everyone in our inner circle. This way to view life is not of our own making. There are many influences, some inner and some outer, that determine this. We live in a society that influences what we wear, how we look, what we need to eat and drink, so life can be merry. We are influenced as to what our social standards should be and what a person needs to do to be considered a success in the world. We are never taught that there is another way to live life: from the inside out. That there is a way to reach our inner spiritual potential and be our true self, not the one that is based in I. We grow up believing that if everything looks good on the outside that's all that matters because that is how we are being judged by everyone anyhow. We are just going along with the program that society has written. The true self is what is there when we start our human existence and what is always there throughout our entire life. The I Self is what our human identification through our Conditioned Mind becomes. Our I Self blocks out our true self. This is the core point of this book.

Stored Negative Energy Flares Up

It really comes down to this: When situations arise, you will either be with what arises and allow the energy to pass through you, or you will store it within your psyche (subconscious) for future flare ups to occur. Once life experiences happen and a person stops allowing the energy to pass through, that stored energy in the psyche becomes a Conditioned Mind Patterns. This stored energy remains dormant until a Conditioned Mind Pattern is activated through some sort of reminder, a trigger. It will come out in whatever reaction the conditioning in our psyche calls for.

Different Conditioned Mind Patterns react in different ways. Everyone's conditioning is different as far as what causes the reactions and how it manifests, but the structure of conditioning is the same. Our Mind Patterns create reactions to this trigger or reminder. The reactions of greed, lust, envy, jealousy, anger, pride, sloth, slander, and so on, are only an outward manifestation of our inner Conditioned Mind Patterns. The inner Conditioned Mind Patterns are the basis of our actions. Without these, the default setting of our mind would naturally be of love. None of our so-called life problems would ever manifest if love were the default setting of our mind.

The Root of All Problems

Ask yourself, if you never had a single need to satisfy your I Self, would you ever have a problem in your life? Would you ever want for anything and, if there wasn't any wanting, would there ever be any disappointments? From where do all your problems derive? Things do happen in our lives that are not pleasant. But if the I Self wasn't there, who would feel the unpleasantness, the disappointment or, for that matter, who feels the pleasure or the elation?

From the beginning of our existence, Conditioned Mind Patterns started to be formed. As you've grown, these patterns have had the potential to guide your behavior, and they will do so for the rest of your life — *unless* you start the practice of meditation. Quieting the mind, or sitting in silence, mindfulness — or any sort of meditation you choose to practice — will help you allow negative energy to pass through and not get stored in the psyche. If you take no actions for change, these reactions to life will be determined for you by these Conditioned Mind Patterns. This energy determines whether love is your mind's default setting or not, which in turn determines the base upon which you live your life.

Here's an example; you're driving on the Highway, just driving along, and you pass a couple of hundred cars. You hardly notice them; you're feeling happy when all of a sudden one specific car catches your attention. This car is the same type and color car as that driven by your first real love. You recall how the relationship ended badly. Her parents never really cared for you, nor you them. As you think back, the emotions of the situation start to arise like it happened recently, but it happened twenty years ago. What causes the vivid recall of that situation with the attached emotions?

It appears in your mind like it happened recently because the energy of the situation was never allowed to pass through, so it was stored in the psyche just waiting to flare up. The flare up causes the emotions associated with that situation to arise: anger, discord, pride, and whatever else it is you are feeling. The problem with this is you were just happy, and something that happened twenty years ago is blocking your ability to be happy now. This situation is not occurring now, but you wouldn't know it by the way you are reacting. Instead of being free and open to have love in your heart, the I Self has taken over and you're living life from a Conditioned Mind Pattern.

This is blocking the energy of love from being the default setting of your mind, and you are now being controlled by your thoughts instead of you controlling them. At this point you are no longer in control of your life. Without your permission you are being told what to think and feel. Look at this for yourself.

Childhood Fears and Mind Patterns

I was unaware of how my Mind Patterns started developing at an early age and progressively controlled my life. This all occurred without my

5

knowledge or permission. For example, I was about five years old and I remember being afraid of the dark. I would have rather not gone to the bathroom than gotten up and faced this fear. At times I would wet the bed. It would make me feel terrible when I would do this, but it was a fate better than taking on my fear. When I would wet the bed I would feel like a baby. And if anyone outside of my family ever found out, I would have been devastated. At about eight years old I finally outgrew bed — wetting, and I would get up and go to the bathroom.

But since I never faced the fear associated with this, a Conditioned Mind Pattern was developed. This became a key diversionary tactic that I used for many years. Instead of facing my fears I would do other things to divert attention away from them. I was also a thumb-sucker until the age of nine because it brought me comfort. Another means to cope with my inner discontentment was biting my nails. I always had this nervous energy that I didn't know what to do with. This is the main reason people tap their foot, or constantly tap a pencil, or chew gum; there always has to be something to do, all because we don't know what to do with our energy.

I would experience a sense of not fitting in with my peers that produced a lot of fear in my mind. I never really understood why I felt this way. Not understanding what these feelings were and how to deal with them, I would act out in some way to divert any feelings the fear conjured up instead of allowing the energy to pass through me. One way I would act out was to isolate myself from my peers because I felt there was less chance they would find out who I really was. And I wasn't about to let that happen. So that was the beginning of my isolation.

Another way I would act out would be to purposely fake an illness on the days that we were having certain test in school; mostly math because it was the subject I struggled with the most. One incident that occurred when I was in second grade: we were going to have a math test so I pretended to be sick. My mom took my temperature and I rubbed my hands together on the thermometer. My temperature read 103°. My mother immediately took me to the doctors and I did the same thing in the doctor's office. I got to stay home for a few days, which allowed me to temporarily divert my attention from the problem. This brought me some relief from the fear. Eventually at some point the mask I was hiding behind was going to be removed and I was going to have to return to school. After three days and much anxiety I returned to school. I took the test and failed.

The fear of having to take this math test was controlling me, and I had no idea this was happening. I was becoming proficient at not dealing with my fears. The action my fear was creating was a direct result of a Conditioned Mind Pattern that had been developed. It was developed because whenever I became fearful of something I didn't allow the energy associated with that fear to pass through so it got stored in my psyche. I didn't know what to do when fear arose because I had never been taught this. Not knowing how to process it, it was processed for me by my ego to form a Mind Pattern for its own protection.

Fear is normal. Ignorance about how to deal with it creates Conditioned Mind Patterns. All children have fear, it's a scary world out there to a child. But unless you know how to process fear and allow its energy to pass through, a Conditioned Mind Pattern will be formed. So anytime I became fearful, a Conditioned Mind Pattern was formed and I became controlled by it. Each time the fear arose and the energy wasn't allowed to pass through, this engrained the Conditioned Mind Pattern deeper and deeper into my psyche. The feeling of fear would be diverted from my inside to an action on the outside. The more fear controlled me, the less of me there was.

Blocking the Flow of Energy

When we are controlled by this conditioned I Self, which is based in fear, there isn't much love around to deal with life. Even at the age of seven I was conditioned to view life from a self-centered perspective. From a self-centered perspective the energy that flows in and out of life puts our instincts in collision with it, not harmony. The walls of my psyche were being conditioned one Mind Pattern at a time.

Another example: as I grew up I really despised not being very athletic. I had some talent, but not enough for my satisfaction. I was always the sixth man on the basketball team or the tenth man on the baseball team.

I wasn't terrible; I just didn't have as much talent as some of my peers. I never acknowledged this and my ego couldn't handle it. By not allowing the energy to take its natural course and flow through, I would just shut down, pretend that it didn't matter, and that it didn't bother me. To me it did matter and it did bother me, but my ego wouldn't allow me to see this; my ego's protection was my true self's undoing.

By suppressing my feelings, the energy associated with these feeling was stored in my psyche. The creativity that is innate in all of us (our spiritual potential, our connectedness with life) wasn't allowed to manifest because of this stored energy, so I found other ways to cope with these feelings. We will develop either healthy or unhealthy coping skills to deal with our emotions. The formation of our Mind Patterns will be dependent on whether our energy flows through us, or gets stored.

By not allowing energy to flow through me, eventually I stopped playing sports. By the time I was about sixteen, I started hanging out with a group in my neighborhood that drank alcohol and caused trouble. Not major trouble — we would break car antennas, bend street signs, graffiti up buildings, or steal bread that was delivered to stores around the neighborhood. This is where my conditioning was taking me; not by free choice, but by the incessant search for something that I could find comfort in; which was created by the Conditioned Mind Patterns. Rebellion, violation, and excess became my life's direction, to find comfort at whatever price it would cost; physically and emotionally. Since I was raised by parents who loved me, I never fell to the lowest depths. If it had not been for the love my parents had for me, who knows where I would have wound up?

Making trouble became comfortable for me. I had found my place in life, or so I thought. More and more as I shut down, I developed these Conditioned Mind Patterns that were teaching me to deal with life from my I Self. With this I Self, there was less and less thought about the consequences of my actions, and more and more thought of how I could stop my mind-created imaginary pain, and bring more pleasure to myself. Just look at this statement; I and myself in the same sentence. Who is the I and who is myself?

If I continued on the troubled course that my life was taking, I would never have reached the fullness of my Creative Potential, and this book would never have been written. The potential would have been there, but it would have remained blocked out by my developing Conditioned Mind Patterns. I would never have been able to experience life as I am now experiencing it. I would never have learned how to love myself or others. I would have never experienced what it means to be in harmony with life, with God.

Life will always be a struggle because of these Conditioned Mind Patterns. They will not permit harmony or cooperation with life. We would always feel like we're going against the traffic. We may attain success and feel content at times, but this will be fleeting as life conditions arise and activate flare-ups of the I Self. This is what the Conditioned Mind Patterns do; they prevent us from experiencing true love, from experiencing the blessings of the miracle of life.

Everyone Builds Walls — Not Just Addicts

Don't think life has to be in total disarray for Conditioned Mind Patterns to be in control. The walls that are built to deal with life are built by everyone. It is through the evolution of our ego that most of this has transpired. But the outside influences — parents, media, news, advertisement, etc. — shape us just as much as our own evolution.

This is just the way many of our human minds have developed. The mind's default setting has become the I Self, which creates so much of our so called problems. Don't think because you are managing your life and it is successful, by material standards, that it isn't conditioned by these Mind Patterns. If you react to something that somebody says or does, where do you think that reaction comes from? If it's not generated from a Mind Pattern (a past experience), then it would not affect you, at all; not one bit. The energy would just flow through. The cause of our reactions is because of our stored energy. Investigate this for yourself. See how your reactions are derived from the past.

Are you really aware of life as the gift that it is? Are you grateful for life itself, or do you want it to be in some other way? How do you treat others? And I mean all others, not just the people in your inner circle. What about the giving of yourself to benefit others? Donating old clothes after cleaning out your closet or giving money to the less fortunate because it's the easiest option doesn't manifest as love, unless it is *truly* from the heart. What of compassion? Do you feel true love for yourself and others? How about giving of your time? Time is our most precious commodity because we only have a limited amount of it. One day we will be out of time. These are just some of the questions to ask ourselves, to help us to see if there is any conditioning that is blocking our heart from being fully open; so the love that is in there can pour out into a world that so desperately needs it. Mind you this is not to say that there is anything wrong with the way you live your life, but look and see if you are getting all that life has to offer.

If you are not getting all there is out of life, is it because you are being blocked by some Conditioned Mind Pattern? Watch the subtleness of these Mind Patterns. Most people don't even realize they exist. They just go about their day being controlled by them, unconsciously.

How about this: you are watching TV and a certain type of person that attracts you comes on the screen. Look at what arises: Where does the attraction come from? It comes from the past, (our conditioning) which will always blocks out our ability to respond or react in the present moment with love. Only when you are present, and do not have the stored energy of the past controlling you, can you have your reactions to life become a response of love.

Another example: you are playing golf, you hit a slice. You instantly get aggravated. But what is it that aggravates you? The slice has already occurred; you can't change it. So what you are aggravated at has already occurred and it can't be changed, but that's exactly what you are trying to do, change what has already occurred, change the past. It can't be done. When you live from a place where you want things to be different than what they are, you are living from a place of discontentment. That's what's causing the aggravation, not the slice. So what is a person to do? Learn to be with the aggravation, to become aware of what caused it, and allow its energy to pass through you. When you let it go, you will then be free to hit the next slice, or possibly a good shot, but it doesn't matter, because you are free. Wouldn't it be beautiful to live every moment of everyday like this? Free. With the right practice, it is possible. The only block is you.

Situations happen that will make you react. The situation activates a Conditioned Mind Pattern, and that is what causes the reaction. This occurs over and over. Somebody does something, or an unwanted situation arises and you react. You do not have a choice in this reaction. You have to do it because that is the way you are conditioned. That is what's there. Even if the situation is not really occurring, and it's just a made-up story in your head, as long as your mind thinks it happened, that's good enough to activate a Conditioned Mind Pattern and cause a reaction.

When you're at work and people start talking about another person, (of course the other person is not in the room), everyone just feeds off the negative energy from each other and any sense of compassion or unity with that other person is blocked off. The operative force of our I Self, which is reacting the only way that it knows, is in full swing. The Conditioned Mind Pattern has been activated from some sense of lack within, so the only thing we can do is make ourselves feel better at the expense of someone else.

Collective energy has a lot of energy to draw you in, especially if you are not aware of it. This seems like it's harmless, but it is not, it blocks your pathway to true freedom; the freedom from the I Self. When we make ourselves feel better by putting others down, what we are really doing is putting ourselves down. How can I operate from love when there is no love to be had? The energy you put out is the energy you receive in return. These are just some of the things that develop when we operate from the ego, the I Self. It's an ego that needs negative energy to build itself up by putting others down, so it can feel superior.

There are also things we learn at a young age from others. Where do we learn to be prejudiced, to be greedy, to hate? Feel free to add to that list. We do not start out our existence with any of those traits, they are learned.

This is the other part of how we are conditioned. Some things are formed from within us and some are formed from outside influences.

Consider a suicide bomber. A person is not born a suicide bomber; they are conditioned to become that way. Take the same person and remove them away from that environment, and bring them up in an environment of love, they will not become a suicide bomber. How could they? The conditioning needed for this to occur isn't there. So love is what they will learn and love will emanate throughout their life. Instead of causing unnecessary harm to themselves and others, this same person with different conditioning will be helpful and harmonious.

As our mind becomes more conditioned, there is less quietness to experience the truth. So our mind just keeps operating from this conditioning. It has to, it knows no other way. It just keeps feeding off its own memory to cope with situations. We stay locked in Mind Patterns that keep our true nature from arising. We believe the world of our thoughts, which aren't necessarily true. They are relatively true, but only to us. Our existence then becomes habitual by letting our Conditioned Minds Patterns control us. The only way to undo this conditioning is to become aware of it. The only way to become aware of it is to study how the conditioning has come about and to learn how to change it.

The reason I had so many problems was that I never learned how to quiet my mind, so I always needed to be busy doing something. That's what the mind does, it make us believe in all kinds of nonsense that really has nothing to do with life. It makes us believe that everything matters, but the truth is not much really matters, no matter what it is. You may think it matters, but if you really look at this, you will understand that it doesn't. Everything, no matter what, is impermanent.

This is one of the causes why many of us use food for fulfillment, and become overweight, or develop other medical problems. It is not simply because we eat too much, or eat the wrong foods. It is because our minds can't be still long enough to understand the impermanence in the pleasure we are seeking. The only reason we are reaching for food is because our mind is agitated. That agitation is why we reach for anything. Whatever form it takes, the thing reached for, is only a diversion that we believe will bring us lasting satisfaction. But it will not last no matter what is used. So we need to find out why we are reaching, and become aware that the cause of our reaching is at the root of the problem.

To me this is where society is at fault; when someone commits a crime the only thing we do is punish the person for committing the crime. We never address why the person is committing the crime. There is a reason for it, it doesn't just happen, it's the persons conditioning. I don't mean what may have happened when the person was a child; I mean why are they still allowing it to control their behavior today? That is what needs to be addressed; until it is, the Conditioned Mind Patterns will run the show and control the behavior; in this case it manifest in the form of criminal activity which will most likely be repeated.

People are not born to be criminals; the influences in their life condition them that way. Nobody is born with a Conditioned Mind; it has to be developed. We may be born with certain tendencies, but those too have to be developed and cultivated to become engrained in our psyche. This is how the default setting of our mind becomes what it becomes.

Because I had parents who loved me and did their best to teach me right from wrong, the conditioning I experienced was different from someone who was possibly abused or raised by non loving people. The conditioning is present for all of us, but a person gets in more trouble when there is less love in their life. People who are well off are also conditioned, it's just easier not to notice when a person is educated and has a lot of stuff. Education and wealth are easier to hide behind because society is more accepting of them. But if love is deficient in their lives, they will have problems caused by a Conditioned Mind, just like anyone else. It is a human state that is very difficult to avoid.

When only the behavior or action is addressed, and the reason we do what we do is ignored, the behavior or action is just repeated. If our minds were quiet we would not need to reach for anything. We would not have a need to engage in criminal activity. If all we have inside us is love then it is impossible for us hate; ourselves or anyone else.

13

Agitation Has Become the Natural State of Our Minds

This agitation has become the natural state of our minds. It is always looking for something to do. It is always looking for the next pleasure. Try this exercise: do not eat or drink anything for two hours and see what arises. Notice how your mind will constantly try and get you to eat or drink something. Try sitting still for an hour without music or TV. Just sit in a chair and be still. If you can't do it, don't be discouraged. It is nearly impossible for the undisciplined mind to do this. Your mind wants to do something, anything, even if it's harmful to you or others. It is just doing what it is conditioned to do. That's all it is, an agitation. That's what causes our Conditioned Mind Patterns to flare up. In a millisecond, the mind gets agitated, flares up, and reacts. If you don't discipline the mind to gain some semblance of quietness and control, this cycle will be repeated throughout your lifetime. Some sense of peace, then a situation arises which causes the agitation; this activates a Conditioned Mind Pattern and BAM, the reaction.

Learn to quiet your mind and you will learn to understand yourself. To be on a so-called spiritual journey is not the discovery of the great secrets of the universe, nor is it to learn if it was the chicken or the egg that came first. What has made the difference in my life being on this journey has been the discovery of why I do and think what I do, and what I can do to stop it; to stop attaching to the things that caused the so-called problems in my life. Not by waiting for some deity sitting on some cloud to do something, but by learning to quiet my mind, by going within. By learning how to sit still and quiet the mind agitations, I can develop the discipline that is necessary to become aware of the cause of the noise in my head that's created by Conditioned Mind Patterns. By doing this, my heart opens and I learn how to love. The more my heart opens, the deeper I can go inside. The deeper I go inside, the more love is discovered. When you become aware and understand the things that make you do what you do, you can stop doing them so you can be free; free to love, free to be at peace with yourself and others; free from the bondage of your I Self.

Quieting the Mind

One method I use to quiet my mind is to sit or lie down and get as comfortable as possible. If sitting, I have both feet flat on the ground and my hands on my lap. If lying down I lay on my back with my hands on my stomach. I start out by breathing in and out at a very slow, deliberate pace. I just sit and follow my breath in and out. The noise in the head will try and divert my attention from the breath, but I just bring it back to the breath. This is what is meant by developing the discipline that is necessary for the mind to become quiet; the timeframe of how long to sit is not important for now. Learning to watch how the mind reacts to trying to quiet it is what is of importance here. This is the key to meditation practice, just watching how the mind wanders and then bring it back to the breath. I do not sit to achieve a certain state of being, or to experience anything in particular. I just use the sitting to discipline an undisciplined mind. Any time I sit I am developing this discipline. This is just one method to try. If this does not satisfy you, try another. You will need to experiment and find what method works the best for you. In the beginning quieting your mind will seem impossible, but with patience and perseverance you will eventually experience a peace in your life that can't be described in words.

The Past Disguised As the Present Controls Our Future

When you learn how to quiet your mind, you will understand the subtleness of the Conditioned Mind Patterns. Without realizing it, you make so many choices based on past experiences. Did you ever wonder why you are attracted to some things more than others? These likes and dislikes are not random. They have been developed over time and are now the operating force in your life.

From the moment you open your eyes in the morning, the past Mind Patterns take over and start dictating to you what you think, feel, and do. That's where the title of this book came from. I was in the gym and said, "Good morning, how are you?" to a woman I see there periodically. Her response to me was, "Well you know, it's Monday." Here's a person who is smiling whenever I see her, so to me her answer didn't really fit her

15

demeanor. I just smiled at her as I was finished exercising, I continued walking to the locker room.

Once in the locker room it just dawned on me that her answer was an automatic response. We've all probably thought this at one time or another: When it's Monday, you have to be unhappy. When it's Wednesday, you are indifferent; there isn't much attachment to Wednesday. But now it's Friday, so you are happy. Then it's Saturday and you are indifferent again. But then it's Sunday and you are unhappy because tomorrow is Monday again. You spend the whole day thinking about going back to work or it being the beginning of the week; unless Monday is a holiday then you can be happy on Sunday. On Monday you can be unhappy because you have to go to work on Tuesday, and if it's going to rain Tuesday, that's a double whammy. This goes on in the mind all the time. It operates this way for different circumstances, not only in our responses to the days of the week, but to any circumstances controlled by our Conditioned Thinking.

As I was changing my clothes in the locker room I just started laughing to myself at how our mind works, then it just came to me that "It's Monday Only in Your Mind." The truth is that Monday is no different than any other day of the week unless we make it so. And what makes it so; our mind. We make the days different by the way our Conditioned Mind Patterns attach our past associations to the present.

This is also how we associate with time. The way we handle time is key to how we live our life. We break our day into segments; a typical day for many of us is broken down like this: The alarm rings and we hit snooze. Already we want things to be different, and we didn't even get out of bed yet. So now we're lying in bed and thinking, "its cold out there." Okay, but we have to go to work, so we get up and go in the shower. In the shower we go over the entire day. Our mind is every place, but in the shower. Next, as we are getting dressed, we think of getting our coffee. Once we get our coffee we are thinking about the drive to work. We are now in the car driving to work and we are thinking about what we have to do once we get to work. Once we are at work we start to think about our mid-morning snack. While we're eating our snack, we think about what we have to do the rest of the morning. Now we're back to work and we start thinking about lunch. At lunch we think about what we have to do when we return to work. When we are working in the afternoon we start to hope that the traffic will not be too heavy on the ride home. On the ride home we think about dinner. As we are eating dinner we think about playing with the kids, or making their lunches for school tomorrow, or whatever. As we do this we start looking at the clock because we have to go to work tomorrow. As we get ready for bed, we wonder what work will be like tomorrow. We lived through our whole day, but yet, not one moment was lived in the moment that we were in. Think about it. It was like we were on automatic pilot.

This is a typical day for many of us, and as we do this, our life is passing us by. Most times, very few moments of our day are experienced in the actual moments that were in. We are usually everywhere, but. Even though in this everyday scenario we continually worry about the future, this pattern is derived from the past. All thoughts of the future come from our past experiences; how else do they become thoughts? From where do our thoughts acquire energy? What makes a thought? All our thoughts are derived from what is in us: our memory, our past.

When you live beyond thought in the present moment, you are not concerned with the trivial nonsense of the mind because what happens will happen anyway, regardless of any thoughts that you have. To ensure a better future we must live in the present. This is the only place where we are free to be with what is; instead of being with the way our limited minds have been conditioned to think it should be.

As our mind becomes quieter, we become more aware of the Here and Now. We start to understand things in a different way. When certain situations arise, we start to become aware of how they draw us in, how they take up all our attention. But it's not the actual thing itself that draws us in; the thing itself has no power. Our mind creates the power of the draw with its labels, for different experiences. If we can refrain from labeling everything that our senses come in contact with, there wouldn't be any draw.

In other words, when we name a thing as "this" or "that," we are drawing on past experiences. Our mind has already come to a conclusion, drawn from the past so we are blocked from the freedom to understand the thing as it actually is. When we can stop the labeling, categorizing, and judging we will start to experience a peace that we have never experienced before. As Jesus said, "*A Peace that passes all understanding.*" And isn't that what we are seeking?

When there is no judgment we can view things as they are, not as we wish them to be. There is no stored energy in this state of being that blurs our vision. In this state we are open to see truth. And when we see the truth, the truth is what sets us free. What are we free from? Free from the bondage of the I Self. Free to be our true self; which has been there from the beginning of our existence.

We all have the potential to access unlimited inner resources, to enhance this journey called life. Through no fault of our own, many of us fall short of getting in touch with our inner resources. We stay attached to a mind that limits our ability to use or recognize these resources. It is unfortunate, life will still be experienced, how can it not be? We are alive, but we will not be living it to our highest and happiest potential.

This is not the fault of any God. It is because *we* fail to tap into our own inner resources. Don't wait for a magical answer from God; you will probably be on your deathbed before you get your answer. You can find your answer now if you so desire, you will discover that being alive is the gift — for one day it will not be so. If you are waiting for something else, you will be missing the mark; which, by the way, is the definition of sin. You already have the potential to soar above the clouds, but only you can take advantage of that. Your evil, if that is what you want to call it, is your Conditioned Mind Patterns, your blocks to love. Your goodness arises when you are free from them.

When you understand how judging and labeling cause you to live from a self-centered perspective instead of from love, this will mean you've had a shift in being. This shift is where the veil of ignorance is removed and your heart opens a little more than it was. By not judging or labeling, the mind quiets and becomes still. The stillness (because the mind settles) allows you to learn a truth that opens your heart. The truth stops the energy from a Conditioned Mind Pattern dead in its tracks, and instantly there is a shift in being because in the stillness your heart remains open. So from the stillness there is truth, and from knowing truth, the shift of being is allowed to occur. There isn't anything you need to do except to be still. Meditation provides the stillness that will assist in this. Because the noisy mind alone blocks this from happening, learn to do what is necessary to bring stillness into your being, and learn to be free. Practice quieting your mind so you can become aware of what arises. In stillness all truth will be revealed.

<u>Reaching Our Potential</u>

Pro athletes illustrate how we can reach our Creative Potential. Anyone who plays for a professional sports team has demonstrated the potential to become a pro athlete. But unless they develop the discipline to train and practice correctly, and unless they're dedicated to reaching their potential, they will probably fall short. The potential is there, and will always be there, but if the person is not doing the things that are necessary to reach his or her potential, there will be little or no progress. Perhaps they can play in the minor leagues, but by not reaching their true potential they will never be truly happy. It will always seem like something is missing in their life. And you know what, there will be.

By not allowing our creativity within to flourish, we never reach our Creative Potential. We live a limited life. Most people never reach their true Creative Potential and so they are never *truly* happy. They are somewhat happy. "You can't be happy all the time, right?" That's what they say. To this day, nobody knows who *they* are. But we believe things prior to investigation . . . and this is where I know I fell short.

We don't ever have to believe anything anybody tells us until we investigate it for ourselves. If we are not at peace, it is up to us to understand the cause of our discontentment. We don't need to ask anyone why we are discontented: we can find out for ourselves. It is each of our responsibility to find out what it will take to become liberated from our Conditioned Mind Patterns.

This is how it is with us; we all have the potential to be totally happy, totally free, but unless we undergo the necessary training to reach our Creative Potential it will never be reached. We will fall short and to fall short is to be spiritually bankrupted. This is what limits our happiness. Our mind never gets quiet enough, so we are always controlled by our I Self, and looking for answers outside of us. The only way we can live a limitless life and be totally happy, totally free, is to live from within, and not be dependent on anything or anybody for happiness. So it behooves each and every one of us to do the things necessary to cultivate our spiritual growth.

In the following chapters I will share with you how, without my conscious permission, my mind became conditioned to think and act in ways that were not conducive to my spiritual well-being; how this conditioning blocked my cooperation with life and hence, any harmony with it. This conditioning caused pain and misery to me and to those around me. Life isn't cruel or painful, but my Conditioned Mind Patterns made me think and feel that it was. I had to really look at how I was reacting to the things that happened in my life. Where did my reactions come from?

I will explain what happened to me, how I became conditioned and how I was able to start the process of breaking free from the grasp of my Conditioned Mind Patterns. How I was given a choice, a choice I never had before. The choice being, to either live the rest of my life entrapped by my I Self (my Conditioned Mind Patterns, where my ego ran riot) or in Freedom; where love is my life's default setting. This choice allows me to choose now, and each day, the freedom to love, the freedom not to cause harm to myself or others, and the freedom to be a benefit to all beings; what more could a person ask.

CHAPTER 2

⚜

The Conditioning Begins (My Adolescent Years)

My human existence started on August 8, 1958. I was named Michael by my parents, and that really was the beginning of my conditioning, my I Self. I say it this way because, as you will see, a large part of our conditioning comes about by the words that we put on things and the noise this generates in our mind. The words and noise make us believe things that aren't necessarily true. Words are very limiting, but that is what the mind prefers, to make sense of life's great diversity and complexity.

The mind doesn't care about truth; it cares about having things arranged a certain way so it can justify what it thinks. Take a simple word like "God." That word has caused more problems than any word since humankind started using words to identify things. What if you didn't attach a certain belief or concept to the word God; would it make things any different? It's the same way with the word I. If there was no I, would it make things any different?

So much of how we are conditioned is associated with words; words that create a world that exist only in our mind. A belief is not a truth; it is just some construct that our mind makes up to help us feel better about ourselves, to explain why we do things, or why we exist. When we let go of these constructs, we find we don't need a created purpose for our existence.

Take a deep look as to how one day we exist and one day we don't. Nine months prior to the beginning of our existence, a man and women performed an act that initiated it. We were named for identification purposes, and this was the beginning of our individuality and also of our isolation from each other. We associate that name with who we are, and that name also causes our separation from each other. As we go through life we grab many other identities that also make up who we believe we are. The more we hold onto these things the more isolated we become. By associating those things with who we are, we lose our spiritual connection to life.

We will lose our attachment to things one day anyway; such is the nature of life. Because everything (no matter what it is) is impermanent, one day we will die; just like that our life will be over. Not because of a decision made by some deity we make up in our head, but because the conditions are no longer right for our bodies to sustain life. What happens to all the things, all the beliefs and attitudes that we were holding onto? Regardless of what was accomplished in our life or what we thought our purpose was what happens to them? We can learn to be in the stillness by learning to let go of our attachment to things. In the stillness of life all things arise. Stillness creates space and without space nothing would exist. So when we are still we can be with what is here, because we are giving it the space it needs to exist. If we are not with what is here, then where are we? Even when we are with what is here, we can possibly attach to that and let that become our purpose. But since what is here is always changing, our purpose would constantly change. When we don't attach to anything, we come to an understanding; we don't need a created purpose.

Schooldays and Early Childhood

I had an ordinary childhood in the sense of the way I was raised. I grew up in Newark, New Jersey to loving parents who gave me every opportunity they possibly could have. I was one of six children. I started kindergarten at the age of five, and I can recall even at that age, my thinking was centered on the I Self. Although I didn't understand this at the time, my feelings were always controlled by this I Self.

There was one girl in kindergarten with whom, for whatever reason, I didn't get along with. Maybe because she was tougher than I was and I was afraid of her. Not knowing how to deal with this, one day at school I took a pair of scissors and cut off a big chunk of her hair. I never thought about the consequences of doing this. This lack of thinking about the consequences became a Conditioned Mind Pattern that caused me many years of confusion and suffering. This was how I started acting out, with a total disregard of the consequences, but at least I could cope with my elusive and confused feelings.

I never understood how to process my feelings, so when a situation evoked a feeling, I developed these coping mechanisms to deal with it. It didn't matter who was involved with these coping mechanism, just as long as I felt better and the feelings I had went away. One of the main feelings that seemed to occur over and over was that I wanted things to be different. I didn't know how I wanted them to be, but just *different* would have been fine. I was never content with the way things were, and I never understood why.

I Felt Different from Everyone Else

I used to think that I felt different from everybody else, but I have since come to understand that I didn't really know how others felt, so that wasn't necessarily true. All I do know is that no matter what happened, I never felt comfortable in my surroundings and this made me act out in ways that would bring me a sense of acceptance. This acceptance never lasted, my discontentment would always return, and another antic would shortly follow.

I can't explain why this was the case. My parents gave me everything that I asked for. I didn't really want for anything. I do know this; my view of life was always from a self-centered perspective. I seemed to always internalize what happened. I always made it about me, whether it was or not. I thought life was the problem, but it was my inability to process it and respond to it from anywhere but the I Self. It wasn't taught when I was growing up, and it isn't taught now; that there is a way to live life from the core of the self, with which we started our existence; not the I Self, which was developed over time through our Conditioned Mind.

I did what I did because of the viewpoint of the I Self. This happened through no fault of anyone in particular; it was just the way my mind had evolved; the way it developed. To be driven by Conditioned Mind Patterns is to be driven by the delusions created by fear; the fear that you will never have or be enough. This is what the I Self does.

Getting Older and Everything Is "All About Me"

The older I got the more I became conditioned to think and react to life situations in certain ways. My mind always made it "about me." All through elementary school I struggled academically, and with the feelings of inadequacy that went along with those struggles, my I Self was building defense mechanisms to cope with life. These coping skills weren't allowing energy to get through; the suppressed, unprocessed emotions were all being stored in my psyche, conditioning my mind along the way.

A vicious cycle was being developed. I didn't have a high opinion of myself and struggled to fit in. When situations arose that would activate a Conditioned Mind Pattern, I would act out the way I was conditioned. I would do things that would bring the acceptance I was so desperately seeking. I would do things that people would laugh at. Whether people were laughing at me or with me, was not a concern of mine, I only cared that they were laughing.

The more they laughed, the more I acted in ways I thought would guarantee social acceptance. My parents were called into school to discuss my behavior issues every year in grammar school. I got expelled in third grade for instigating chaos throughout the school; I got thrown out of class for being disruptive. Instead of standing outside of my classroom like I was told, I roamed the halls and caused havoc. All my friends thought I was so cool, and I loved it. The teachers didn't think I was so cool, and they mandated another trip to the principal's office and another visit from my parents.

When I had trouble understanding the subject we were going over in class, I would divert my feelings of inadequacy with behavior that suppressed such feelings. Except for the incident in kindergarten where I cut the girl's hair, I generally didn't involve others physically in these disruptions. My Conditioned Mind Patterns didn't produce direct anger, but rather behavior designed to help me find social acceptance. The truth is that nobody, including me, really knew why I was the way I was. Who would have thought it would take me forty-nine years to find out why I did what I did when I was an adolescent?

Throughout my adolescent years, I acted out in order to gain the acceptance that I was so desperately seeking. One time, I was in eighth grade, I found a text book in the playground and a teacher told me to give her the book. I knew I had an audience so I ripped the book in half and told the teacher, "Here, you can have your book," and threw it in the air. The laughter from the people who witnessed what I did was well worth the trouble I got into — or so I thought. This prompted another visit by my parents. I had to apologize to the teacher in front of the whole class; I got one week detention in exchange for the laughter.

I could never find anything that I was really good at. I had no special talents to speak of, and this tore me apart inside. When people would go on stage at the end of the year, for making the Honor Roll, I would have given anything to have been a part of that, but I didn't have the wherewithal to do it. I really loathed "being average," and the torment this caused me manifested in my creating skills that were not conducive to being in harmony with life. I would always get an unsatisfactory on my report card in the category of "growing in self-control." My self-control was nonexistent; I would act upon whatever impulse arose, as long as I had an audience and it brought me pleasure and acceptance.

Another incident I remember was in gym class, auditioning for a school show performing gymnastics. One of the demonstrations was the long horse jump. I was actually pretty good on the long horse, but my self-esteem was so low I really didn't think I would have a chance to make the team. And God forbid, if I gave it my all and then I didn't get selected, I would have been crushed. So I purposely tripped myself up so people would make a big deal about it and feel sorry for me. This was another one of the Mind Patterns I developed that stayed with me for a very long time; doing things to make people feel sorry for me.

Behind this seeking of approval, acceptance, or pity was a compulsion to just go along with the crowd. I was literally dying to belong, instead of succumbing to the isolation I so frequently felt. Even if I thought about the consequences of my behavior, the euphoria of acceptance and being part of the group always outweighed them.

The Greatest Diversion Yet — Other People, Especially Girls

One great diversion I found was, there was always some girl who liked me, and this provided for me, a new way to find acceptance. I would go after any girl who showed an interest in me, even if I didn't like her all that much. I wouldn't really try to go after anyone I really liked because I feared rejection. It was better to settle than to go through that. The friends I had at the time were into sports and not into girls, so it gave me something that separated me from them. It was the one thing I found that made me feel good.

Having a girlfriend became a valuable measurement in my sense of self worth. This Mind Pattern continued well into adulthood. I always had to have a girlfriend, which would allow me to divert attention away from me. When I had sex for the first time at the age of thirteen, it really separated me from my friends. I would brag to them about this like I'd accomplished some great feat. I did something that none of them did, and it made me feel awesome. I sensed the shallowness in this, but at least I found something that I was better at than my friends. Unfortunately, this was another one of the Mind Patterns I developed that stayed with me for a very long time. Using people for my self satisfaction became a way of life for me. I was slowly developing these Mind Patterns, one at a time, to cope with whatever was going on inside of me.

Because no one really understood my behavior, the self-centered conditioning was getting engrained ever more deeply in my psyche. This self-centered conditioning was becoming the normal operating foundation of my existence; for my way of coping with life. Needless to say, it was a faulty foundation. My walls were going up one incident at a time; yet I and those around me were totally unaware of what was happening.

Trying to Protect Myself from Getting Hurt

As I grew up, my defense mechanisms for coping with life were being put into place to prevent me from getting hurt. They were being perfected. Although I looked like everyone else outwardly, inside I was in a constant struggle. Up until the point that I was about twelve years old my troubles had mostly taken the form of diverting behaviors, like being the class clown, or faking an illness, or doing just about anything that would bring me attention to divert my fear.

With puberty, though, I was discovering things outside myself, like alcohol, gambling, girls, pornography, and stealing, to name a few, which could divert any feelings of inadequacy or fears that arose; and I started using these things as a way of escaping. Whenever I became fearful, lonely, and isolated I went searching for something to bring me pleasure and relief. This was just the beginning of my search for endless pleasures, endless relief.

The object being used to bring us fulfillment is not important. The object doesn't matter. Everyone uses whatever is convenient to bring the fulfillment he or she desires. Every social class has its objects of desire, and it doesn't matter what they are. A Conditioned Mind knows no social status; it just blocks out our ability to experience our true nature, the social status or object is immaterial.

Since I was not a very good student and I was not adept in sports, the process of coping with the feelings that I didn't measure up, had me looking for something to divert these feelings, to project it outside of myself. Whatever the cost, I sought to create some false sense of a good inner feeling. I didn't realize this was happening at the time, so I just kept looking outside myself to bring me inner fulfillment.

The older I got the more my search for inner fulfillment grew, and the more that search involved other people. My behavior started becoming more self-destructive, to myself and others, as I was using alcohol, amongst other things, to squash my feelings. I would use girls just to get sex. I would lie to people to get whatever it was I thought I needed to feel good. I was around twelve or thirteen when I made a conscious decision that, even if there was a God up there somewhere, it wasn't doing anything to benefit my life, so I was going to take care of myself.

Santa Claus God

I was raised as a Roman Catholic. My parents tried to make me go to church every Sunday, but since I never felt a connection to this God I was learning about, I wouldn't go. My mother would give me money to put in the collection basket at church, but I would go to the park across the street instead. I would buy a pint of milk and a donut with the money she gave me. And when church was over I would go in and get the weekly pamphlet and bring it home.

My formal religious training had no bearing on the decision to turn my back on God; it was the view I had of God. This is where my weakness lay: I wanted a Santa Claus God, one that would grant me my wishes. And if God couldn't do that, then where was the need? I was now going to take care of me by whatever means I could come up with. I was going to bring as much pleasure to my life as I could. And whoever got in the way would have to suffer the wrath of my I Self; this wrath being based in self-centeredness meant I would do things from which only I would benefit, without any regard of how I would affect others. I arrived at these conclusions without knowing my Conditioned Mind Patterns were in place, and they were making most of, if not all of my decisions for me.

I have since come to understand what I was really looking for was a magician, someone or something that was going to make my life the way I wanted it. My thinking was really distorted. My belief was: I wasn't smart,

I wasn't good in sports, I didn't have any special talents, I was just an ordinary person, I didn't like it and I wanted things to be different. Since God wasn't taking care of me, there was no need for God or religion, so I took matters into my own hands. My I Self, with its Conditioned Patterns, was in full control of my decision-making process. You can see how a belief is just a construct created by the mind: None of what I believed was actually true, but unfortunately I didn't know this at the time. I thought it was true and I gave these beliefs the energy they needed to control my life. This is what brought me to my understanding that a belief is just noise in my head; a hindrance to my freedom.

As I continued living my life in this manner, things were just getting more confusing for me. The more confusing it got, the more withdrawn I became. The walls that I was building were just reinforcing my conditioning. The more my conditioning became the operative energy in my life, the more isolated I felt. This isolation from those around me, is just the outward manifestation of what was occurring in my head. This created view allowed me to see only how different other people were from me. That is what my I Self view created: differences in others not unity. The more differences my I Self created, the more isolated I grew. I was creating a perception of reality that was destroying my life and I didn't know it. I just kept closing down more and more, not letting any energy flow through me, this didn't allow letting anyone get close to me because my heart stayed closed. The moment I became uncomfortable with a situation, my defense mechanisms would come into play and defuse the discomfort the only way my I Self knew how, the way that had been learned; diverting the attention outside of me. It was going to be many years later before I would learn how to stop living my life like this.

Love and Friendship

I had many so-called friends around me, but no one was ever considered my best friend. It is hard to live from the I Self and have close relationships, unless someone has something that you want. Since the nature of the I Self is isolation that is what my mind's default setting was. Not that I wanted to be like this, but there really wasn't any choice. The I Self creates a dual identity by separating us from each other and from ourselves. That is the essential nature of the I Self.

Blocked by my Conditioned Mind, I never really learned what true love was. My distorted view of life, derived from a self-centered perspective, disabled my ability to learn to love unconditionally, so honest relationships were difficult to establish. I learned only to look outside to fill some inner desire and that inner desire was always selfish in nature. My attraction to the object of desire, whether it was a woman, a substance, a car or whatever; was to satisfy my I Self, which will always block the ability to feel true love, and to form true relationships. True love can only be experienced from the inside, and unfortunately I was conditioned to look outside. And so another vicious cycle formed.

This is one of the main reasons relationships didn't exist in my life. My relationships didn't come from the inside, from the heart, so how could they last? The main foundation of life, which is love, wasn't there. If a relationship isn't based on unconditional love, and conditions change, there is separation because the connection to the other person is lost. The connection is lost because our focal point, our energy, is on our differences and we become isolated from each other. When our connection to each other is based in the form of a thought and the thought changes, therein lays the cause of the separation. An example of this would be if a relationship is purely based on a physical attraction. The physical attraction is thought based, with that being at the core of what establishes the relationship, it will be very difficult to sustain because of all the negative energy that surrounds the other parts of the relationship. Eventually both partners will tire because as desires change and physical appearance change, there will be nothing to hold the relationship together. To go beyond that, to establish a deep relationship based on unconditional love, there has to be a connection to each other that doesn't involve thought. It is the same connection which you get when the mind settles enough to understand, we are one species living on one planet.

Living from the Head, Not the Heart

True love can only come from the heart, but we live so much of our life from our head. Most of us have never learned to love unconditionally. How could we, if we have a Conditioned Mind? That means we put conditions on everything. To love unconditionally is to love no matter what; when we learn how to do this we will be doing our part in making this world a better place to live.

Think about it: Where does all our hate come from? We are on this tiny planet, spinning around in this huge galaxy, and we treat each other like we are all from a different place. We are one race, the human one, on one planet. Until we start acting this way, things will continue to get worse in this world. When you learn to live from the self that has always been there, you become one with life, you are in harmony with it, and you are in harmony with all beings. This is a spiritual law that happens when you do the things that put you in cooperation with life. The only way to cooperate with life is to establish love as your mind's default setting. Stop hating and you will love. That is the way things change.

My Conditioned Mind Patterns were in full swing and there wasn't a damn thing I could do about it. My walls were becoming a fortress. I thought they were being formed by my mind to keep things out, but what they were actually doing was creating a prison that kept me locked in; locked into Mind Patterns for forty-nine years that did nothing, but block out the innate goodness that is and was always there. I just needed to learn to unblock it.

Object-oriented Life

Living from this I Self, everything I wanted and everyone in my life became an object; something to be used by me in whatever capacity I saw fit. This world was here to be used for my satisfaction or to fill a necessity I thought I had or needed. Other people's feelings didn't matter. If you had something that I wanted I would do anything to get it. I would make every effort to get it, no matter the cost to you or me. What was yours became mine.

I do not make light of my role in any of the things that occurred in my life, but how can a person be held responsible if he's acting the only way he knows? The selfishness that the I Self breeds doesn't allow for compassion or the feelings of others. This made for a very lonely existence. In my heart I would have given anything to have a genuine relationship with a woman, but my I Self would not allow me to be anything but selfish, and to use everything and everybody to fulfill my desires. I know society wants to hold people responsible for their actions, but most of us are living like we are being pulled around by a leash. We are controlled by our Conditioned Mind Patterns. We think we are controlling our lives, but upon further review, we may see things in a different light. Take a good look at how much control you really have.

Today I do not react to life the way I did for forty-nine years because I know the origin of my past behavior. I am aware of the Conditioned Mind Patterns and the way they controlled my life. I understand how they were formed and how they were the cause of how I acted. I know it wasn't my true self who did what I did. I know I was driven by my Conditioned Mind.

These Mind Patterns don't go away just because we become aware of them. But as the mind becomes quieter, the pull our Mind Patterns have upon our psyche decreases. So it is necessary to continue the practice of meditation, so we can continue to quiet our mind. In the quiet, when the noise subsides, we become more aware of our Conditioned Mind Patterns. As we become more aware of our Conditioned Mind Patterns, we will understand how they control our life. We will be able to let go of our guilt and remorse because we will understand they are only generated noise, created by our Conditioned Mind. We know that given the choice, we would not have acted the way we did. But we never had a choice, until now. When Jesus said *"Forgive them for they know not what they do,"* maybe this is what he meant? People are unconscious (conditioned) and don't even know it. They act the only way that they know; the way they have been conditioned.

It was the Pharisee's fear of Jesus that made them act the way they did. It wasn't Jesus; all he did was preach about love. Their reaction to him was caused by their conditioning, which allowed fear to be the controlling energy of the situation. Fear driven energy is so powerful because it acts as a direct threat to the ego and anything that threatens the ego is in for war; sometimes to the point of annihilation and crucifixion. So when fear arises, the Conditioned Mind Patterns will use any defense mechanism in its arsenal to cope with it. Once the threat is gone the ego feels safe and smug. The I Self is satisfied . . . but not for long.

A "Behavior Problem"

My conditioning continued on all through grammar school. Except for one teacher in sixth grade, who actually took the time to work with me one on one, no one understood what made me behave as I did. I don't know if she understood or not, but with her working with me one on one, the feelings of inadequacy didn't materialize within me. Because I understood what she was teaching the misbehaving was not present. I actually made the Honor Roll once in her class.

Unfortunately she was the only teacher to handle me in this manner, so to the other teachers I was deemed "a behavior problem" and that is how I was treated. Their assessment of my behavior was correct, but they had no insight into why I was behaving disruptively. My disruptive behavior stemmed from my inability to know how to deal with my feelings; the teachers didn't understand, nor did I, that this was not the way it had to be.

By not having the knowledge or the tools, my teachers didn't know how to properly address my behavior issues. So I was not only affected by my conditioning, I was being affected by their conditioning. I understand today how much influence other people's conditioning had upon me. Someone in my life with insight into my conditioning could have changed my whole perspective. But there wasn't anyone in my life who understood this, so I became a person who was controlled by my fear-driven Conditioned Mind Patterns, and I acted out accordingly.

This is not to blame anyone for what I became; it is just to show how much of what we do and what we become is influenced by the scope of others around us. What others believe becomes what we believe. Or sometimes, in defiance, we choose the opposite just because we hate what others believe or are.

When all is said and done, we become conditioned by so many outside influences and we think we are making choices. I can really see how my conditioning drove me. When situations arose I just did what I was conditioned to do. Like stated earlier, who in their right mind would choose to live like this? Who would choose a lifestyle that would lead to their own destruction? I'm not saying that somewhere in my heart I didn't know that what I was doing was not very good for me — but I didn't have the power or the knowledge to change it.

My walls were in place and until I learned to let the energy pass through instead of storing it in the psyche, life was going to continue to be a struggle. The more my intellect runs my life, the more of a struggle it is. Our thoughts are our only true bondage. No thing outside of us can keep us from our true self, unless it is allowed to. The only reason we allow it, is because of ignorance. Why else would we create this self-created prison?

The value of knowledge and control was really stressed one day while I was talking to my fourteen-year-old son about what I was learning. He said, *"Dad this should be taught in school. This is so much more useful in dealing with life, than Algebra."* Algebra has its place, but when I was fourteen I was already gambling, smoking marijuana and drinking occasionally. That was how my Conditioned Mind Patterns responded to feelings that I didn't understand. I was never taught how to properly process those feelings; I guess it was assumed that I knew how. Well I didn't know how and I don't think knowing Algebra would have helped me much.

Ignorance of our effect upon children is legion in our society. We are not aware of our own conditioning, so we're unable to properly influence others. When all you can think about is you, how can you properly influence others, particularly the young and vulnerable? This ignorance persists constantly; just watch how parents get involved in the sports their children play. At little league baseball games they yell and scream at teenage umpires as if they're professionals, not that being a professional makes it okay to yell at them. Or they act as if their child is going to play in the Major Leagues. Even if your child does one day make it to a professional level, what does that have to do with you today? Their life is their journey, not yours.

At games, parents constantly yell at their children from the stands to do this or watch that. Do they really think their child is listening? Ask them to clean up their rooms at home; do they listen then? What makes you think they are going to listen to you yelling like a lunatic from fifty yards away? This is our conditioning and this is how we are conditioning our children.

Helping Our Children

So what can we do to wake up and investigate our own lives? If we can get our lives in order then maybe we can help our children. This may be interpreted as strong language to some people, but if you choose to remain in your ignorance, there are consequences for you and your children. If someone would have taught me about this when I was a child, in all probability my life would have been much, much different.

Our children are not our possessions. They are not objects we own, to mold a certain way so we can find satisfaction through their accomplishments. We need to find ways to enhance their Creative Energy so they can become who they truly are; not what we want them to become. How many of us use our kids this way, to make ourselves feel some sense of satisfaction, to give us a sense of purpose? When we have to rely on conditions being a certain way to make us feel a sense of accomplishment, what is it that is lacking in us that makes us need this?

Our sense of well-being has to be based in love for it to be genuine. We are here to influence our children with this love, so they grow up to influence others with love. What happens to them throughout their life is for them to decipher and learn from. When we awaken to the understanding of how our Conditioned Mind Patterns block love from arising in our own lives, then and only then will we be able to be the influence to our children, and to all beings the Creative Intelligence intended us to be.

As I was gradating from eighth grade and was about to enter high school my journey was now entering a stage in which I had access to many more things to create diversions. This outside reaching and relief was becoming more and more necessary, as my self-centered conditioning became more and more the default setting of my thinking. Most of my childhood innocence was gone by now, and it was going to take many years to learn that is where I needed to return if I was ever going to live my life *"as intended."*

CHAPTER 3

Teenage to Young Adulthood Conditioning

After grammar school I attended the neighborhood high school, which opened a whole world of opportunity for my Conditioned Mind Patterns to flourish. The walls that my ego had created to cope with life were solid by now, and my I Self was in full swing of running the show. Gambling was becoming a larger part of what I used to divert my feelings, so I didn't have to deal with them, but it was only another object. With the I Self running the show, the only thing that mattered was satisfying the sense of lack in my life by using whatever means I could to find to subdue this void.

Wine, Women and Song

I was fourteen, and besides gambling, I was being exposed to much more destructive solutions to deal with my inability to cope with life. Alcohol, marijuana, and women became the other means used to satisfy my I Self. This combination brought me the release I'd been seeking. Actually these diversions alleviated much of the confusion I endured for a long time, but little did I know they were also the creator of my confusion.

I would use escape mechanisms and diversions for most of my life. I wasn't drinking every day yet. But the older I got, the more accessible alcohol became, and the more it became the main solution to all my problems; even though all my problems were delusional, created by my self-centered Conditioned Mind. I have come to understand that the objects we use to find release (whatever they are) are all just part of our conditioning.

Whether we use drugs, alcohol, gambling, becoming successful, dieting, working out, shopping, going out to eat, going back to school, worshipping a God, giving money or old clothes to the less unfortunate, or volunteering — we can all add our own thing, not wrong in and of themselves — but if it doesn't come from our heart, and is derived from self-centeredness, it is just a form of delusion, of self justification. Our minds use such things to try and make ourselves feel better. We use these outside things to also justify our existence, so we can give our life a self-created purpose. It is all part of the object-seeking compulsion of our Conditioned Mind Patterns. It's all part of the created story to satisfy our I Self.

When I really looked into this dependence upon outside reinforcement, I understood how it grew from an inner sense of deficiency. And because of this deficiency, I wouldn't attend any social function without using some form of substance. I wouldn't go to a high school dance without drinking alcohol; most of the time I would get so drunk I wouldn't make it to the dance. If I did make it, the only way I could start a conversation with a woman was, to be somewhat intoxicated. I always found any social setting very difficult. Why; because of my low self-esteem and fear of rejection. But what caused this fear and low estimation of me; it was my distorted view of life based in self-centeredness.

Lying to People Became Second Nature to Me

I would lie to people even if I didn't have to, just to make myself into something I wasn't. Lying became second nature to me. This is the world my I Self created. There wasn't anything real in this world, it was just my created perception of the way I *thought* it was. It was only a thought which was created by my Conditioned Thinking. This is how the ego works; it makes up its own reality, not based in truth, but based in delusion, so it can constantly be fed. In fact, it has an incessant need to be fed. This is what caused me to seek an outside solution; this constant hunger of my ego. This delusion created the story of something lacking in me, and the subsequent, spin-off story.

The Truth Sets You Free

When truth is discovered you realize there is nothing lacking in you. You are perfect just the way you are. Nothing that the mind makes you believe can improve what God has created. Only your mind thinks it needs improving. With this realization you see there isn't a need to find an outside solution. In truth, there is never a need for an outside solution. When this truth is realized your heart stays open, and with an open heart, new Conditioned Mind Patterns can't be formed.

As I went through high school my conditioning was in full survival mode. The void inside (my self centeredness) just grew larger and larger. I was gambling heavily and drinking alcohol as often as I could, almost every day. The friends that I'd played sports with were no longer in my life. I was surrounded by people who were doing the same things as I was doing; men and women alike. It was as if life was one big party, a party that I never wanted to end, and a party I couldn't allow to end.

I was bouncing from girl to girl. I wasn't attending class and would go to school just to hang out. I didn't play any sports in high school, but I did go out for the baseball team my junior year. I made it to the final cut, but I didn't make the team. This crushed me, but I would lie to myself that I didn't really try to make the team. I lied to myself often. This is a perfect example of how unprocessed emotional energy accumulates in our psyche when it's not allowed to pass through. You never totally get over something until you learn how to allow this.

By the time I was seventeen, my world was all about satisfying my inner void or lack. I used whatever I could to accomplish this. That is what I was conditioned to do and that is what I was doing. Any social event I attended required some kind mood-altering substance. I could not be with a crowd of people without using something. Fear would grip me, and if I didn't have anything to create a diversion I would make an excuse to leave or not even go.

Drinking Until I Passed Out

At my prom I got so drunk that I passed out. This happened often and was a major problem for me. Many days I woke up not knowing what I did the night before. I would go out with hundreds of dollars in my pocket only to wake up in the morning, broke. Or my clothes would be torn up, or I would be cut up. I hated how I felt when this happened. This caused immense feelings of guilt and remorse, and the only solution was to start drinking again as soon as possible, so I could block out these feelings . . . pure insanity.

This insanity was created by my own mind. My mind told me to drink. It was the drinking that was causing my problems. The next day my own mind told me that the thing that caused all my problems, drinking, was my solution. If that is not insanity then what is? Here's the kicker, my mind didn't just use alcohol like this; it was using everything like this.

Leading a Horse to Water

I didn't deserve to graduate high school but I did. That was only because my father worked with my Principal's father and they were very good friends. From the time I started high school up to the time I finished, the only thing that I valued was satisfying my inner desires. My parents tried to point me in the proper direction, but without my cooperation what could they do? The saying *"You can lead a horse to water, but you can't make him drink"* was very fitting for me then. I wouldn't and couldn't listen to anyone. I didn't have any answers except one, and that was to satisfy my I Self. I would drink, gamble, and carouse with women. I would lie, cheat, and steal if that's what my I Self needed to do, to feel satisfied. That was the only answer my ego was looking for. Don't allow anything or anybody to get in the way of doing what was needed, because the alternative was to feel pain and suffering, and my ego wasn't going to allow that to happen. What a hypocrite the ego is. It creates pain by trying to protect us from it. And the thing used for protection is the same thing that is creating the pain. Unbelievable!

On a few occasions I tried to change my ways, but since I didn't know I was conditioned to do what I was doing, my attempts failed. I would try to not gamble, or use alcohol, but after a couple of days of not doing them, I would give into some trivial excuse used to justify going back to what I was doing. I had no idea my attempts to change had to fail, because I was unaware of my Conditioned Thinking. It suppressed my knowledge or ability to change. Changing my life's direction meant I had to change the conditioning that was pointing me in the direction I was heading. Without having the knowledge or the tools to do this, change could not occur. I had no idea there was even a way to change.

Some people are fortunate not to be as conditioned as others, but if you really investigate the reason you react or act the way you do, you will understand that everyone is conditioned to some extent and *we all* do things automatically. Either we learn to control our mind or we continue to let our mind control us. It is one way or the other. We don't become "a little awake." Although our awakening is a process, the initial shift from unconsciousness to consciousness, is all that is needed to start the process. And either that happens or it doesn't. Consciousness is the realization that we have been sleepwalking and we are now aware of this. It doesn't mean life becomes perfect and nothing will ever bother us again. But it does bestow awareness on us of what causes us to become bothered.

After high school my life continued to be controlled by the Conditioned Mind Patterns. I lived my life like one big party. I had to ingest some kind of substance, and was under its influence, all my waking hours. This had to be done, so I didn't have to feel any of the feelings that arose. I didn't have a choice in this; it had to be this way. I was eighteen at this time, and my life was heading in a downward spiral, and it was going to get worse.

I enrolled in a community college only to never attend a class. The fear that gripped me crippled any attempt I had of living a so-called normal life. So I dropped out before I ever went to one class. I then enrolled in an Air Conditioning and Refrigeration School, thinking a trade would be better suited for me. I was actually doing okay for about three weeks, when they started the Theory of Electricity course. That is when the math started. It involved Algebra and Geometry, neither of which I took in high school. Math brought out the worse in me. So I would sit in class, and I would be full of fear that I was going to be found out that I didn't belong there. It made me feel like I did in grammar school; inadequate, confused and isolated.

So what did I do, I turned to my solution which was to go out on break and smoke marijuana. It didn't help me learn the Theory of Electricity, but it did make me feel better. So I did this for a couple of days, then I started smoking marijuana before class. I had developed the mind-set that if one is good, two are better. Within two weeks I was going to the Meadowlands Racetrack instead of school, so I was finished with that.

I was using my father's car and I didn't want him to discover that I dropped out, eventually he did and I couldn't use his car anymore. I have since found out that I did have the ability to learn Algebra, Geometry, and Trigonometry. I just needed to be shown how it was done, one-on one, like in the sixth grade instead of in a classroom setting.

Merry-go-round of Drama and Chaos

A lot of things transpired in the years between the time I was seventeen and twenty-six years old. When I was seventeen my father bought a restaurant. The restaurant afforded my conditioning many opportunities: There was an endless supply of wine, women, and money, to say the least. And since my mind had been conditioned to believe that everything in this world was in it to be used as I saw fit, more and more people were being affected by my conditioning. My life was a merry-go-round of drama and chaos. I was using my fathers business to fill my needs in whatever capacity my I Self deemed necessary, and that included bouncing from relationship to relationship. The restaurant's array of waitresses became my personal harem. I was also using the cash register as my very own ATM machine, but I was only withdrawing, never making deposits. And there was an endless supply of alcohol. Who could ask for more? I was twenty years old and my life was a total mess, but I pretended that I had it all together.

I'd describe my relationships as virtually nonexistent; there was plenty of consensual sex, but not much else on an emotional level — at least on my part. I know some of the women I was involved with cared for me, but I couldn't have cared less at the time. It wasn't about them; it was about me. This is a very sad and lonely place to be, believe me. I never understood how to really be in a relationship with anyone. That would mean I would have to care about someone else too, and that wasn't going to happen with the way my mind was conditioned. I didn't want it to be that way, but it was the way I had developed, and it was the only way I knew how to be.

I would use my girlfriends to fulfill any number of personal needs. I only had a car periodically, so when I didn't have a car I needed to be with someone who did. Or if my parents were getting on me for drinking too much I would have to find a woman with an apartment, so I wouldn't have to listen to them. It was always about fulfilling my needs.

Broken Relationships and Broken Promises

What I experienced during this period of my life were car accidents, fights, broken relationships, broken promises, and so much confusion and chaos. There was always chaos, which I thought was just the way life was. There was always a story my mind created, and it justified anything that happened, or anything I did. It was never my fault; the ego doesn't allow us to look within and accept any blame. It was always someone else's fault. It was just the way my perception of life had been developed; to always blame someone or something else. This way of perceiving things created all my chaos. Perception is 99.9% of our reality created. The other .1% is truth, and in my case there wasn't any.

My relationships with others, or lack of them, were very difficult for me to cope with. I was close with three brothers and two sisters, until my addiction to drugs and alcohol took hold of me and became my focal point. The connection to my whole family became distorted. Because I never felt like I was a part of anything, I always seemed to be on the outside, looking in. I really had no clue about how to deal with people, and all this ignorance did was create fear of others, which isolated me more. I avoided involvement with others, to avoid emotions and feelings, theirs and mine. I even felt isolated in bars until the substance I was using took affect.

I could not maintain any kind of relationship with women or men; I didn't know how to. What really made me feel the worst were all my broken promises; so many broken promises, to so many people. I always meant what I said; I just didn't have the wherewithal to follow through. I would just drown out the feelings of guilt, remorse, uselessness, shame, and confusion associated with these broken promises by taking and using my diversionary substances, using the solutions that were created by my Conditioned Mind Patterns.

When life's default setting is self-centered fear, all we can do is satisfy our own needs and desires. Even though at times the heart may have been willing to keep the promises I made, there was no way my I Self would allow that to happen. For example, I'd be living with a woman; I would call and tell her "I'll be home right after work, around ten o'clock." I would stop at the bar across the street to visit a friend. I would intend to have only one drink, but I would be out all night, and never even call my girlfriend. Do you think there was a choice here? With the I Self there isn't any room for anyone else. That's why, as they say, the road to Hell is paved with good intention; my heart may have been willing but my I Self was not. The guilt, remorse, and shame that this caused, ate at the core of my being.

Never intending to be this way or to do the things I did, but not knowing that there was any other way out of the downward spiral, I would cope the best way that I could: by blocking it out with as much diversion as possible. I'd use anything that I could find, to keep all the feelings and emotions that go along with this way of living in check. I felt like there was nothing I could do, but go along for the ride; a ride I wouldn't wish on anyone. This is how so many people live; maybe not to this extreme, but still controlled by their Conditioned Thinking nonetheless.

That's what happens with our Conditioned Mind Patterns; they take us along for the ride. They say "jump," and we ask "how high?" You don't think this is true, but when was the last time a situation occurred, when you felt you had been wronged and you didn't react automatically? You don't even have to be wronged; you just have to think you were. How about if you were right about something and someone disagreed with you, was your reaction controlled by you or did the reaction happen on its own? All this I-am-right-and-you-are-wrong stuff occurs just to satisfy the ego, to prove its point. To be right is only important to our ego. In the grand scheme of things, how important is it? What does it all really accomplish?

The Unexamined Life

If you are honest about this, I would venture to say that many of your reactions happen on their own. So if you don't think any of this pertains to you, really look at some of the reactions you have when things don't go the way you want them to. It doesn't matter what your background is, there is some level of conditioning in your life, whether you want to admit it or not. Not admitting it is part of being conditioned.

Do you find yourself judging someone as this or that? How about gossiping? What about if you smoke cigarettes, why can't you stop? Eating too much? Spending too much money? They are not adding one thing to your life that will benefit it, but yet you still do things that bring harm to you. Why? Because you are just along for the ride, the ride you get from your Conditioned Mind Patterns. The ad says "Just say No," but if there wasn't any conditioning you wouldn't have to say NO. You just wouldn't do it. So get off the merry-go-round.

You see, it is not just the way it is, and you are not just the way you are. You can say that if you want to and continue to be controlled by your Conditioned Mind, or you can learn how to change the conditioning, and really take control of your life. You really do have a choice, you may not choose to make it, but you still have it.

I would do things that I didn't want to do and not understand why I was doing them. I would bet thousands of dollars on football games and

45

have ten dollars in my pocket. Or I would go to the racetrack and bet every penny I had, only to lose all my money and be broke for the weekend. Then the lying and scheming would begin and I would use anybody I needed to. And who told me to behave in this manner but my own mind. Take a long hard look at this. Learn to understand how your mind is at the center of every decision. Understand there is no one to blame for the way your life is except yourself. Look how your ego attaches to anything that it thinks it needs, even if the thing is destructive. It doesn't matter whether it's a substance or behavioral, it will use whatever it needs for its survival.

At my father's restaurant, there were many pleasurable resources that were there to be used at my disposal. Many of us are conditioned to think that acquiring these pleasures are the keys to happiness, but they actually wound up being the very things that were causing my problems. Again and again, the vicious cycle spins. My ability to maintain a certain lifestyle, with an endless supply of resources, was a problem that kept me locked into my conditioning a lot longer than I would have been, had those resources not been available to me. This is a key factor in keeping many of us unaware of our Conditioned Mind Patterns. Hiding behind success or using money as a measure of self-worth, makes it very easy to not look at what is really going on in our life.

I lived this unexamined life until my father sold his restaurant in 1986. Once the restaurant was sold, it really put a hindrance on my vast supply of resources. The problem was I was both physically and mentally addicted to them. When situations change and the demands exceed the supply, the I Self will do anything to get the needed supply to satisfy the demand. Whatever it takes, it will do. This led me to the next part of my life which I call The Fall of My Empire.

CHAPTER 4

The Fall of My Empire;
The Adult Years

I use the word addiction mostly to refer to the attachment to the I Self. We focus on the glaring substances, or behaviors that sustain our unhealthy lifestyle, and we say this is addiction, but we ignore the less subtle Conditioned Mind Patterns because they don't seem as glaring. The less subtle ones are just accepted because they are not obvious. But they control us as much as the glaring ones do. Either way, whether they are glaring or not, we are controlled by them, and we indulge them at the cost of our happiness and freedom.

What the Mind Calls "Reality"

The common denominator here is, that a great range of substances or conditioned responses are all used as a coping mechanism to deal with a reality, created only through our conditioning. Whether we feel compelled to drink alcoholically or to become an athletic or financial success, we are still in the grip of a Conditioned Mind Pattern. The key here is to understand that when the conditioning was formed, it trained us to use whatever it could to satisfy a craving that was created through these Conditioned Mind

Patterns. Just because it isn't a debilitating addiction doesn't mean we are not being controlled by our Conditioned Mind.

The mind creates all of this and calls it reality, but whose reality is it? The addiction to the physical is real, but the reason for the addiction is not. You are not physically addicted to anything before it is ingested, so where does the need to ingest a substance come from? It comes from a need to satisfy a never-ended craving, to satisfy a never-ending desire created in the mind. This craving takes on many forms, and takes so many people to their graves.

This craving causes suffering if it isn't fulfilled, and this same craving causes suffering if it is fulfilled. This suffering is caused by the delusion that things need to be a certain way in order for us to be happy. And if they aren't, or even if they are, we suffer. So if things are the way we want them, the delusions makes us think we are happy. But eventually things have to change; such is the nature of life, and this causes us to suffer. When things aren't the way we want them, our I Self can't handle it, so what usually follows is an eruption of our ego. Either way, we are never satisfied.

We all pursue fulfillment of our cravings; the only differences are the things we use and the degree to which we use them. This is the reason our Mind Patterns are formed; to satisfy our never-ending desire to have things a certain way, a way that we think will bring us happiness; a way that is pursued by everyone.

A state of constant craving is the only way our I Self (the ego) can survive. Some of us get so depressed by constant suffering and craving of relief, that the only alternative is suicide. We can't take this lightly, this is real. This is what was happening to me. Even though I didn't know it, my I Self was doing whatever it needed to do to survive. It will even kill itself and bring about its own annihilation, if that's what's necessary; if that's what the conditioning demands. It would seem that suffering is what our conditioning was developed for.

Living from this conditioning makes for a very unhappy existence. Even if you think your life is okay, which it may be, if you are barely conscious, you will never experience what it is to be truly free, until you understand how controlled you really are. Deep down inside, no matter what you accomplish or attain, you will never be at total peace because of your attachment to your I Self. This I Self deceives us into believing that there's no other way to live. It makes us believe that we are in control — but are we?

Just About Unemployable

I was now twenty-six and my father sold his restaurant. I tried working for the new owners, but that lasted about a week. I couldn't stop drinking because of the way my conditioning controlled my life. I was just about unemployable, so I quit. Unfortunately, with my low self-esteem, I always worked in the restaurant for my father because it was safe. I never had the courage to venture out and try new things; besides, the restaurant was my empire.

I never really developed any skills. I was conditioned to always take the easier, softer way in life, and that is what I did. So I just worked in the restaurant and continued to satisfy my incessant cravings, just to survive. The problem this presented was that, although I had an ego the size of a Zeppelin, my self-worth was nonexistent.

The truth was I couldn't get through a day of work doing the basic things required in a restaurant, without taking some form of substance. This is what I had become. Not that I wanted to be this way, but it's the way it was. My I Self became more operational than my true self, the self that was there at the beginning of my life, and all through the havoc my I Self created. As this I Self pushed my true self more and more into the background, my self-worth diminished more and more because I become less and less in touch with reality, with truth. Since my I Self is not real, in the sense that there is no real substance to it, and its key ingredient is delusion, what did I have to draw on in a time of crisis, or in a time of real need in this state of delusion? Nothing there is real, so I had nothing to draw on. This was the reason I had no self-worth.

So now I was unemployed, and the whole purpose of my life to this point, had been in fulfilling my desires to satisfy my I Self. None of my desires was to benefit anyone but myself and those desires weren't really a benefit for me either. I was twenty-six, unemployed and living at home. My downward trend was now like a whirlpool. I had a hard time facing my parents, so I would isolate myself in the basement until no one was home. Then I would sneak into the house to take a shower and change my clothes. I just didn't want to face anybody. I would avoid confrontation as much as possible. I had the attitude that if everyone left me alone I would be okay. If there wasn't any confrontation, then that worked out just as well as if everybody was leaving me alone. I embraced isolation, but inside I would have given anything to experience love. That is what my heart was yearning for.

Not realizing how I was hurting the people who loved me, I found my life was a mess, I had no idea how this had occurred, or if I could do anything to change it. I really tried to change things, but it never worked out. Things were destined to remain just the way they were. That's exactly what I believed at the time. This self-destructive direction my life was taking was strictly this way due to the mind-based sense of my I Self being stuck as my mind's default setting. Ever since I was a child, these make-believe fears and desires just went round and round in my head. I built my walls to deal with these fears, and I constantly tried to keep them from arising and tried to fill my world with pleasure. It was always about satisfying me. The pleasure that I was seeking was always at the expense of others. So here I was twenty-six, living in the self-created prison of my mind, lonely within the created walls of my Conditioned Mind Patterns, miserable and afraid.

I had no idea what was going to happen next. Fear had me in its grip, and the only thing I could do was go to the neighborhood bar and drink until the noise in my head would stop. It took a lot of alcohol to quiet the noise, but it was the only way I could get through the day.

A Sudden Death

The restaurant was sold in September of 1986. November of that same year my oldest brother Nunzie, died suddenly, at the age of thirty. The cause of his death was attributed to a heart condition he had, that no one knew about. The only thing I want to say about that is, his lifestyle didn't make for a harmonious life for someone with a heart condition.

I can't say if my brother had an addiction problem or not, but I do know he lived life in the fast lane, and that had a large influence on some of the decisions I made early in my life. I was attracted to the way he lived, and I wanted to be like him. He always had big cars, like a red Lincoln Continental, and gold Cadillac Eldorado. He wore nice clothes, silk suits in the latest styles. He always had beautiful girlfriends. It seemed he was always broke, but yet, he always had money. To a large degree I did become like him — but fortunately, *I didn't die.* His death was the springboard that pushed me into seeking help.

I always looked up to my brother, Nunzie. We had a lot of fun together. He was a big Frank Sinatra fan and one day we went to a restaurant in New York and actually met him. It was pretty cool. Happy times like this were becoming pretty much nonexistent. I didn't get into trouble every time I drank alcohol, but every time I got into trouble, it was associated with drinking alcohol. Needless to say, my brother's death shook the entire family.

At the time of his death, in the frame of mind I was stuck in, I was of no support to my family. I dealt with his death the only way that I knew how; find something to hide my feelings behind, so I didn't have to deal with it. Use the skills that had been developed to build up my walls. As I recall, my family even had to come and get me from a bar; what an epitome of self-centeredness. My parents actually said to me that they "always thought it would have been me who they'd have gotten that call for." All I could say was: "Not me, I would never let that happen." It was pure insanity to even think I had control over such a thing. That's the thing about being unaware that the mind is conditioned; you aren't in control, but you think you are.

Although I am accountable for my actions, I understand now how I was not responsible for them. How could I be? I was being controlled by a force (my mind) that I didn't understand. A force that had been conditioned by so many influences, that the real me underneath didn't have a chance.

Should I really hold myself responsible for something which I had no control over?

When the mind is conditioned to react to things in a certain way, how can we hold ourselves responsible, and for that matter how can we hold anyone else responsible for what is done? People, including myself, just do what we are conditioned to do. You don't know what you don't know. All behavior is learned, and until one learns how to re-train the mind to operate from a place of love, not much internally will change. You can change a lot of things on the outside that will present the facade that you are changing, but the only true change comes when a person learns how to love. You learn how to love when you learn to stop reacting to life from the Conditioned Mind Patterns, and you allow what is here to be. I often joke that I only made five mistakes in my whole life, but I made them over and over. My Conditioned Mind Patterns controlled my life, so this was not far from the truth.

Everyone Read Me the Riot Act

After my brother passed, I continued living with my parents. They told me they'd had enough of my antics, and if I wanted to continue on the path of self-destruction and kill myself, they didn't have to watch me do it. So they gave me an ultimatum and tried what some folk call tough love: Do something about my drinking problem, or get out of their house. The choice was mine. Although my real problem was my I Self, to my parents, drinking was my problem, it was, to a degree — at least that's what it seemed.

A couple of weeks before my brother's death I started working construction for one of the few people left in my life who tolerated my self-centered behavior. The job included medical benefits. I didn't want to be homeless, so I decided to go to a rehabilitation center to get my parents off my back. I had no knowledge whatsoever about what I was getting into. So off I went. I was in this rehab center for twenty-eight days. For me it was an eye-opening experience, but not to the point where I was willing to change my whole life. I got an education about what addiction was, but I didn't understand how most of anything they said in rehab applied to me.

So it wasn't long after I returned to my parent's house that I just picked up where I left off.

When There Is Nowhere Else to Turn

Very few people really understand what is needed for a complete transformation of our spirit. A steep degree of ego deflation and high degree of intention are required for the most difficult undertaking that a person may ever do in his or her life. Most of us won't do it. Through our conditioning, we'd rather keep pursuing what we know, than start down the road of the unknown. We will only go down the road of the unknown if it is absolutely necessary. Only after all our other options have been expunged, and there is no where else to turn will we start looking within for our answers. Up until we get to this point with our conditioning in place, we will always look outside for our answers. We just aren't allowed to look within. And it is our own mind that keeps us from our answers; as long as the Conditioned Mind Patterns are in place. Our egoic mind has to operate like this, it is a must. For it not to do so it would have to look inside for its answers, and that would cause its own destruction.

Understanding this now, I see how my entrenched Conditioned Mind Patterns remained in place, regardless the twenty eight day stay in the rehab center. All the defense mechanisms I had developed to cope with life were not going to change because I took a break for twenty-eight days. I could have gone away for twenty-eight years, and unless something happened to reveal that it was my Conditioned Mind Patterns that had to change, I had no chance, but to continue using my developed solutions to life.

The next two years were really a struggle, because I was being fully controlled by my Conditioned Thinking. Now, though, I had some awareness (just a little) due to the education I received at the rehab center. There were periods where I was actually not drinking or using any mood altering substances. During these periods I would feel great, but eventually the Conditioned Mind Patterns would flare up and BAM, the cycle would start again. It would always start with one drink, maybe a quart of beer at lunch. Maybe I would have another quart on the way home. I would do this for a couple of days, and then the compulsion to drink would set in, and I was off on another spree. I would miss work, not go home, and the worse thing of all, I was blacking out almost every time I drank. It was the only way I could be free of the guilt and remorse I was feeling. None of this would have ever occurred had I had the ability, through an understanding of my Conditioned Mind Patterns, not to take the first drink. But my Conditioned Mind Patterns still saw alcohol as the main solution to my life's problems.

Finally my friend at the construction company had enough and fired me. I was in and out of my parent's house during this time. I was allowed to stay there during the periods of abstinence from drinking. I periodically attended twelve-step program meetings, which showed me there were others who struggled as I did, but I was still steeped in my conditioning. Even though my coping tools weren't working so well, they were all I had. Since I was still being controlled by my Conditioned Mind Patterns I was still operating under the spell of the mind-based sense of my I Self. Self-centeredness breeds self-centeredness.

A Symptom, Not the Cause

Many events took place in this two-year period. By attributing the cause of my problems to alcohol, I concluded that all I needed to do was stop drinking. One would think that this would be the answer, but it was not. It would take me twenty years to learn this. One year after my twenty-thousand-dollar-rehab stay, in a luxurious setting complete with swimming pool and tennis courts, I found myself in another rehabilitation center. During this period I was dating my future wife, Maureen. Her mother helped me get into this rehab. This one was run by the State of New Jersey, and this time I was admitted to a rehab center for indigents.

I did another twenty-eight days in this rehab center. When I came home, in no time I was behaving the same old way, doing the same old things. So long as I lived from my Conditioned Mind, this was the only possible result. Changing for the betterment of self will occur only when conscious steps are taken to cultivate change. If I am not doing what is needed to bring about change, it simply won't happen. Although I was attending twelve-step meetings after the rehab with more regularity, I still hadn't gotten to the point where I was one hundred percent willing to try a different way of life. The insanity and chaos in my life continued for about ten more months.

Part of the problem that kept me locked into my old, habitual way of thinking had been my conditioned beliefs. Our mind uses different Conditioned Mind Patterns to construct different beliefs. Such beliefs become our limitations to true freedom, and they keep us locked into the bondage of our I Self. Mind Patterns employ such constructs in whatever way is necessary, to block out emotional pain. Our Conditioned Mind will use a construct of God in this way. It makes us look for some God outside of ourselves, which we can use to make our world fit nicely into a comfortable little self-created box. Or our Conditioned Mind will use God so we have something to blame for our troubles and the troubles of the world; all constructs that limit our ability to know what is *truly* going on.

Living a Make-Believe Life

We invent our world around this so-called deity that can't be seen. We build a make-believe life around a make-believe God so we can have a make-believe purpose. When it is said to "do the next right thing," we think this God is happy with us because we are doing the next right thing — whatever we create that to be. And because God is happy with us, we will go to heaven. I don't know where or even if there is a heaven, but I do know because of the limitations caused by my beliefs, created by my Conditioned Mind, I was living in an I Self-created Hell.

I was now twenty-seven years old, and I was bartending in a neighborhood bar. I knew my life was in complete disarray, and I still didn't have a clue why this was so, even after the rehab. I wasn't living in my parent's house anymore because they asked me to leave again, but this time they were not letting me back in unless I stopped drinking for good. I always had the intention to stop drinking for good, but it never lasted — because I never stopped for me. There was always some condition associated with my stopping. It was either to get back into my parent's house or to get them or someone else off my back. But this was about to change.

I was sleeping wherever I could, mostly over at the bar owner's house. He was kind enough to put me up. I would often sleep in the bar and open it in the morning. My relationship with Maureen at this time was turbulent to say the least, but for reasons unknown to me; she never fully cut our ties. I was living this merry-go-round life, without the ability to stop it, so I could get off.

"Something Has Got to Change"

One day, which was no different than any other day, just like that, for no particular reason, I woke up and a thought popped into my head that "Something has got to change." At this point I knew I had enough. I was tired; tired of the struggle, tired of the fight. Tired of what my life had become. I gave up. I knew the way I was living was not working too well, and I became willing to try a different way.

That willingness was the key to the change that was about to take place; without it no change would have occurred, no matter how limited it was. A new direction for my life was about to begin. Although I didn't know it at the time, I was about to change my entire existence. I would change from a course of self-destruction to cultivating the true grounds for change. When something like this occurs it is a modern-day miracle.

CHAPTER 5

The Delusions of a Conditioned Mind

Since my old way of living wasn't working, I finally become willing to try something different; pain will do that to a person. I started attending the twelve-step-program meetings every chance I got. I would attend between seven and ten of those meetings a week. If anyone would have asked me at the time if my old way of living was done, I would have told them, most assuredly, yes. I didn't think I would ever go back to living the way I did. Little did I know the only thing that changed was one of the solutions my Conditioned Mind developed, wasn't being used as a mechanism to cope with life anymore. All I did was substitute using a substance as my solution with something different.

New Cravings: Surprise, Surprise

Now I was going to meetings and my cravings switched from drinking to meetings. It was definitely a healthier substitute, but a substitute just the same. My coping skills were still dictated by my Conditioned Mind Patterns, it just wasn't using a substance as one of its coping mechanisms.

I did stop drinking, and I haven't had any alcohol since June 18, 1987. But my Conditioned Mind Patterns were still in control. When a person is controlled by Condition Mind Patterns, if the conditioning is not identified, nothing will change. Jesus himself could have tried to help me, but as long as I was being controlled by my Conditioned Mind Patterns, the results remained the same. This is a Conditioned Mind Pattern Law, not really. ☺

Twelve-step programs are an excellent source of strength and support for people who want help, because they develop awareness of the Conditioned Mind Patterns. This awareness leads to liberation of bondage from your I Self. The Twelve Steps are one way to teach what those Conditioned Mind Patterns are, how they've operated in your life, and how you can be released from their hold.

The first step addresses the main substance that's become the escape mechanism. The remaining eleven steps are designed to help participants determine what their other coping mechanisms are; when we discover, one by one, all the forms of our bondages, we become more able to live from our true self and stop living from our I Self.

As my recovery process continued I went to meetings for support and camaraderie. I was getting involved in the twelve-step program and helping others, to the best of my ability. I was doing this for me. Not to get back into my parent's house or to get anyone off my back. I wanted to do this, and I was doing what was necessary to attain this state. I was living again at my parent's house, and they began to trust me. I actually got a job. Maureen and I maintained our relationship through all of this, and we started seeing more and more of each other. For the first time in a long time there was some semblance of stability in my life. I was doing all the things I thought were necessary to improve my life. And my life was improving, on the outside.

I was attending about ten meetings a week, and I became very involved in the program. I also started exercising regularly. I was very busy, so there wasn't much idle time on my hands. I was doing great, or so I thought. Unbeknownst to me, the changes that were occurring were of an outer nature only. There is nothing wrong with this, but when one has a problem of an inner nature, as I did, and the changes that are made are external, the problem doesn't go away. Outside, it appeared that I was doing much better. One day all this outer stuff would not be enough for me to sustain a contented existence.

I understood my malady intellectually as physical, mental and spiritual, but I didn't grasp this at the heart level. So despite recovery from alcoholic drinking, my Mind Patterns persisted. In the midst of recovery I got into an argument with my father. I was feeling pretty smug about myself; I'd been abstinent from alcohol about five months. And I developed this little chip on my shoulder. While I should have been grateful just for having a roof over my head, I was not. I don't remember exactly what the argument was about, but he told me point blank: if I didn't like it there I could leave. I wasn't making much money at the time, so I wasn't about to leave voluntarily. I realized I needed to keep my mouth shut, and I was allowed to stay.

Clearly, I wasn't changing on the inside. I wasn't really learning about myself. I stayed controlled by the Conditioned Mind Patterns. I was still the person I had always been; I just wasn't using mood-altering substances as my coping mechanism. I was using other mechanisms to cope with life. As I see it now, the outer progress I was attaining just deterred me from seeing what was really going on: The default setting of my Conditioned Mind was still very much intact. I wasn't having nearly as many problems as before because I wasn't under the influence of alcohol. But my life was still out of control.

At that point, instead of being totally immersed in my Conditioned Mind, I experienced occasional flare-ups. As in the incident with my father, the flare-up was brief and soon extinguished. I never explored or understood why it occurred in the first place so they were never truly extinguished. And so it went for roughly the next twenty years.

The twelve-step program has methods in place that help people learn and change behavior problems, but since I only understood it at the intellectual level, my change was minimal. As I continued my abstinence from all mood-altering substances, I kept attaining more material possessions and so my life kept getting better . . . so I thought. These material possessions became the gauge for my success. The only thing abstinence from alcohol ensures is: if you are abstinent you can't get drunk and, therefore, the troubles caused by inebriation go away. It's impossible to get a ticket for drunk driving, or have an alcohol-related accident or incident if you're not drinking alcohol. Life just naturally gets better, on the outside.

The Seven Deadly Sins and Anger

I didn't understand that my behavior was still driven by Conditioned Mind Patterns, which I have come to see as the defects of greed, lust, envy, sloth, jealousy, gluttony, pride, and anger. I still didn't understand why I acted the way I did. I do know this; I always looked outside for an answer, never inside. I never discovered what triggered my flare-ups. I was studying the twelve-steps to the best of my ability, but I was only addressing the events themselves that had taken place in the past; I never looked at the cause of those events. I memorized the twelve-steps and as stated earlier I understood them intellectually, but they never reached my heart. My heart remained closed and my thinking remained anchored to the mind-based sense of my I Self as its default setting.

After a year of being on this path, an acquaintance from my neighborhood offered me an application for a promising job that had the potential to become a new career. This was just one of the many benefits of this new way of living. I am currently at the same job, twenty-three years later and counting. I work for a Public Utility. How ironic that the same course that I feared so many years ago, the Theory of Electricity, was required for my current job. And when someone took the time and showed me how to do it, I passed with flying colors.

This job has been a great boon, but also just another outside measure of my success. Remember, the ego is only as happy as its most recent attainment. My life was run by my ego, and this is the reason I was never grateful for anything, because my ego was never satisfied. The egos nature is to want. You can be grateful only when you are content with what you have, not with what you are going to get. Wanting is not from our true self, this is our I Self doing what it does best.

Until I understood this, I couldn't be happy. It was not the true me that had flare ups or lived the way I did. Be real. Who would choose to think and act in this manner? If I had a choice, do you think I would have chosen to be ungrateful and ignorant? Not unless I was mentally ill or programmed by a Conditioned Mind. I just did what I knew how to do, nothing more nothing less. Not a good or bad choice, not the right or wrong choice; there wasn't any choice.

Anger, Apologies . . . and More Apologies

Here's another incident that illustrates how my conditioning still ruled me. I was still living with my parents and decided to cook dinner for six people. There was Maureen, my sister Anne, who was bringing a five-year-old girl with her, and two other people. I was making pasta with beans in red sauce. The little girl wanted plain pasta. I freaked out for no apparent reason. I started ranting and raving about how you need the right amount of pasta for a certain amount of beans. This all occurred instantly; all she did was ask for plain pasta. I didn't go through any thought process. I just had a reaction. There is no precise recipe for what I was cooking. This reaction was just a story created instantly by a Conditioned Mind Pattern.

Needless to say, everyone got up, looked at me as if I were crazy, which I was and left. Here I was with two pounds of pasta in a bowl, a nice salad, which I had taken care to make, a table set for six people, sitting alone, trying to justify how I reacted. Did I choose this reaction? Was this a choice that I made? Did I want to act like a raving lunatic? I think not. I eventually got up and did say I was sorry to everyone. And we all sat down and enjoyed the dinner. The little girl even got her bowl of plain pasta.

This typifies the kind of incidents that occurred over the next twenty years; different circumstances, but the same self-centered reaction. Another time, for example, at work our cleaning woman brought two dozen custard cups for all of us to enjoy. There were four of us on a shift. We each ate a few. One of the men was going to take some custard cups home with him.

Well, I planned on taking them home, and when they went missing I lost my temper and made a fool of myself. Whenever things didn't go the way I planned I would always react in anger. So here I go again, apologizing for the way I acted. These reactions were automatic; they occurred without thinking. This happened more than I care to remember; my Conditioned Mind Patterns were always in control.

Since I never understood why these flare-ups occurred, it always seemed they would just happen. Whenever there was an association to something that activated a Conditioned Mind Pattern, a flare up would occur. The association is the trigger. It doesn't make a person react only negatively; such associations also entice us to seek pleasure. Your association with a given object, circumstance, or being, produced by a Conditioned Mind Pattern, compels you to want it. You feel, "I must have it." This is the same Conditioned Mind Pattern that produces anger, but this other type of association uses pleasure. We all have too many associations to manage, so working on any one in particular is not going to do the trick. For a flare up not to occur, the Conditioned Mind Pattern itself needs to be changed. You will need to recognize the associations and identify the Conditioned Mind Pattern in order for them to change.

Trying to Fill the Void

Do you see how deeply seated the Conditioned Mind Patterns are, and how they hold you in captivity to the I Self? The whole nature of the Conditioned Mind Patterns is to satisfy an I Self that feels a sense of lack; a lack that it will try to fill, one way or another. This lack is the energy that causes the Conditioned Mind Pattern to be formed. It was this sense of lack that was controlling my reactions.

I have come to understand that flare ups occur because our ego, operating through our Conditioned Mind Patterns, doesn't allow us to flow with the energy of life. So it either erupts in the present or is stored, waiting for a future trigger to activate it, so a flare up can occur. But whether it manifests now or later, a Conditioned Mind Pattern is being formed.

When these flare-ups do occur and our ego attaches to them, the story in the head starts and the drama begins. Once a Conditioned Mind Pattern is activated all sorts of things happen. We go through many different emotions. Feelings arise that cause us to justify our actions, which present themselves in any form that is necessary for the situation: Anger, rage, jealously, pride . . . . The list of capabilities for the undisciplined mind is endless.

It starts with a thought. If that thought is allowed to pass through — and by 'passing through' I mean that we do not attach to it — then that's it, you're free. If not, the next step is it starts to attach to the ego, which creates the story. It then has to run its course until it reaches a conclusion. It will then return to your psyche to become more engrained. The Mind Pattern will be that much easier to activate next time there is an association. And it will become much more difficult to let the energy pass through. You will attach to the thought and let the Conditioned Mind Pattern form, or you will not attach to the thought and allow the energy to pass through.

Embers and Ashes of the Ego

In short, even though everything quiets down during recovery from substance abuse, it only seems like the big fire is out. The embers of the ego are just waiting for the right condition to arise so they can flare up again. This happens again and again, due to the deep-seated Conditioned Mind Patterns, which have been developing in our psyche since the day we started our existence. Conditions arise; we react the only way we know, hoping to protect ourselves; the story starts; it runs its course, dies down, and then it lies in waiting for the next set of circumstances to activate our Conditioned Mind, so it can flare up again. It will never go out completely until we learn (and it has to be learned) to extinguish the ego's embers for good.

This is a problem because the ego creates havoc as it runs its course. There are too many scenarios to write on paper. This affects not just the life of the individual having the flare up, but the life of everyone associated with the individual. It's truly mind boggling. If you are honest with yourself, you will understand how many people are affected by a simple act like driving a car. How you go through an array of emotions just driving to work, and if your conditioning is deep-seated enough it can erupt into "road rage." All the mind wants is for there not to be any traffic, ever. It gets agitated when somebody is going to make a left turn and you're behind them. It wants everybody driving just the way you want them to. How about red lights? Do you always have to catch every single one? If people just adhered to things the way we wanted them to, driving would never be an issue. But does the driving cause the distress or is it the Conditioned Mind, wanting things to be a certain way? Wanting things a certain way is the cause of our distress.

When we learn to be with what arises instead of listening to our mind trying to arrange everything to its liking, we will be free of the I Self. When we can accept the red lights in life as we do the green ones, we will know we are on the path to freedom.

There are guided meditations that can be used to help you in this adventure of learning to quiet the mind. It doesn't matter whether you lie down, sit in a chair or take whatever position you choose. You just have to be comfortable and make sure you are not disturbed. Listen to what the guided meditation tells you, and practice listening to it until your mind starts to quiet down. You will eventually experience life in a different way if you keep practicing this. This truly is an adventure which, when embarked upon, will bring results beyond your wildest dreams. To be free of attachment is what meditation can lead to. This has been my experience.

CHAPTER 6

Society's Delusions

I was twenty-eight years old at this time and never really accomplished much up to this point of my life. So when I started out on the journey of recovery from addiction, I didn't have much self-esteem. I had no real skills to speak of. All my Creative Energy had always been blocked off by my I Self and I had no idea what I was capable of doing. Whenever challenges arose I would always find ways to deal with them, so I would not be exposed for my self-created inadequacies. Mind you, this is just what went on in my head. It wasn't the truth, but my conditioning led me to believe these lies. I hid behind my Conditioned Mind Patterns facade; lies, lies, and more lies. And if I couldn't tell myself the truth, how was I going to be truthful to anyone else?

<u>Twelve Steps in the Right Direction . . . But Not There Yet</u>
Now, though I was doing things that was helping my sense of self worth. My self-esteem was getting better because I was cooperating with life to a certain degree. Naturally, just by not drinking, things were getting better on the outside. My life on the material level was coming together. I was working at this new job and I bought a car. I'd been dating my future wife for a couple of years, and soon we'd be married. I was very involved in the

twelve-step program. I was doing the things I thought were needed to live a productive life (by society standards). I didn't understand that all this change on the outer level meant little without the understanding that it was the inner change that needed to take place.

I even went through the Twelve Steps, the way they were explained to me by someone who was trying to help me. Unfortunately they didn't have the deep impact on me that they would have twenty years later. At this time I used them strictly as a self-help tool, not a tool to form any connection to life or to my fellows. I knew nothing of any Conditioned Mind Patterns that were controlling the way I behaved.

As life progressed on the material plane, material possessions became my focal point. After four years of my new way of life, I married Maureen. It was a wonderful day in my life. We are still together, and she deserves more credit for this than I. She really is a gift to me, I am grateful for her. The more things I did that adhered to what most other people did, the more I thought I was doing what I was suppose to be doing. I wanted to do these things. I just didn't know my happiness needed to come from within and not from these things.

At the time of my wedding my father was sick. Shortly afterwards he passed away. It was a very sad day indeed, to say the least. To lose the rock of my life was not easy to go through, but I would say to myself that at least he saw me straighten out my life. The mind is very cunning. My father passed away, and my mind was still making it about me. That's how the mind operates. Even when faced with death, we justify things to make ourselves feel better. The mind always looks for ways to bring itself comfort. It constantly tries to arrange things to its liking. It creates delusions; it's the greatest magician we will ever know. The delusions created are the delusions we live by.

Look how we react to death. When we attend funerals, we cry, but who are we crying for, not the individual who has passed, they do not even know we are there. Maybe the family does, but look how quickly we move on with our lives. We cry because we want things to be in some other way. People die, it is a fact of life, but we don't like to talk about it because it shows how impermanent our little world really is. We would rather ignore death than face the reality that we are going to die one day, we just don't know when. Our egos don't like to face truth, so we make up all kinds of cliché's to make ourselves feel better. That is the only reason these clichés exist; to make ourselves feel better. If a person is old and they pass away, we say things like "They lived a good life," or if they are sick, we will say something like, "At least they are not suffering anymore." But in reality, who are we saying that for? Who are we comforting?

"It's All Their Fault!"

I was married about a year when we started looking for a house. For me this exemplified the next step in my outer process of becoming a productive member of society. On the inside, I knew it was more important to buy our own home because this would allow me to isolate and be less involved with other people. We were living in a four-family house and I was having a difficult time with it: I had no control over what the other families did. One family would constantly smoke marijuana on the front porch. How could they; didn't they know I was in recovery? The reality of the situation was, I was envious and would have given anything to be able to do what they were doing, if I could have gotten away with it. I knew I would have lost all I had acquired up to this point, if I'd given into that desire.

Another family would put their garbage in the hallway for hours and it would really smell terrible. I couldn't stand it, but I didn't know how to constructively interact with people, or how to handle confrontation very well. I would just stuff my feelings deep down inside, instead of confronting someone, which would create resentments. I knew how to handle my resentments, by pointing the finger at others. We needed to buy a house as quickly as possible, so I could get away from what I was feeling, and stuff them as far down in my psyche as they would go. My solution was as before: fix an internal problem with an outside solution. This was no different. My mind created this. It made me believe that if I changed the things that were bothering me, I would be happy. This is the delusion the mind creates. Unfortunately at that point in my life, wherever I went, there I was.

Blaming Others for Our Unhappiness

This is just a part of our Conditioned Mind Patterns, to keep blaming others for our inner discontentment. I was blaming the other people in the house for my unhappiness. This is how our delusions are created, looking outside for answers; the looking itself is the delusion. I don't know if I really wanted to buy a house, but I knew I wanted to get away from these people because it was their fault I was not happy. So if my living arrangements changed, then I would be happy, so I thought.

We found a house and moved in, fourteen months after being married. No more four — family house, but now there are neighbors. Not many issues arise. We are far enough apart that what we do doesn't really affect one another, so my ego was in check as far as that was concerned. Work was a different story altogether. My people skills were very limited, which is to say, if people just left me alone or if they did what I wanted them to do, I was okay. But when they didn't, my Conditioned Mind Patterns became activated.

I used people my whole life for my benefit. So I never developed an ability to cooperate with others. My own inadequacies just kept isolating me from others. All because when a person lives as an isolated individual he or she lives from only the I Self. It blocks any unity we can have with another human being. When the ego is in control of life it makes you believe there isn't anything that you need from another person unless it is to benefit you. As long as you are operating from the I Self and not the true self there can be nothing, but separateness between individuals. That's the way it has to be, there can be no unity, no compassion, no real love for anyone, including yourself.

Owning a Home Will Keep You Busy

I was thirty-three now. I had not had any alcohol or any other substance, for five years, but I was still reacting to others with many of the character traits that had been developed over those drinking and my so-called partying years. I seemed to be better than I'd been, but that was due mostly to staying busy more than to any inner change. Owning a home will keep you busy. That is part of the dilemma; when you are busy there isn't much time to look at yourself. But what happens when the busyness stops? Without the diversion of the busyness the Conditioned Mind Patterns take over. Maybe you justify that you deserve a reward for working so hard. So you sit back and take your pleasure, but if you really look into it, you will see the emptiness that the so-called pleasure brings you. Whatever forms the pleasures take, before you know it, it's gone, so now it's time to get busy again.

The mind will try keeping pleasures alive for you. That is what the mind does, it creates Mind Patterns to hold onto things that brought pleasure in the past so it can try and recapture this pleasure over and over. Why do you think the same behavior is repeated again and again? The mind is trying to find things that make you feel good. You wouldn't do things that make you feel bad, or would you? When you are busy this searching does not occur. It is when the busyness ceases that the mind becomes restless and needs to search for the delusion of pleasure.

Look how our mind does things to make us feel good, only to use it against us. The same mind that uses the pursuit of pleasure turns around and then makes you feel guilty for doing what it made you do. Think about it. Use your own circumstances. That's how the mind operates. It creates the delusion of pleasure and then counters it with guilt. It creates the delusion of peace, but the thing that brings you peace is used to cause your discontentment. See this for yourself. As long as you stay busy this doesn't occur.

But what if one day you are forced into inactivity, what will you do then? Hopefully it will not be when most of your life has passed, and you see that all your busyness was just wasted energy. Because you were too busy to take the time to learn not to be controlled by your Conditioned Mind you do not know how to be still. Now what? Learn to truly enjoy the life you have been given because, as I have stated before, "One day it will not be so." My experience has shown me that promotions on my job, a wonderful family life, new cars, vacations, are all good things, but they're not going to put me in harmony with life. These are not the things that will bring happiness. Only when you are free from the hold of your Conditioned Mind Patterns will you enjoy the things attained in life and the happiness you so *truly* desire.

Inner Torment

My inner torment was eating at me most of the time. Not all the time, because when I was preoccupied with some activity at least my mind had another focus. And as long as my mind was busy I didn't think about how I was feeling. I may not have been doing things that were conducive to my spiritual well-being, but it was better than feeling discontented. Being busy creates a diversion, but it doesn't fix the problem. It's only a temporary solution to the problem.

In a new town I was still attending the twelve-step program, but I was not going to as many meetings as before — maybe to only four a week. I was still coping with life through my Conditioned Mind Patterns, so my defense mechanisms were firmly in place. I was still in the grip to these Conditioned Mind Patterns that nearly destroyed my life, but I was still unaware of this.

I continued to feel great resentment of people, past and present. Someone in the twelve-step program suggested that I do two of the steps that directly deal with other people: "Made a list of people we harmed and become willing to make amends to them all," and: "Made direct amends to such people wherever possible, except when to do so would injure them or others." I became willing to do this. I mention this because willingness is so vital in our process.

I paid back everyone I owed money to. I met with people I had harmed and made amends. I felt better, and I was glad that was over with. I thought I would never have to do that again, but I was wrong. Because the Conditioned Mind doesn't need a substance to be self-centered, it was just using other things to create drama in my life. There wasn't nearly as much drama as when my life was consumed by alcohol and drugs, but there was drama nonetheless.

I had willingness, but my lack of understanding kept me ignorant to what caused me, and causes many of us, to suffer unnecessarily. Needless to say, my list of harmed people grew. When you become a productive member of society, it does not necessarily ensure that it is good for you. Materialism is good for society. If not approached with the proper mindset it can lead to bondage and further conditioning. That's what it did to me.

That's why this is not about merely changing our thinking from negative to positive. The positive can be a block just as much as the negative; if you're using it to form your identification. If you're using the positive to make a construct of who you are, then you will think you can create your sense of well-being. Through the Conditioned Mind Patterns, whether it is positive or negative, this is what most of us have been trying to do our entire life.

Ignorance and Suffering

It is through sheer ignorance that we do the things that cause us to suffer. Who would choose to suffer? But if you don't know there is a choice, then there isn't a choice . . . and you suffer in ignorance. I'm not talking major issues here. Suffering is very subtle. How about just not wanting to get up in the morning? Or complaining because it's snowing outside and you have to shovel it. Or talking politics? Or working out six or seven days a week because you think if you look good, and enough people tell you that you look good, then you must be "doing good". This is all part of the delusion created to make you think you are okay. What would happen if you got hurt and couldn't workout, would you still be doing okay? Or would you suffer because you can't workout anymore? Our suffering is always caused by not accepting what is and wanting things to be different.

The mind can't look inward to find an answer without practice and that is why it constantly looks outside. Your true sense of well-being can come to you only when your mind is quiet. If you do a good job at work, is that everything that defines you? What happens when you make a mistake, then who are you? Your true sense of purpose isn't derived from anything that you do. It is derived from the stillness that only comes when you learn to quiet the mind. Our I Self needs a purpose for existence. The true self does not, because it exists whether you have a created mind purpose or not. A created purpose is a created delusion.

One day we are living on this planet, and then one day we are not. What goes on in between and why? The mind constantly tries to figure this out. Since I'm trying to stick to my experience I can't say what will happen to me when I die, nor am I really concerned. I don't really know which of the religions has it right, maybe they all do, and maybe none of them do. I do know this though; I have studied teaching of Jesus, of Buddha, of Hinduism, of Taoism and many others. I have read many different books on different philosophies and religions. What I have found is so long as the default setting of my mind is self-centered; my life will be a struggle. I must learn to understand and control my mind so its default setting becomes one of love. I do not have to believe anything to understand this. The only obstacle to my freedom is looking and waiting for something on the outside to fill an inner need, and that will never happen.

It wasn't until I started doing the meditation practice necessary to allow these great teachings to infiltrate my life, that my mind became quiet enough, so I was able to understand the teachings and what was really going on inside me. I really started understanding what I was reading. Knowledge was becoming wisdom. I didn't make this quote up, but I use it often: "I have met the enemy and it is me." To me, this about says it all.

In a Hundred Years, This World Will Have Different People

After I was married for three years I felt the need to really conform to society's standard by starting a family. I had a wife, the career job, a house, a car, no dog or white picket fence, but I was on my way. So it was time for children. I don't mean to sound glib, or to devalue any of these blessings. My loved ones and my home are very important to me. But when I first sought them I didn't understand their value. They were the basis of my life, to the measure of my existence and progress. I have since learned that things, circumstances, even loved ones, will never bring the inner fulfillment that I was seeking, no matter how many wonderful things

happen. Remember this, that one day you will be separated from then
All is impermanent, whether you like it or not. In one hundred years,
or take a handful of people, this entire world will have different people on
it; billions of people, all different, Only our memory will be alive and that
will only last until the last person who remembers us dies. So what is it
that you are holding onto that you think is so important?

As my life progressed I didn't give much thought to what was
happening. I was just following the path I thought would lead to a successful
life. Materially I was doing what was needed to become the productive
member of society that I saw other successful people become, but this is a
measurement of society's, not one that will necessarily bring happiness.

The Good Life

My wife and I are now blessed with a daughter and she is beautiful.
I've been abstinent from all substances for seven years. I'm thirty-six.
My external world is going well, but my behavior is still based in self-
centeredness, so I am not doing things that are conducive to my spiritual
well-being. I am still gambling, frequenting pornography web sites, and
doing whatever it was I needed to do to satisfy the cravings created by my
Conditioned Mind Patterns. I am as happy as I could be with my life being
controlled by my Conditioned Mind Patterns. My outer life is exactly the
way I wanted it, but for reasons not yet known to me, my inner life is still
a struggle.

Besides my family and colleagues, there weren't many other people
in my inner circle. I wasn't even attending all the twelve-step meetings I
told my wife I was attending because most of the time I didn't go inside.
I started smoking cigars and often stayed outside. I barely attended, until
I wasn't going in at all. At least when I attending meetings regularly I
wasn't all caught up in my self-centeredness. I may have used meetings
largely as diversionary solution, but without them I was totally consumed
by my I Self.

So without the meetings my Conditioned Mind Patterns retained
complete control of my life; how could they not? All my actions or reactions

73

came from the mind-based sense of my I Self. Every decision had my I Self at its core. It would appear that I was doing things for people, but how was that possible? I didn't know this at the time, but when I look back, and when I do it is for reflection purposes only, I can see how a person is either God-centered or self-centered, and at that time in my life there was no God. Need I say more?

Two years after my daughter started her existence, we were blessed with a son. Now life was complete, by the measurement of society. We had a girl and a boy. What more could anyone ask for? Yet inside I was still missing the final piece of the puzzle, I didn't know where to find it or what it was. I was never at peace with myself. I was okay with my outer life, but not with my inner life. I was still looking for that inner peace, but I didn't know how to attain it. To my dismay, the Conditioned Mind Patterns that I had cultivated and developed to cope with life were still in charge. I was not doing things to support my life in a healthy way.

Fortunately, I never started drinking again, so the chaos that goes along with that never threatened my family life. I did start playing golf, and to say I became obsessed with it would be an understatement. I live a half mile from a golf course and I was playing three to four times a week. When I wasn't playing I was practicing. Since I am a shift worker when I played it didn't affect my family because my wife worked and my children were in school. But I wouldn't tell my wife every time I played because I knew it was excessive. It made me lie, and not only about my score. I felt good only if I played well. Sometimes when I was working the day shift, I would wake up at 3 a.m. and practice for an hour or so before going to work. The point to all of this is to show how golf just became another obsession. It took hold of my mind and controlled me; just like so many others things in my life.

The I Self thoughts, based in my Conditioned Mind Patterns, had to constantly manipulate things to keep the outward appearance of my life looking like I had it all together. This is what the Conditioned Mind has to do. It has to make everyone, including myself, believe that everything's okay. It has to make me believe there's nothing wrong inside me that something from the outside wouldn't fix. That's why I would constantly lie, so I could keep up the appearance that everything was going great. But who was I really lying to?

Is a Cigar Just a Cigar?

By now twelve-step meetings were nonexistent in my life, I now became obsessed with cigars. I will do and use anything to keep my mind busy. I really believed that all I had to do was stop using certain substances. I understand now how going to meetings for support helped me in the beginning, but by never addressing the causes of my behavior, I never understood the hold my mind had on me; how much noise it created to keep me in its grip, to keep the truth out.

Of course, the last thing in the world our mind wants is for us to learn how to quiet it. Why do you think it's so difficult to do? The mind wants control. There is no fight when the mind is in control. You are of no threat to it. But then you learn that if you really want to be free you will need to learn to meditate, so you can learn to understand the inner workings of your mind and allowed it to settle. Quieting your mind will be the most difficult thing you will ever do in your life, but it will also be the most rewarding thing that you will ever do for yourself and for others.

I had a few minor medical procedures done during this period that required pain medication. This was very difficult for me, as one of my previous coping mechanisms was the abuse of pain medication. Although I had taken medication in the past for different ailments, there was never any abuse since I stopped drinking alcohol in 1987, but this was about to change.

The mind will use anything to take away our pain, whether the pain is physical or emotional. We may pick any substance or activity — Vicodin, Codeine, tobacco, nicotine, wine, food, golf, sex, gambling — our conditioning will incorporate it into a craving. So although I initially took the medication as prescribed, it was only a matter of time before I would not. This is not a choice I would have made had I a better understanding of myself. Since I didn't, I used the medication more frequently than had been instructed.

My aliments were legitimate, but I was abusing the amounts of medication I took. This was a very subtle abuse that took years to develop.

I had never really understood how things controlled me, and this left the door open for all kinds of problems. By not understanding the way my Conditioned Mind always used things on the outside to fix an inner problem, my abuse of medication was inevitable. I was so accustomed to being controlled by my Conditioned Mind Patterns; when the time came it just used a substance other than alcohol as a coping mechanism.

Our ego will use whatever the weakest links in our psyche is. Not all people have Conditioned Thinking that gravitates towards anything as devastating as drugs, alcohol or gambling. But if you look closely you will notice something else that has a hold of you, be it work, food, shopping, sex, your appearance, cars, money, prestige — feel free to add your own item to the list. Remember, the substance is irrelevant; the hold it has on you, and how it blocks the ability to love is what matters.

All this was occurring unbeknownst to anyone. I appeared to be controlling everything that was going on. By controlling, all I mean is I would not allow things to totally get out of control. I could not control my conditioning, but I did seem, somehow, not to let things slide to the depths of total despair. I would gamble with only a certain amount of money, and when it was gone I would stop. I never physically cheated on my wife, but I would go on porn sites. When I would steal something it would be with an excuse at hand, to be used if I got caught. An example being: I would put a case of water under the shopping cart in the supermarket. At checkout if anyone would have questioned me I would have said, I forgot it was there. If I didn't get questioned, I would just walk out. All this was done to satisfy a thrill created by my ego. It was never about the thing. It was done to satisfy a craving; the craving of the thrill. Once the craving was fulfilled, it would feel like it never happened; so it was onto the next thrill. It was all to get over, to feel like I was getting away with something. This "get-over" attitude, this "If I don't get caught, then I didn't do it" lie, had been cultivated at a very young age. Today the most important thing for me is: *To thine own self be true.*

I think attending the twelve-step program earlier helped me, even though I'd stopped attending years ago. Their principles did keep me from becoming completely destructive. But since my Conditioned Thinking had me in its grip I only changed somewhat. Without being aware that I was conditioned, I was fighting a losing battle. Although most of what I was going through was in my head, I was now physically dependent on the pain medication. I tried to stop taking it, but I could not.

CHAPTER 7

The Beginning of the End

I never understood the driving energy behind my behavior. From as far back as I can remember I did what was necessary to stop the fear, the loneliness, the feelings of inadequacy, and isolation. Whatever came up inside was alleviated by an outside cure or distraction. I wasn't a bad person; I was just doing what my mind had been conditioned to do. Things could have been different, had I been aware of the conditioning. I don't know what the difference would have been, but I do know that the less a person lives their life from the Conditioned Mind Patterns, the more love that person has; which manifests itself as kindness, peace, understanding, patience, tolerance, unity, and compassion. It's unfortunate, but not many of us are aware to live life from here.

We Don't Change When We Don't Know What Needs Changing
I was forty-five years old and was becoming more and more withdrawn. My Conditioned Mind Patterns were more and more in control of my actions, and reactions to life; almost to the point of my own annihilation. There wasn't any connection to anything in my life that didn't start with the letter "I." The I Self never lost control of me, even though at this time I had been abstinent from alcohol for seventeen years. This is what happens when

all we do is focus on a substance instead of why we need a substance in the first place; we don't change because we don't really understand what needs changing. We can be abstinent for years, but it doesn't mean we've changed. If the I Self is still running the show, there is no change.

It is not very clear to most of us that our behavior is caused by something. We just accept it as it is, saying that's just "the way we are," or "I asked God to remove this or that and it's still there." If that's what you are waiting for, then just accept the way you are because you are not going to change. God is not a magician; the only one that is going to change you is you. The change occurs when you start cooperating with life and learn how to quiet your mind so you can learn to stop acting from your I Self.

You can serve others forever, but if it's from the I Self and not from the heart, it doesn't cultivate love. It may give your life a purpose, but does it make you truly happy, truly free? I was controlled by a mind that constantly convinced me I was seeing "reality." My mind said to me, "I didn't need to look deeper; after all, I had my beliefs, why rock the boat? "If it ain't broke don't fix it . . ." but it being me, was broke, and I just didn't know it.

We can fool ourselves profoundly. If you would take the time to learn how to meditate, you will understand the deep, inner workings of your mind. This discovery will be so beneficial that you will opt never to do without it. You will make it one of, if not the, most important part of your life. You can't learn how to open your heart so you can be filled with love until you learn what is keeping it closed. Do you think you learn that by staying busy?

From my experience, I have found if you learn how to quiet your mind through the discipline of meditation, you will learn things about yourself that you could not have imagined were even there. This has nothing to do with anything materialistic. This is allowing the creativity that has been suppressed for so many years by our Conditioned Mind to arise. It will surface when you learn to be silent and still. Most of us are clueless as to who we truly are. This is not through any fault of ours, but a by-product of ignorance and ignorance alone. There's a whole other dimension to life that most of us never experience because of this ignorance. We shouldn't blame

God for our troubles; we are here on this earth, that's God part, that's the miracle. What is our part in all this?

A Life of Quiet Desperation

My life was picture-perfect on the outside, but inside my I Self and my true self were constantly struggling. This is always what creates our struggle. Without the I Self there would be no struggle. I didn't understand this at this time; I was not happy, and I didn't know why. My entire life was a blessing, yet I didn't feel blessed. My circumstances couldn't have been better, but I felt very little internal peace. I was coping, as many of us do. The innate goodness that is in all of us had not surfaced to my inner being. It was in there somewhere, buried beneath all my mind-generated noise. I was really at wit's end, and I wasn't sure what was going on with me.

I was going to more and more doctors for my so-called ailments. At this point I thought my ailments were real, and I can tell you this, they were real in my head. Our mind can make us believe anything. And there was no one in my life with who I was sharing this, so my stories were validated by no one, but me. To say the least, I was in trouble. My newfound obsession, golf, was not working anymore. I found the only thing more impermanent than life itself was my ability to maintain a consistent golf score. Discontentment was now the normal operating mode of my life, and it was all self-created by my Conditioned Mind.

The only thing that relieved my discontentment was the pain medication, so I was taking it as often as possible. There were times where I would cry out to this imaginary, magical God in heaven somewhere to help me. I would ask why this was happening to me and to please fix me. But how could God help me without my cooperation? When no relief came, because I wasn't doing the things necessary to allow relief, my I Self would just tell me: "See, there is no God, you need to take care of yourself. Take another pill."

I had put all my eggs in one basket, the basket of the material world, and when the basket was dropped, all my eggs broke, and nothing was left. The whole structure of my life was based in this material world so I could attain material possessions for my pleasure; yet they didn't provide anything useful to enhance my spiritual well-being. I felt no fulfillment through anything I owned or because of anything I accomplished. I was as empty inside as I had always been. Do you think this was a choice that I choose to be like this? My Conditioned Mind was spiraling out of control, and I had no idea what I was going to do.

I was looking for peace, but didn't know where to look. That's what the Conditioned Mind Patterns do; they make you look for answers in all the wrong places. I knew I was in trouble. I started searching the Internet for topics associated with peace, happiness, and bliss; I would type in search words like "spiritual bliss." I found a website called Pure Silence and became very interested in it. There was something there; I didn't understand it, but I knew it had something to do with the answers I was seeking. I could not grasp exactly what it was saying because of the noise going on in my head, but I just sensed that it was truthful. Unfortunately I didn't know how to apply what I was reading to my life. I would return to this website often.

My Pain Medications Become Habit Forming

One more year went by where I was led aimlessly around by my Conditioned Mind Patterns, still going to doctors, even getting prescriptions filled on the Internet. Then I had to get my gallbladder removed. This was the turning point. This is when any resistance I had to not taking pain medication stopped. I had no other option, but to use it, no matter what. Now whenever I ran out I would just go shopping on the Internet. I found Tramadol/Ultram, a medication purported to be non-narcotic, non-addictive, but "can be habit forming." I really don't know what that means, "non-addictive, but can be habit forming," but soon it had me in its grip.

I took this medication strictly to satisfy a physical craving. I'd originally taken it to alter my mood, but it wasn't doing that anymore. I have had many physical cravings in my life, but the danger with this one was its potential to kill me. I could not get off it, no matter how much I wanted to. I tried and tried, but I couldn't get off it by myself.

This struggle persisted for two years. I focused my whole existence on not running out of this medication. Now tell me, where was the self in all of this? The I Self was fully in control, whether I wanted it to be or not. Why is it that I *thought* I had to escape from life to begin with? Why didn't I have the ability to cope with life? Why hadn't I developed coping skills based in love? Why was I so self-centered? Where did all this originate from? When did it start and why? What made me do the things that I did, and feel the way that I felt?

My conditioning was in place many years before I reached this point in my life. I had many questions, but to me the most important question of all was; Why did this happen? The answer I found was: it was driven by my self-centeredness, my I Self. All my problems that ever occurred in my life were all derived from my I Self. No I Self – no wanting things different – no wanting things different – no problems.

A Moment of Grace

On a day which wasn't much different from any other — I was driving pass a wedding and I had a moment of clarity: I asked myself, *"If I continue on this road, how am I ever going to be there for my children? These are the most important years of their lives, and I need to be there for them."* I made a decision right then and there that I was going to get off this pain medication. I was going to do whatever it was I needed to do. Although I wasn't aware of this at the time, *my life as I knew it was about to change, forever.*

This clarity came from my having a thought about someone other than me. It was probably twenty years since I'd *truly* thought of anyone else. As far back as I can recall my thoughts were always centered on me. This is our Conditioned Mind, our I Self at its best. Just this one thought of not thinking of me, saved my life.

Now some people may say God planted this thought in me, and that may be true, to an extent. As I understand it, love overcame my conditioning for one split second — the love of my children. Where it arose from I don't really know, but it did. At the moment when those thoughts occurred, I was willing to do what was necessary to cooperate with life instead of fight it. All my life I was always in collision with my true self (with love). The self that was there when my existence started, before my ego, my I Self, took over. At my moment of clarity, my true self (love) arose to overcome my Conditioned Thinking. I am eternally grateful for this. It doesn't benefit me or anyone else to attach a belief that something outside of me did this; all I know is because of what happened to me at that moment, my entire life changed forever. God is just a word. What happened to me in that moment, words cannot explain.

Birth Pangs of a New Life

The next chain of events that took place signaled the beginning of the end, the end of life as I had been conditioned to live it. I started looking on the Internet for a place to go to help me get off the pain medication. Since I tried numerous times to stop taking the medication and had failed, I knew I couldn't do it on my own and I needed help. It all came to a head one day when I came home from work and my wife asked me if I was drinking again. She had done a search on our computer's history, and she had discovered the sites I had searched, looking for help.

An indescribable slew of emotions opened up inside me and I told her what had been going on. I knew I'd hurt her in so many ways, and the pain that ensued after she confronted me was unbearable. I knew my wife was hurting, but I didn't know what to do. As my wife went back in the house, the floodgates of years of pent-up emotions just opened and I started crying uncontrollably. Years of living a lie, of causing pain and suffering to myself and to others, of reacting to life from a place I never understood nor could I ever control, were about to cease. This was definitely the end. At the time I really didn't know what it was the end of, but I knew I needed to find a way to live differently.

I called my brother-in-law who lived across the street from me because I was scared. I didn't plan on doing anything to hurt myself, but I didn't know what I was capable of. In this frame of mind I didn't want to risk being alone. So he picked me up and we drove around for hours and talked.

The way I understand it now is, years and years of these pent-up emotions were finally melting away the blocks to my heart. It was the first time that I could recall being honest with myself — and that's the first step if any change is to occur.

I had no idea what was going to happen to me, to my family, or my marriage. I did know that my old way of handling life was over. No matter what happened to me from here on in, I was going to find out how to be at peace. I wanted to live, but knew I could not continue on the road I was on. Mind you, I have never considered taking my own life, but I often thought if I didn't wake up one day that would have been okay.

After about four hours I regained my composure and went back home. I very gingerly approached my wife. I told her I was so sorry for all I had done, but I knew what I needed to do was to leave her alone so she could sort through what was going on inside her. I also needed to focus on what I needed to do to. Even though we all affect each other in life, everyone still has his or her own process of dealing with things. Wherever that process was going to take my marriage, I was willing to live with it and the consequences of my actions.

The next step was to make the necessary arrangements for me to get off the medication. I felt terribly worried about my marriage, but even more concerned with getting off this pain medication. I knew, that had to be my first priority, or there wouldn't even be a chance for my marriage to work. I realized there was a reason why I ended up in the predicament I had, and I was going to find out why it happened. I understood part of my problem had been in my thinking I could do everything alone, that I didn't need anyone's help. But now, I was ready to ask for this much needed help.

I called my Employee Assistance Program at work, which went a long way in my willingness to reach out for help. This was the beginning of breaking the hold my Conditioned Mind Patterns had on me. Without asking for help, there wouldn't have been any freedom. Freedom does not come from holding on, freedom comes from letting go.

My ego always told me I didn't need help, but I finally knew better. The reality of it all is this: we are all dependent on each other, whether we want to be or not. From the clothes we wear to the food that we eat, understanding that we need others is a huge step in deflating our egos. To know of myself, I am nothing and can do nothing was all the beginning I needed. So much of my conditioning had to do with isolation. Asking for help allowed me to connect with people. This connection wasn't there when I was living from the mind-based sense of my I Self.

Cooperating with life means being amongst people — working with, playing with, living with people; this is the foundation of all spiritual growth. Our sense of well-being emanates from within when we're in harmony with other people. When we aren't in the me-me-me, mode of our ego, we are free to enjoy this world and the people in it. We are in harmony with life instead of living from a conditioning that is ego-based, and is always making us feel like we are going against the traffic. That's how it always felt to me, like I was always going against the traffic and when I was really self-centered and isolated, I was also going uphill. It didn't have to be that way, but I had to learn how not to make it so.

<u>Twelve Steps – Take Two</u>

I went to a hospital so I could be medically detoxed. Physically, this took three days. It was the beginning. I went home and started an Intense Outpatient Program to help me stay away from drugs, so my head could clear up. Although my mind was very foggy, something told me to get back to the twelve-step program that I attended previously. I called a friend from that program and fortunately he was still involved in it. Between the IOP and the twelve-step program, I was getting the necessary support to overcome my dependency upon the pain medication. Very slowly the fog in my mind began to lift. I was taking it one day at a time; I really didn't have much choice. The clearer my mind got, the better I felt.

But certain questions kept surfacing over and over: Why did this happen? Did it have to happen? And the most important question: Was there a way to change? I knew I had to find answers. I knew those answers had something to do with the website called Pure Silence.

In my heart I knew self-centeredness was at the core of all my pain; but I still didn't understand why I needed outside things to feel better inside. It wasn't a physical pain; it was strictly an aching in my heart caused by my self-centeredness, which was caused by my Conditioned Mind Patterns. This much I understood, my self-centeredness was my problem, and I needed to find out how not to be controlled by it, if I was ever going to be happy.

I was fairly young, twenty-eight when I originally stopped drinking. Because of my drinking I never attained any sense of accomplishment or material possessions. Everything I did up to the point when I attended my first rehab was to feed the beast (my ego). Self-centered, unconsciousness, selfishness, ego — give it any name you want — but the bottom line was my mind had been conditioned to satisfy my self-created demons and there wasn't a thing I could do, but to feed that beast. I had thought the beast was addiction, but in truth the beast was my I Self. My own mind created the pain and it also created the self-destructive solution. That's how it had been conditioned to work, and it did its job to perfection.

After I originally stopped drinking my life progressed nicely on the outer layer, but I was never grateful for anything. Nothing satisfied my I Self for long. As I attained one thing, my ego quickly moved onto the next thing. I took everything for granted, like it was supposed to be the way it was. I have since come to understand that my mind was still locked into the Conditioned Patterns that had been developed perfectly since childhood. What happened to me was the inevitable expression of this unchallenged conditioning.

What changed me was this understanding: through my Conditioned Mind I had based my entire philosophy of life on attaining things. I belonged to a world of objects. I believed that this was what life was about; to bring pleasure to my being and to avoid pain at all cost. When I had more things than I ever imagined having and it still didn't bring the fulfillment I so desired, what was I left to do? I knew this was the end; the end to an existence that I never understood.

I started to become aware of things in an entirely different way. I wasn't adding to my old way of thinking. I started developing a new view of life.

I understood my old one didn't work. I saw for the first time that life is a process with which I could cooperate, and that I didn't have to depend on anything outside of me for my happiness. My happiness was inside me, I just had to learn how to allow it to transpire.

I began to understand that it was not up to some God out there somewhere who I was conditioned to believe would bring me fulfillment. God wasn't going to perform some sort of magic act to take away all my problems and make me happy. God wasn't going to make everything okay, and I wasn't going to get everything I wanted. It didn't mean I couldn't be happy, all it meant was that I now had something tangible to work with; something I could see, my self-centered behavior. This new viewpoint which was being created from reading books on different religious philosophies was helping me to develop an understanding of why I did what I did and why I was the way that I was. I also understood if I wanted to change I needed to do certain things. It was up to me, what a relief. No God to blame. It wasn't anybody's fault, it was just the way it was, and I now had the answer I was so desperately seeking.

God and Saint Peter

I have found through experience there is not an entity outside my being trying to destroy me, or one that is trying to save me. It is my own ignorance that blocks my ability to know truth, which blocks my ability to love. That's what the Conditioned Mind Patterns do. That is their sole purpose; to block love. That's what would have destroyed me if I didn't wake up and become aware of what was happening.

I often joke about God watching over us and talking to Saint Peter. God says to Saint Peter, "Look, I've had enough with this species. I think I'll just create another flood and start over with them; we'll see what happens this time." Then Saint Peter replies, "Why should we do anything? Just give them a little more time; they are doing such a good job of destroying themselves." There is no one to blame for what is happening to us as a species or as a planet. It is our own mind that is making us do the things that we're doing, and we are destroying ourselves in the process.

87

CHAPTER 8

Awakening

As I was attending an Intense Outpatient Program and going to twelve-step meetings, I was getting the separation from the pain medication that was needed to clear the cob-webs from my head. When I was out of the hospital about two weeks, I found myself arguing with a twelve-year-old boy about a roller hockey game we were playing. My eleven-year-old son was playing in this league, but there weren't enough kids to fill out a team for this game. I was playing goalie just to fill in. Here I am, forty-nine years old, and I am actually antagonizing a boy about his not wanting to change teams to make them more balanced. He wanted to play on the team with his friend. I was calling him "a baby," among other derogatory names.

My Way

All of a sudden something clicked in my mind. The only reason I was verbally attacking this twelve-year-old boy was because I was making his actions all about me. I was the one who suggested we change the teams, and when he didn't oblige, a Mind Pattern was activated. I felt horrible. I apologized to this boy right away and knew I needed to change the way I reacted to things triggered by Mind Patterns. I needed to find out why I reacted the way I did. I was starting to recognize that it happened when I didn't get my way. From this moment on, my self investigation ramped a notch.

I would search the Internet for anything to do with peace, bliss, nirvana, enlightenment, spiritual awakening, and quieting the mind. One thing I started to notice was everything I read was associated with the mind. Everything was based in learning about the mind and how, through discipline, you can learn to control your reactions to your thoughts. A very important site to me was The Divine Life Society, which was based on exploring the teachings of Hinduism. It taught me about how my mind, not the devil, was the root of all my evils and if I wanted to be free of those evils I had to learn to control it. This placed responsibility solely on me, and for that I am grateful. No more waiting for a magician to perform a magic trick to make me all better.

In a twelve-step program we review and identify our past behavior. This inventory helps a person become free of that past and go on with his or her present. The steps take you through this process, and it's often referred to as "cleaning house." The first time I did this was many years earlier, when I identified how my behavior harmed others. I never identified the causes of that behavior and why I reacted the way I did, so my behavior stayed the same.

Here is the major difference in how the steps affected my life during my second phase of involvement: By identifying the causes of this behavior, I now understand that it can be changed. I called my friend from the program to now go over, once again, my past behavior. But this time my self-centeredness was the foundation of my inventory. I wanted to learn the blocks to my progress, character defects that rose to the surface in my harmful words and actions towards others. What was not allowing me to be in harmony with life? I wanted to find out why I was so unhappy when I had everything I thought a person could want.

You can dress this up and say what I was doing was learning how to be at one with God, or I was doing the things necessary to allow the Spirit in, whatever words you may be comfortable using. For me, I understand it as simply identifying my self-centered Conditioned Mind Patterns. They were the true nature of my malady. When the Conditioned Mind Patterns are activated and cause a flare up, there can't be any harmony, and I suffer and cause suffering to others. It is that simple. Not easy to digest, but simple.

When you act from self-centeredness, you suffer. I have seen this played out over and over; in me and in others, this blocks any real connectedness you can have with life. It creates a void which is the absence of God or love, if that's how you want to think of it. For me, it is the absence of love. Why was love absent from my life? It was time to find out.

I wrote down the behavior that was causing me the most trouble. I focused solely on the behavior associated with my self-centeredness. I went over this with my friend and, lo and behold, just like that the pain, shame, guilt, and remorse I felt about my most glaring flaws were lifted. They lost their hold on me. This is where identifying the true cause of my problems was so important. Without the honest and total identification of my self-centeredness, I wouldn't have been aware of the behavior that needed changing. Now I had something real I could see. This wasn't something make-believe or mystical. I knew I had to stop living from my I Self, this *truly* was the beginning.

Desiring Change

Mind Patterns just don't go away because we identify them; I had to honestly want to change, from my heart. A real internal battle ensued; deeply entrenched Conditioned Mind Patterns don't go away without a fight. I now started understanding the hold my ego had on my psyche. I started reading books on learning how to quiet my mind through meditation practice. As I practiced some of the methods from these books, my mind started to settle. This allowed me to understand how certain occurrences activated my Conditioned Mind Patterns. So instead of allowing them to control me, I was able to learn how not to give into them. I was able to understand the noise in my head for what it really was; just noise. This perception created space between my thoughts, and my reaction.

For the first time in my life I understood why I did what I did. I felt a new sense of choice: I didn't have to succumb to my Conditioned Mind

Patterns. I didn't have to give into them. Now mind you, this was just the beginning, there were many things that had a hold on me, but this is what a spiritual journey is, a discovery of the things that block out Universal Love.

When I say I didn't have to give into them what I mean is I didn't have to attach a story to the thought that arose in my head. That's really all there is to it, but it is the hardest thing I've ever had to do. Thousands of years of evolution followed by forty-nine years (for me) of Conditioned Thinking; good luck in changing habitual thinking. But that is what I was changing, the attachment of a story. It is never the thought the causes a problem, it is the story attached to the thought. Sometimes they are short stories, sometimes they are long stories, and sometimes they are epic novels — filled with all kinds of drama, but nonetheless they are still just stories created by you.

Where do all these stories originate from? Our Conditioned Minds Patterns give them energy. They are all self-created; the only reality to them is what you provide. You have no control over the thought, but you can control what you attach to it. This is unknown to the majority of us, and these attached stories are our prime source of suffering. Without the story, which we create, there would be just a thought. How much of a problem can a single, unattached thought really cause? It's there and if you don't attach to it, it's gone. Just like that. Like a passing cloud.

Here is an analogy that illustrates this point very clearly: Imagine you are the sky and the clouds are your thoughts. As the clouds pass through, you will hardly notice them. If you attach and build them up it becomes cloudier and cloudier, which means less and less sun shines through. Before you know it the sun is completely blocked out, and there are just clouds. Underneath all the clouds the sun is still there, but you can't see it. When you learn not to attach to the clouds, the sun will always shine. This is your innate goodness that is always there.

I started reading anything I could about spirituality. I'm not even sure how many books I read in a three-year period, but it was quite a few. I started noticing a common theme in all the books I was reading: Each one was a little different in some methods and beliefs, but they all pointed to the same place: To be free you can't be self-centered. You will either be selfishly self-serving or you will be lovingly serving others. When you are selfishly self-serving you are disconnected and isolated from life, you are not in harmony with it. When you are lovingly serving others and that includes yourself, you are cooperating with life and are in harmony with your true self.

Of course, what resonates for me may not do the same for you, so you need to find your own path. But I assure you of one thing: if you honestly want change and are willing to do the necessary investigation, you will be amazed at what you may find.

Words of Wisdom

A book that helped me in the beginning was one that my wife gave me. The name of it is *Awakening to your Life's Purpose — A New Earth* by Eckhart Tolle. From this book I gained helpful understandings. The most important was how my ego always needed to be fed, and never stayed satisfied. When it did get satisfied, it was time to move on and try to acquire the next satisfaction. It seemed to me that I had to obey, but it was only because I didn't know I didn't have to. I also learned why I was unable to form any kind of lasting relationship with anyone, male or female. It was such a valuable wealth of information. It gave me the ability to understand the false power of my I Self, feel compassion for myself and become able to *truly* forgive myself.

Knowing Right from Wrong, But Choosing Wrong

In my heart I always knew right from wrong, I just didn't understand why I always choose wrong. I know I am accountable for all the harm I caused, but I had no awareness of why I was doing what I did. I finally found something that showed me that I was just doing what I had been conditioned to do. Self-forgiveness lifted a burden I had been carrying around my whole life. I never understood why I did what I did and I just buried the guilt, shame and remorse deeper and deeper in my psyche.

Understanding this cycle was so freeing. It helped me break the hold guilt, shame and remorse had over me.

I returned home from my three day stay at hospital in September of 2007. I was going to the twelve-step meetings regularly and by mid December the Intense Outpatient program I was attending would conclude. Through my EAP at work I was afforded the opportunity to get well without having to report to work. This allowed me the time I needed to really look at myself.

I would go to the meetings for much-needed support. While I was there, I would feel good. But when the meeting would end the noise in my head would take over. I didn't quite understand what was happening. I knew there was a cause, and I was determined to find it. So I kept investigating why this was occurring, and very slowly answers came to me. My friend from the program would constantly tell me to take it one day at a time. Like I said earlier, it is such a valuable tool. I stated practicing meditation and, with my mind becoming quieter, I started practicing living my life by those words. This was really helping in alleviating so many of the difficulties that were all created by my mind.

Reading, Discovering and Changing

I started changing. I was discovering what, in myself, was creating my difficulties. I kept reading and discovering. The more I read, the more I discovered about myself, the more I discovered, the more I changed. The more I changed, the freer I became of my I Self.

Without my ego in total control I experienced moments of true freedom, I felt happiness I had never experienced before. I wanted more and I knew I could have it, as long as the core of my yearning wasn't to satisfy my ego, but was to be a benefit to others. My starting point was to be free so I would not suffer anymore, but this new insight was opening my heart. My attention was now on how to benefit all those with whom I was associated. I didn't want to cause suffering to anyone ever again. This is the love that is in all of us, when we remove the blocks and let it shine through us.

Really Celebrating Christmas: True Freedom

It was now Christmas Eve. My family celebrated at our house. This was very important to me, that particular year especially, because it emphasized to me that my wife didn't leave me when I relapsed — and this again is to her credit. She stayed with me, and I know it could not have been easy for her, considering how much I'd hurt her. She knew, even back when we were first dating, what she was getting into with me. But she saw something there; she saw the goodness even as it was blocked out by my addictions. Her older brother didn't especially see me that way; in fact, I was at the top of his list of men he didn't want his sister to date.

I know what hurt my wife the most were my lies. I told her "everything was okay" when it wasn't. I was taking pills without her knowing anything was wrong. Maureen's staying with me helped so much. It allowed me to focus on recovery without too many distractions. This Christmas Eve stands out because it was one of the first times I noticed how I was changing.

On previous Christmas Eves I would always have been busy doing something. Whether it was cleaning up, emptying garbage, getting ice, etc, I used being busy as a diversion because I didn't know how to just be. I was always uncomfortable with myself. As long as I was busy I was okay. I couldn't just sit and enjoy the moment. I had to always be doing something.

I reflected back, and saw this pattern over and over in my life. We have a built-in-pool in our backyard, and the standing joke was I knew exactly how many river rocks we have in our yard, because whenever we had people over I was always busy fixing the rocks. I couldn't just sit and enjoy anything and I never knew how or why, until now. I thought, like many people do, that the constant fussing, fixing things, doing yard work, or house work was just the way I was. I have since found out that this is not so. This was just the way I was conditioned to be. It was part of my defense mechanism, to cope with my feelings of fears or inadequacies or any other false feelings. If I was busy I didn't have to look at myself.

I was having a difficult time of sitting still because my mind never stopped. It was always thinking, doing, scheming. It wouldn't shut down, but

I did understand by now what was happening. I started to get little glimpses of quietness. Some space was being created between my thoughts. Very little, but it was a beginning. I knew I was onto something, I saw the results with my own eyes. I was changing. It became clear to me the reason I'd done what I did for so long was because I was controlled by my Conditioned Mind Patterns. I knew that until I learned to quiet my mind enough to become aware of these Mind Patterns, I would continue to be controlled by them.

Jesus said *Know the truth and the truth will set you free.* To me this meant I have to learn to still my mind so the truth can be seen. To be without stillness is to be without truth. This truth I speak of is only found in this stillness. It is not some idea of truth you make up. When you really know truth you will be able to reach your true spiritual nature. Without truth there will always be noise. To live in a world of truth is to be free of anger, sloth, envy, greed, lust, pride, jealousy, hate, and the most important fear. Fear is the most important because all the others are generated from our own fear.

So my experience that one Christmas Eve was so important; being able to actually see the results of the work I was doing. It was the most comfortable I ever felt without using an outside diversion. I didn't have to do *anything*; there was nothing to accomplish, nothing I needed to do. I just went with the flow, not controlling, not trying to arrange everything to be perfect (in my mind). I was just enjoying my family and being content with what was there. It was very freeing not having to do anything, and being able to just be, and not be controlled by my Conditioned Mind.

On that Christmas Eve I felt peace. This sense of belonging I felt made me realize I was just like everyone else. I was just an ordinary person, with a job, a wife, and children. I had a great family who loved me. It was the best feeling I ever had in my life. I didn't want anything to be any different than what is was. This was *truly* a miracle.

Sitting Still and Finding Quiet

I was sitting in quiet as much as my life would allow. I would sit in a chair, on my bed, on the couch, or wherever I can find quiet. The important thing to me was I was learning to still my mind. For me, there is nothing mystical or magical in learning to quiet your mind. I just had to be persistent because I understood quietness was not going to happen overnight. I just had to do what the Nike commercial says "Just do it". I was getting better and better at it. That is how my discovery of myself was occurring. It wasn't coming from a mystical union with God or from a sudden burst of knowledge, it was occurring by being still. My mind was settling. And by being still I was learning what it meant to be with God. This is not a feeling; it is just being with what is there in the present moment.

When you start to try and sit still you will know how hard it is to achieve one moment of quietness. You will think it is useless, that you will never be able to do it. This is natural. It's not that you can't do it; it's that you never learned how or ever found a reason to do it. Once your mind starts to quiet you will become aware of how you have been conditioned. You will notice how the noise in the head is just this conditioning. You will see what arises and how Conditioned Mind Patterns hold you in captivity. When you start to become aware of them, you can change them. Not overnight, but a little at a time; one sitting at a time.

It's hard to change what you do not see. Persistence is the key. Sometimes it feels like you are taking one step forward and two steps back, but remember, Rome wasn't built in a day. It will take possibly the rest of your life, if ever; to be totally free . . . but what's the rush? This is not being done to attain anything; it is being done to discover in you the things that hold you in bondage to your I Self, so you can discover what blocks your ability to love.

I was sitting whenever possible, but I had also found I had to integrate the practice of quieting my mind throughout the day. The more awareness I had of the noise that was going on in my head, the more I understood how my conditioning was running my life.

Today I always start my day by reading short meditations or listening to guided meditations. Depending on the amount of time I have, sometimes I do both. I do this either while I lay in bed or I sit in my living room when I first wake up, before starting my day. My mind is usually unattached to thoughts in the morning. For me the morning is when my mind is at its quietest. All attachment is noise, so before the hustle and bustle of the day starts, it is a good time for me.

You will find your own time. I have no set routine. I have no special techniques that I use; my current job requires I do shift work, so it is almost impossible for me to get into a set routine. I try different things to become aware of what works the best for me. Sometimes in mid-day I see the noise and I just go and sit. Everyone is different so everyone needs to find his or her own path. I do know I am changing, and just the fact that I've written this book, something I'd never thought of doing, is amazing in itself.

A Visitation Brings Peace

In February of 2008 I had one of the most profound experiences I've ever had. I was visiting a Catholic monastery; I was sitting on a chair in a room with some instrumental music on. On the wall was a 3-D picture of Mary holding Jesus. As I was just sitting looking at this picture I felt overcome by a deep sense of Presence. It wasn't something mystical or magical that I felt, I was overcome with a peace that I had never experienced before. I just knelt down on the floor in gratitude and started crying. At the time this happened I knew in my heart that I was going to be okay. I knew this was real, this wasn't something created by my mind. I stayed on the floor for about twenty minutes crying and filled with peace. Then someone knocked on the door and I just got up and answered the door.

I was a changed person inside. It was powerful for me. I really knew I was going to be okay, and what a blessing. I share this for one reason only — to let you know that in meditation anything can happen. Most of the time when I sit, I just get quiet, that alone is amazing. Each experience is different. Sometimes I can get really still, and sometimes my mind wanders, but I am always learning, developing discipline.

What is of importance is to realize each time you sit it is a new experience. It has nothing to do with any previous sitting. It is not a comparison or culmination of some past experience. Each experience is unique unto itself. If you try and recapture something that happened once before, you will always be chasing that experience. This is what we do with our life. We look for some past pleasure to bring us a present satisfaction. Understand, this is just a story (noise) being created by your Conditioned Mind.

Our fulfillment is in the sitting itself, regardless of the experience. Just experience the experience and don't add anything to it. To try and recreate an experience is just another way for our minds to use our past Mind Patterns, to hold us in bondage. Look and see how you are always drawing on past experiences to provide present joy. Think about it, when you want a scoop of ice cream; it is the memory of the past pleasure the ice cream brings to you that causes the craving. The craving isn't from the ice cream, it is from the pleasure you think the ice cream will bring; the ice cream is just the object used, anything can be substituted for the ice cream. To me this awareness was mind-boggling.

The more I sat and meditated, the less I reacted when things happened. This was a slow process, but I was aware of changing; a little at a time. The Conditioned Mind Patterns were so engrained in my psyche; they went back so many years that I knew I had to be patient. Old habits die hard, and they don't go away easily.

I had a conversation with my children about what happened to me and how I was going to try to live differently. I always reacted negatively whenever something happened in life. It was the way I had been conditioned. Up to this point in my life dissatisfaction and complaint were natural. I didn't know there was another way to be. My first impulse was to always say no and yell. So I explained to them what I was trying to do. I told them I was learning not to react and yell the way I always had. I told them that, hopefully, they were going to see a difference in me, but it was going to take time. I thought being negative and always yelling was just the way I was. I didn't understand that it was the way I was conditioned, it was not a choice; until now.

When certain conditions arose I would get drawn in and react the way I had learned and been conditioned to. But the quietness has allowed me to become aware of this pattern and create the space needed not to react.

This is the space between the condition that arises and the space before the reaction occurs, a millisecond. Most of us don't realize there is space between a thought and a reaction, but there is. The problem is it happens so fast . . . and without a quiet mind we will never experience this space. This causes us to react unconsciously to life as conditions arise. We are controlled by life like we are a puppet. Life produces the conditions and we react automatically because of our Conditioned Mind.

Space Between the Thought and the Reaction

When a thought occurs and space is created, that split second in between the thought and reaction is all that is needed to stop the reaction. Here's a vivid example that revealed this to me: It was the summer of 2008 and I was taking my fourteen-year-old daughter to Long Beach Island in New Jersey. She was going to stay with a friend overnight. She needed to take her own bedding. We were about twenty miles from home when she told me she forgot her bedding at home.

The plethora of emotions that I went through in a split second was unbelievable. What caused all this was prior to even getting in the car to go to the shore, I had this whole trip planned out in my head. I was working the night shift so I had to leave my house around 4:30 p.m. to get to work on time. It was around 10:00 a.m. so I had plenty of time to drive her to the shore and still get home in time to take a nap before going to work. It would have been a three-and-a-half to four-hour drive, round trip. This is the story that I had created in my head. So when she told me she forgot her bedding it messed up all my plans. The anger I felt was beyond description, but I didn't react. The anger was there alright, and my mind frantically wanted to react, the way it always had, yelling and screaming; that's what my mind had been conditioned to do. It constantly tries to arrange life to its liking, and when life doesn't cooperate it tries to force the matter. It has no choice because that is the solution that is there. But I didn't react, and as the anger subsided I just turned to her and said, "We'll just turn around, go home and get the bedding." No yelling from me, no crying from her.

It was just a flare up brought on by a Conditioned Mind Pattern. It didn't control me. I didn't react. What freedom!

Although it seemed like a long time, this took about one second to happen. The space between the Mind Pattern thought and the reaction was there. This space allowed me not to react. I was not controlled by this Mind Pattern that had been in place for so many years. A pattern was broken. We turned around and got the bedding. On our way to the shore we actually talked about what happened. How different the energy in my car would have been had I reacted like I normally did! The difference in the energy in my car created a whole different environment for me and my daughter. The energy that was brought into the situation was of love. The new space allowed me to understand that I was angry because things weren't going according to the plan my mind arranged. My ego didn't like when this happened, so it acted accordingly. My I Self was trying to make it about me. Fortunately, the created space allowed energy to flow through me and I become aware that the circumstance wasn't about me; it was about not reacting and not hurting someone else. This is another spiritual law. When the energy isn't stored in our psyche we are free to love.

This showed me the value of what I was practicing. This lesson taught me why I was practicing meditation. What I mostly experience when I sit is peace, quietness. I watch my thoughts and I allow them to just pass through in and out, without attaching to them. No story, just thoughts. A lot of times I use my breath to divert attention from my thoughts. I know this is a scientific fact that our minds can't think two thoughts at the same time. So I'm either controlled by my thoughts, or I am aware of them and am not letting them control me.

Finding Your Own Quiet

You will have to find what *you* need to do to quiet your mind. Do some research and practice with different portals. Find your spirit, the place within that you can call home, where you can go amidst the storms in life. Find the things that allow you to cooperate with life. Even if I am in a room full with people, I close my eyes so I can focus on something to stop my mind. It just takes a second to stop creating the story. Sometimes I will use my breath as a focal point. Sometime I use the noise in the room, to just listen and be with what's there.

The drive with my daughter was so important because it showed me first-hand that my practice was working. I was really changing. This was real. I was probably, for the first time in many years, doing things that put me in harmony with life. It wasn't so much that I was learning to love as much as I was learning not to hate. I wasn't learning patience; I was learning what caused my impatience. I wasn't learning who I was; I was learning who I was not. This was very important for me because I didn't have to add anything or find the magical formula for fulfillment. All I had to do was stop doing the things that were creating my difficulties. I would ask myself if what I was doing benefited my life or not. If not, why do it? I felt so much gratitude for what took place with my daughter. After I dropped her off at her friend's house and began returning home, I started crying. These were tears of joy that were melting away a heart that had been iced over for way too long.

The space between my thought and my reaction didn't occur when you may think. It seems to have been created at the moment my daughter told me she forgot her bedding, when I didn't react. But it was created during my time of sitting, of practice quieting my mind. It is in the practice that you will change. That's when you get in touch with your inner self (your potential) and break the Conditioned Mind Patterns cycle. The thought and the reaction happen so fast, it is impossible to stop it through your own thinking. It has to come from your place of quietness; which is established through your sitting. Find where that place of peace is within you. True change always comes from within.

As the "Squirrel Cage Mind" Becomes Quiet

Things like this continued to happen to me. I was reading and learning. I was changing daily and continued to change. I read many books that encompassed spirituality; some solely on the teachings of Jesus. The teachings of Jesus have been very important to me. Joel S. Goldsmiths, founder of the *Infinite Way* website, has also provided a valuable tool in my development. I didn't read these books once and then move on; I read some of them two and three times. I was studying them and they were all helping me to identify the things in me, in my thinking, that were blocking love from my life.

I read, and I practiced. I knew that learning how to quiet my "squirrel cage mind" – that's one of the terms I use to describe a mind that never stops, was pivotal for my life in allowing the true essence of my being to become the default setting of my mind. It was something I could do each moment of each day if I choose to, but I had to learn how to do this. Saint Paul said *"Pray ceaselessly."* I understand this as when I lose my connection with life, I need to use the tools that are necessary to bring me back to my place of peace. Sometimes it is as simple as saying, *"that's enough"* to my thoughts, just to stop them. Sometimes I use the simple phrase "I AM." Or "I am not my thoughts". This works for me.

Whatever you find to stop your incessant thinking; use it to cultivate the things in your life that can allow you to be at peace. The more you pray the less chance there is to lose your connectedness. Taking a breath is a part of this. Why do you think you see people taking a deep breath when they are preparing to perform certain task? It is because by taking a deep breath, the mind stops and your natural instincts are allowed to take over. To me, a deep breath is a form of prayer. Anything used to stop our mind can be considered a prayer. It makes you at one with what is happening around you in that exact moment.

People don't think their way to heroic deeds, the thinking would stop them. The mind would say, *No way, I'm not doing that, I might get hurt.* But when you are not thinking, then your true self arises and anything is possible. That is my understanding of acquiring the ability or faith to move mountains.

Our mind is the creator of our world, and most of what we create is a delusion. Take a bottle of water that is filled half way. You can say it is half empty or you can say it is half full. Labeling it half empty or half full is relative and opinion-based. It's an assessment. The truth of the situation is there is just water in the bottle. The opinion of "half empty" or "half full" can be debated; that there is liquid in the bottle cannot validly be called into question. Well it could, but that would just be from ignorance. Nobody can truly argue with truth. So labeling the content of the bottle as half empty or half full is just a created delusion.

If you pointed upwards and said, "That is the sky," would anyone argue with that? That is how you know it is truth. The mind creates what you see and feel. But what you see and feel is not necessarily the truth. When you start understanding this by learning to quiet your mind, truth will be revealed to you. You will start to see things as they really are; not as you have perceived.

CHAPTER 9

Understanding My Self

I was getting more and more in touch with my Conditioned Thinking. My thoughts were still going round and round in my head, but fewer and fewer flare-ups were occurring. The less the flare-ups occurred, the less this meant I was reacting from my I Self. There were situations that caused more reaction than others and this is what I started getting in touch with. I was using my children as a sounding board. I would ask them how I was doing, and they were telling me I was doing better. I wasn't yelling nearly as much and I seemed happier. My son told me, "Dad you don't yell at stupid stuff anymore." This was all the proof I needed to know that I was on the right path. This was real progress. We think we only affect ourselves when we are being controlled by our Conditioned Mind Patterns, but so many people are affected by our reactions. That's exactly what would've happened when my daughter forgot her bedding for her overnight stay. How different the situation would have been for both of us, had I reacted the way I always had.

Road Rage Revisited

Another example you may relate to: Another driver wants to switch into your lane. You may not want to let them in, but they are going anyway. Now your anger arises and anything can happen, depending on how attached you are to not letting them in. You get angry at them because they are cutting in without your permission, and they get angry at you for not letting them in. What would happen if you just let them in? No anger would arise. The energy would not be stored in either of your psyches and both of you would be free of any Conditioned Reaction. That's how change occurs, one situation at a time. You can substitute the traffic example with anything.

I have come to understand that it isn't just negative energy that causes reactions. Even positive energy can be a hindrance if it doesn't come from a place of love. If all you do is work all the time to provide for your family, but neglect them in the process, this makes you a good provider — but not necessarily a loving provider. What good does this do for anyone? It's not about finding the positives in life; it's learning how to just allow what happens in life to pass through you. Then you can respond to things as they arise instead of reacting to them. That's exactly what happened when I was driving my daughter to the shore. I wasn't trying to be "the little engine that could." I acknowledged the anger that arose. But because I've practiced meditation, space was created and I didn't have to react. I responded like an adult, in a loving fashion. It wasn't in a "positive" fashion; the response was of love. I wasn't saying "I think I can, I think I can." Rather, I didn't want to bring harm to my daughter by yelling and making her cry. My intention came from my heart being open to someone else's experience.

Our process is not a race to get somewhere. It is slow and sometimes painful to be with what arises. Years of diversionary tactics take a long time to undo. First we have to learn what we need to undo. It is difficult to understand this, but if you ever want to change *you will have to understand* what needs to be changed. Before I understood the workings of my mind, I realized my view of certain things was not right. I realized it was distorted. This distorted view didn't allow me to do what was necessary to be in cooperation with life. This view is what I discovered was at the core of my unhappiness.

I knew if I wanted to be happy I needed to change my outlook. I had to learn to see the truth (the view of love) and this view is what produces happiness. Happiness is a by-product of a view based in love. This view wasn't some belief that I had to make up; it was being with what was here. What is here is truth. Not my perception of what is here, but what is actually here. What is actually occurring in the present moment is what's here.

So the main cause of not being happy was my distorted view; a learned view which conditioned my mind to view life through its distortions. I developed this conditioning, with all the feelings and emotions that go along with it. Before I could start living from another view I had to understand where the distorted view came from. It came from my Conditioned Mind Patterns. And the right view comes from my heart, which when opened, emanates love.

Being Present

The heart is always of love, always unconditional. No strings attached. The distorted view comes from our mind, our self-centeredness. It is painful learning to keep our heart open, but the other option is to keep it closed. By keeping it closed our walls of protection would remain, and we would just keep dealing with our conditioned reactions over and over. So the choice is to respond from love, or to react from our self-centered fear, the creator of our walls, and the conditioner of our Mind Patterns. So I was learning how to become aware of the truth of each situation because I understood that truth was going to be the key to my freedom.

I was noticing daily growth, daily change of my view of life. I was becoming more aware of these changes. It was not me that was changing things; it was the quieting of my mind, that's what was changing my view. I was just watching when I was viewing life from the core of my I Self and then I would do something to change it; something as simple as a deep breath would change the direction of my energy. I would do things that would return me to the present moment. The difference in the way I was, as opposed to what I am becoming, is remarkable. Every single thought I had in previous years was either in the past or future, and it was always about me. Now I saw that freedom could only be had by living in the present moment.

This is really what the process is for me: To learn how to be present. It isn't about me merely helping others; what if there were no others to help? It isn't about being successful, or being a productive member of society. It isn't about anything. It is learning to live in the present moment so my mind can expand to experience Universal Love and share that love with all beings. When I am present I can be with life as it happens, if there is someone to help, than that is what I will do. But it is not my purpose. This is what I AM is. I am not this or that. I AM; I don't need to add anything to it.

I AM

I mentioned "I AM" previously. It is discussed in a wonderful book written by Nisargadatta Maharaj. *I Am That* is its title. Reading this book opened up another dimension of looking at my existence. It is not existence as the world knows it; that existence just keeps you in bondage. The world's existence is about things. Living in a state of I AM leads to an existence that goes beyond the limitations of our mind. This has been such a help in stopping the squirrel — in-a-cage mind in its tracks; I use this often. When the mind is going, and I just say "I AM" and don't add anything to it, the mind's endless racing stops. This settles my mind. I just sit with I AM and don't attach anything to it. The labeling of things is what hinders our spiritual potential from arising.

The Unknown Keeps Us Growing

When I think, *I have everything figured out,* nothing new is allowed in. The known is always limiting. The unknown is what allows us to grow. The mind loves to label things. It is a labeling machine. It has been conditioned to know; if it doesn't know it will keep looking until it does, it will keep trying to find an answer. It will make things up, it will lie. It will constantly try to arrange life until it figures out an answer, whether that answer is true or not does not matter to the mind, as long as it finds an answer it is satisfied with.

This is where I AM comes in. Just by adding I AM the mind stops in mid thought. It is an incomplete sentence, and the mind doesn't know how to deal with that. It can't find the solution to the story it is trying to create. Without a story there's no drama. Remember, the thought doesn't create anything. The mind attaches to the thought and the story is what's created. In reality the story is already written in your psyche, but it needs a title. You create the title. "He cut me off, she said this about me, my boss doesn't like me, or the world is unfair." These titles and our stories are created all day long. The thing they all have in common is this; they all originate from our I. It is from our I that all these stories are created. Without I, there would be no stories.

I AM Anchors Me in the Present

All the mind wants to do is create a false existence that is based in pleasure. That is why when there is no pleasure, the search for it begins. And who wants the pleasure? I do. Learn to really sit with I AM, understand that regardless of what you attach to, it will one day be gone, no matter what. This will make you view life in a totally different light. Sitting and meditating is a solid practice, but what do I do throughout the day when sitting isn't possible and the mind becomes agitated? I can't draw on the sitting I did in my morning meditation, so what do I do? What I do is just close my eyes for a few seconds, wherever it is I happen to be, and say I AM.

This is a truth, that always is, and it doesn't need anything added to it. It is my true self, not the self I thought I was. I don't need to be sitting in meditation to be with I AM. It is self-sustaining. It needs nothing for its survival. It just is. Come to understand this truth by examining what is it that makes you who you are? The constant of life is it is always changing, the constant of I AM is it is always the same. I AM is always the same because it can't be altered or enhanced.

Cravings are created by our mind agitations. Smoking, divorce, jealously, scheming to make more money, eating to satisfy a craving . . . the list goes on and on. The story starts from the labeling. Once something is labeled (the title) then the drama begins; with I AM none of this occurs. I'm not saying that overcoming a craving is easy, it isn't. It goes against everything we have been taught. We have been conditioned to defend ourselves, to always make the other person the bad guy, to always push away pain for pleasure. What it comes down to is this: how free do you want to be? If you practice a little, you will have a little freedom. If you practice a lot you will have a lot of freedom. If you practice all the time, you will have freedom all the time. It is possible, and it is totally up to you, but how free do you want to be?

"Wear the World Like a Loose Garment"

Have you ever heard the phrase, *"Wear the world like a loose garment."* If I want, I can be free and not be controlled by my Conditioned Mind Patterns. But I have to learn to let go of them and live life from a place of peace.

You may experience periods where there is a semblance of peace in life, but once certain conditions arise, BAM — you are drawn in and your peace is gone. Just like that. So where is this so-called control you think you have in your life? What happened to your peace? Did you decide it was time not to be at peace anymore? You were just at peace, and now you are not. Once the drama begins, the ego takes over, and the flare up has to run its course until the ego has had its fill. If the conditioning has a lot of history attached to it, its fill can last a long time and end up anywhere. Many people end up in jail, have car accidents, etc. whatever form the conditioning takes on produces so many problem. So many tragic things happen when this occurs, and it can all be avoided if you take the time and learn to *"Wear the world like a loose garment"*. Take the time to understand it is just a Conditioned Mind Pattern that was activated and all it did was run its course. You were just along for the ride.

Through Death I Found Life

May of 2009, my father-in-law passed away. I knew my father-in-law about thirty-five years. The day before his passing I went to visit him in the hospital. I was at his bedside and we shared a very special moment, one that will be with me until my own passing. Although there were many people that had come to visit him in the hospital, we were alone. I could see he was much more at peace than the previous days. He was holding a set of rosary beads in his hands. I held his hand and because of his faith as a Roman Catholic I asked him, "Pop, did you make peace with Jesus? He answered yes. I was reminded of a saying I heard many times in my life that Jesus said "*Whenever two or more are gathered in my name, I am there.*" I am not implying that Jesus was with us in that moment, that would just be an interpretation, but there was a Presence with us. I just held his hand for a few more minutes. People came back in the room and I just squeezed his hand and let go.

The next day my father-in-law passed away. It was a sad day for my entire family. It happened so fast, it was hard to believe he was gone. I made a vow that day that I wasn't going to wait until the day before I died to find peace. I have made vows like this before, usually when I heard of some kind of tragedy in someone's life. This time it had a deeper impact on me. I knew it was not going to fade away.

My father-in-law had been diagnosed with COPD (Chronic Obstructive Pulmonary Disease), and it never occurred to any of our family that in seven months he would be gone. I think his passing had such an impact on me because it was a culmination of many things that happened in my life up to that point. So many people with whom I'd grown up were now deceased. My father-in-law's rapid decline from vibrant health to death made life's impermanence impossible to ignore. It showed me how precious life is because one day, just like that, it will not be so. I had never given this much thought, but now I saw that our greatest gift is life itself. This gift is not dependent on conditions, unless *we* make it so.

Nothing needs to be added to life for it to be a gift; just the fact that we are alive is truly our gift from the Creative Intelligence. And so I had another shift in my view of life, and another erroneous view fell by the wayside. The fact of death showed me life in a new way.

If you had one week to live, you would have to let go of whatever you are holding onto. You do not have a choice in this decision. You can hold on as tight as you want, but in a week, like it or not, you will have to let it go — no matter what it is. That's how it is with everything: people we love, objects, our beliefs, everything. Why not learn to let it go now because you never know when the last week of your life will be? A saying I like to use is "Live each day as if it will be your last, because one day you will be right."

Love Is the Basis of All Change

I was reading more and more. I was studying the teachings of Jesus, and coming to understand how love was the basis of all change. I was also continually studying Hinduism and Buddhism, along with the twelve-steps. I was attending five to six twelve-step meetings a week. I was sitting, learning to quiet my mind as much as possible. The more my mind settled, the more I understood the true nature of what my distorted outlook of life had been.

I was learning from the teaching of these different religions and philosophies. I didn't practice the rites or rituals of these traditions, nor did I attach any belief to what I was learning. I just focused on the teachings, the similarities. They all taught love, each in different ways, using different words. But love is love anyway it is said.

The beautiful thing about all of this was: What I took from what I was readings were the things that I needed to cultivate change of my distorted view. Hinduism was teaching me how my distortions originated in my mind. More importantly it was showing me a way to be free of these distortions. Buddhism was teaching me many of the same things as Hinduism, but for me, at a deeper, personal level. The Buddha which means the "Enlighten One" or "Awakened One" was a human being, in form, like you and me. He was inspired to find the cause of our suffering and a way to become free of that suffering. This is what I wanted.

Our Conditioned Mind Patterns discount anything new, no matter how distorted the old idea is. Even if the old way of thinking is destructive, our mind will hold onto it just because of its familiarity. I understand this as the main cause of why I repeated the same destructive behavior over and over; the mind doesn't like change unless it is the one arranging the change.

The denial (due to our conditioning) that's associated with our ego is what keeps us locked into our self-centeredness. The ego tells us we have been living our lives a certain way for such a long time and we are coping just fine, so why change? The question you can ask yourself is: Are you truly happy and free? I don't mean having periods of tolerating life. I mean, are you truly happy? If you can't say there is true joy and happiness in your life, the only person who can discover why, is you. What are you attached to that's keeping true joy from arising in you?

When we are living in a way that we think our way is the right way, and there is no other way; that is what I call "Contempt, prior to investigation." When the mind is in control, and the heart is closed, our Conditioned Mind is calling the shots. Our heart can't open when all we think about is ourselves; this is a direct result of our conditioning. To be willing to listen to someone else, to think it is possible that we don't have all the answers takes a level of humility that can't be attained if our ego is in control. Ego and humility can't coexist in the same moment. This would be like love and hate coexisting in the same moment. Each moment is either of Love or it isn't. It is the same with truth: it either is or it isn't. When there is truth, I can't help but to feel humility, because I know of myself, I am nothing and I understand the emptiness that the I Self offers. It is only when I am free of my I Self that I can be in cooperation with the Creative Intelligence of Universe; that is when I started realizing there is nothing I needed to do, nothing I could do to enhance my life. I just had to realize that life was controlling me, I was not controlling life.

When we realize life is in control (which it is, regardless of whether we allow it or not) instead of thinking we are in control, we will reach a level of humility that allows us to be in harmony with it. When we are trying to control things even if things worked out exactly the way we planned, we still wouldn't be in harmony with life. With the I Self in control there isn't anything beside the I Self to be in harmony with. We would be operating from our I Self, to satisfy our I Self which is derived from our I Self, so how can we be in harmony with anything besides our I Self.

It's Either Love or It's Not

I would always judge things without really knowing any of the facts. My preconceived ideas and beliefs kept me locked into my attachments to things, which caused my suffering. The very things my Conditioned Mind made me believe I needed for my happiness were the very things causing my unhappiness. It is just a facet of our mind. It is what it has been conditioned to do. I started investigating my life because I was tired of just going through life, just getting by. It was like life was a chore. My feelings and emotions were being thrown around like a rag doll. I wanted to find peace and that meant searching for truth. I wanted to find out why I had everything I thought a person could want, and yet I wasn't happy? I wanted real inner happiness, not some idea of happiness made up in my mind.

Quieting our mind allows this truth to emerge from behind the walls that were created by my I Self, to keep it out. That's what happens when we have a closed mind, we do not allow truth to surface so we remain marred in ignorance. This is the only thing that keeps us disconnected from each other and from life itself. "Contempt prior to investigation" is really ignorance in disguise, created by some idea that it is not possible for someone else to know more than you. Someone may have a different view of life that may actually work better than yours, but you want to hold onto your view no matter how many problems it creates, because that is what you know. We all have our strengths and weaknesses, but when we use our strengths together to bring love into the world then we are working in unity with Universal Energy. This is the *true* measure of any action: It is either of love, or it isn't.

Opening the Heart to Love

I have learned to open my mind to new views of understanding, by reading and meditating. I found Joel S. Goldsmith's *Practicing the Presence* priceless. It provided a totally new understanding of life and about me that I never had before. It didn't make me believe any one thing in particular; it opened up for me an understanding of who I am. Not at an intellectual level, but at a personal, spiritual level.

What was written was based in truth. How did I know it was based in truth because it produced a clear understanding, and not some make-believe interpretation? A clear understanding of anything based in truth will always produce love for others. Truth will never produce anything to do with our I Self. There can't be anything, but love, when there is a clear understanding that is based in truth. This is the beauty of truth; Love is its base.

To me it doesn't matter whether Jesus is the Son of God or not. What matters to me is my understanding of what Jesus taught. I understand the love he has for me and for humankind. To me that is what's important. What does it matter if Buddhists wear orange robes and shave their heads? I do not necessarily have to wear special clothes or get a certain haircut to understand The Buddha, or anyone else for that matter. To me the teachings are what matters. I am not saying there is anything wrong with religion or rites and ritual; there is immense value in them. What I found for me is rites and rituals are not a prerequisite to practice how to identify and learn how to change living from my Conditioned Mind Patterns.

In the words of Buddha, Jesus, Abraham, or Allah whatever name of a spiritual teacher you choose — the Conditioned Mind is dominant prior to conscious investigation. You react from some past influence, something you heard, or something somebody else wrote, and you read it and believed it. You never investigated it, you just made up your mind that this is the way it is. This is prejudging, a form of spiritual prejudice. Even if you investigate it, and it works for you, this does not mean that is the way it is for everyone. Our world is filled with different instruments and God is the master musician.

You will have to investigate this for yourself to discover what works for you. I do know this; with a quiet mind, "Contempt prior to investigation" is not an issue. I am allowed to learn all sorts of new things that were previously blocked by my Conditioned Thinking. That is true freedom. Not to be in bondage to some belief that there is only one path to liberation, and if I don't believe in that way I'm doomed. I was doomed my whole life until my heart opened and allowed the light to shine. I would be afraid to call what happened to me anything specific, for fear it would close my heart and thus I would return to the control of my Conditioned Mind Patterns. With the heart open, prejudices don't arise. This in turn allows the sunlight of the spirit to guide my life. This is what I needed to remain free, to live from my heart instead of my Conditioned Mind Patterns.

Understanding "The Second Thought"

There is nothing wrong with intelligence when it's used properly. If it is used to benefit others, then it is being used properly. This is what being in harmony is. I needed to fill my head with new things, which required a lot of reading on my part. I integrated what I was reading with my intelligence and my heart, and I was able to notice the truth in it. This takes a great deal of intelligence. We take what we learn and bring it to our heart, so what we learn can become a benefit to all beings. This is being in harmony with Universal Intelligence.

What was happening now was all the teachings were pointing me to the same destination, the quiet mind; to be of the spirit, to understand what emptiness means, how everything is impermanent, so why attach to it? I was investigating why the mind becomes agitated in the first place, and why it needs something to quiet the agitation.

I remember an incident when my next door neighbor's dog was barking around 4 a.m. I was awakened by the barking and the first thought in my head was, if that dog doesn't shut up maybe I'll go over there and shut it up. I thought this automatically; I awoke from a deep sleep and this was the first thought I had. How much control did I have over this thought? Do you see how much power these Mind Patterns have? I have since come to understand I am not responsible for the first thought that comes into my head. But here's the pivot: if I am being controlled by a Conditioned Mind Pattern I am not responsible for the story (the second thought) either. Once I understand the conditioning, I then become responsible for the second thought, which is the creator of the story. I can then learn how not to attach to it.

Fortunately, I was practicing daily and to that I attribute my next thought, which was: "That's what dog's do, they bark, can you just be with the barking?" This is how my thinking was changing. I accepted that's what dogs do, they bark, I fell back to sleep. I don't know if the dog stopped barking or not, but I do know when I woke up about four hours later, I had a realization that for most of my life I had always wanted things to be different then what they were. I saw how this chronic dissatisfaction created most of my so-called problems and it all stemmed from this; wanting things to be different. As I lay in my bed I just started reflecting how this was true for most of life. It wasn't what happened to me that was the problem; it was me wanting them to be in some other way. WOW!

If I was stuck in traffic, not wanting to be stuck in traffic was the cause of my problem. It wasn't the traffic . . . and who was it that didn't want to be stuck in traffic? I didn't, my I Self. If I just sat in the traffic and didn't want it to be different, than what would happen? I would still be in traffic, but not attached to it. If you look into this you will understand how this holds true for everything. The mind wants to arrange everything to where it creates for you alone a perfect world, but that perfect world exists only in your mind. It wants every traffic light to be green and when it isn't, the Conditioned Mind will get agitated and a flare up will ensue. The degree of attachment to this conditioning, determines whether you have a flare up or a raging eruption. That's what causes "road rage" — an eruption of a Conditioned Mind Pattern.

It can be avoided by being present with what is occurring at that exact moment. A lot of what transpires in our life is due to our anticipation of the future. When you are sitting in work thinking about going home or some place you need to be with the hopes there will be no traffic, this is setting yourself up for your flare-up. Once you are on the road and there is traffic, the negative reaction follows. It has to; it was set up by you to occur. There is no choice, but for that energy in you to react negatively. You can dissipate the negative energy by being with what is here or you can continue to want things to be in some other way. That's your choice.

When you are present with what is here, as opposed to wanting it to be different, you change the whole dynamics of your dealings with any situation. The energy used is transformed to put out flare-ups instead of fueling them. The situation doesn't change, how you cope with it does. It is another scientific fact that our human bodies are pure energy. Where you channel your energy determines what happens. Energy cannot be created, it cannot be destroyed, it can only be transformed. Its direction determines your transformation from a self-centered being to one who emanates love.

Change Is Constant

How does an individual like Adolf Hitler get his power to inflict so much harm to so many people? Not from his words, they are in and of themselves powerless. It is people attaching to his words and giving them the energy that's needed to allow their emotions to fester. That's what gives the words the transforming energy. You can't have a riot with one person; you need the energy of others to incite a riot. Jesus preached love and the angry crowd wanted him crucified. The angry energy feeds off itself and others. Love does that too. I am sharing my experience to possibly help someone understand, there is a way to bring more love into your life, and into the life of others by changing the way you look at things.

One thing that has helped me keep my mind free of Conditioned Mind Patterns is to not make this journey "about" anything. What I mean by that is this is not about changing my wife or children. It is not about trying to change anyone or anything. It is not about trying to change the world. It is not about anything in particular except the journey itself. What this process has afforded me is to allow everyone in this world and everything in it to be exactly the way it is. The awakened spirit isn't about being free; it is allowing everything its freedom.

The mind is always making life *about* something. From the time the alarm rings in the morning, it becomes about getting up, about getting ready for work, about the cup of coffee (got to have it), about the ride to work . . . etc. This occurs constantly throughout our day. Our mind needs to create making life about something; it uses this to create our reality. A reality that is based in thought, which creates our perception, this isn't true reality. This is created from our I Self because the mind is not comfortable unless it is thinking about something. Creating a world about this or that causes all our problems because of the instability of this created world. Nothing is real in this world because it is based in thought. Thought has no substance to it, so there is no foundation. If your house is built on sand there is no solid foundation to weather the storms.

The mind either holds onto things to the end, whether they are based in truth or not, or it just goes from one thing to another looking, searching, until it can grab hold of something. Then when the next thing comes along it will let go of that and grab hold of the new thing. In each incidence the foundation is faulty. Our mind thinks it is creating stability, but with our impermanent lives, what can we truly consider stable? The only thing that is really stable in life is that there will be change no matter what, and that change always occurs in the present, never the past or future, that is a given.

People act upon their Conditioned Mind Patterns when they are unconscious, before they have embarked upon investigation. If you make life about changing people or about saving them you may find yourself quite frustrated. People change when they understand there is a need to change. Most of us don't understand this need because we don't see truth. Our mind makes us believe there is no need to change; that everything is okay just the way it is. This is what the mind makes you believe. So you can't change anything if you don't know it needs changing.

Our conditioning holds us in its grip, no matter what outside sources are trying to change us. It isn't until we come to our own realization that we need to change that we will take the necessary steps to do it. A thief steals and has to keep stealing. That is what he is conditioned to do. His I Self is never satisfied, or he would stop stealing. He has no awareness of the need to change, so he keeps doing what he knows, no matter the consequences. He may end up in jail, but when he comes out he immediately starts stealing again. What makes the thief not change? What keeps him entrapped in his life-style? If you like, you can substitute the stealing with something more in line with what you identify with.

The world is full of individuals who are conditioned like this, who only think of themselves. They are not at fault; the default setting of their minds is self-centeredness. This is what keeps us unaware and locked into our old way of doing things. The I Self doesn't want us to change because that would cause its own destruction. So this view of self-centeredness must change if we are to change — and that motivation has to come from the individual alone. All the reading and preaching in the world will not make an individual who is living from their I Self start living from their heart. Not unless something happens for the allowing of their transformation that will open their heart.

Saint Francis of Assisi said *"Preach the gospel everyday and when necessary, use words."* Be an example instead of talking about a set of ideals. Our example is more powerful than our words will ever be. There is so much freedom in this because when we are the example we are not attached to anything. This is when we are truly free, when there is no attachment.

Remove the Ideals and Agenda, Remove the Bondage

Just changing your energy pattern from I Self to Presence (the present moment) is all that is needed to become the example of Universal Love, not the mouthpiece or cheerleader for it. When you take away the ideals and agenda, you take away your bondage and your limitations. Attachments limit your ability to love. When you are not attached, what you are left with is I AM. Not I AM this or that, just I AM. You will never experience being freer then that. It sounds too simple, but it isn't.

I don't know if there is any one thing I can pinpoint specifically as being more important than another as far as the readings and teachings I've discovered are concerned, but if you investigate this for yourself you will find what is needed to transform your mind's default setting from being self-absorbed to love. Before this journey began, the love and compassion I now feel for others was never there. A quiet mind creates an open heart, so I can emerge from behind the walls I created for my protection, the walls that turned out to be my prison that kept me isolated in my own mind.

Taking Responsibility for Seeking Answers

There is such an extensive array of information at our fingertips if we are willing to look for it. If we are willing to investigate the source of our behavior and reactions, we can find answers. I have learned when I stopped being ignorant about why I behaved in the manner that I did and started taking responsibility for my feelings and emotions associated with that behavior, my eyes started opening and I was presented with a real opportunity to change. I stopped waiting for God to make me all better and took this responsibility into my own hands.

Do you think God is up there somewhere saying, this person gets this and this happens to that person? I always blamed God when I didn't get what I wanted. I have found it more realistic and beneficial to honor life; whatever the Creative Intelligence of this vast universe is and learn to cooperate with it. This helps me creatively manage what happens to me instead of just accepting it as "I guess this is the way God wants it to be." God is love, how could love allow me to suffer? By saying God gave me free will; I was using that as an excuse because I was ignorant to the real causes of why I was acting the way that I did. How about I do what I do because of the way I had been conditioned! I became a product of my environment which was mostly unconscious. That is what kept love from being the default setting of my mind.

Another saying that I used was "God is testing me." Did I really think God was testing me? What does God need to test me for? If I pass, do I get a better seat in heaven? Do I get to be higher up in the angelic chain of command? There is only one thing that caused me to fail at life and unfortunately it was also the cause of all my misery: it was my self-centered perspective. That's not God's testing of me or causing me to fail, that's my Conditioned Mind. When enough of my blocks are uncovered and love becomes the default setting of my mind I will never feel like I am a failure or like I am being tested again because I will understand there is no such thing. Those feelings are self-created and are derived from my I Self, not from love.

Please investigate this for yourself. All your answers are within you already, you just need to clear the blocks and you will be in harmony with what is there. Not with the future or the past, but the Here and Now. That's all there is, everything else is just the story you make up. You have all your answers within you; you just have to learn to ask the right questions.

Ask the questions that will allow you to cooperate with life. The will of God are those things that cultivate love and harmony in your life. Find and remove the things that block that love. Do you think God's will is something else?

Change the Conditioning, Change the World

I have worked shift work for twenty-two years. I have always struggled on the night shift; to the point of experiencing borderline depression. People have told me to get off shift work, but I knew if I ever wanted true freedom I would have to learn to be with what is here. I can keep trying to find my peace by changing outside things (that is what I always did) or I can find the reasons why I felt like I did. One day as I was sitting in quiet it just hit me, the reason I had always struggled with the night shift was this: from the moment I woke up in the morning on the day I had to work the night shift, all my thoughts were about me. From what I was going to have for dinner at work, to planning my day around taking a nap, to not doing too much around the house because I had to work. This is the way my mind had been conditioned to think, the way my Conditioned Mind Patterns kept me in bondage to my I Self.

Once I identified this Conditioned Mind Pattern I had something to work with. Every time my mind would try and create the story about me going to work I would tell it "Shhhhhh" and it would stop. This was amazing. I can't begin to tell you how much happier I am and how much better my life is because of this one moment of awareness. Also how much better life is for those around me, because my conditioning doesn't just affect me, it affects all those around me — from the teller at the bank, to the gas station attendant, to the people I work with and especially to my family. Change the conditioning, change the world. If this happened to me it can happen to anyone. All that is needed is willingness to work in harmony with life. When your mind becomes quiet you will become aware of the things that block this harmony.

The quieter my mind becomes, the more my Conditioned Patterns are revealed. The more they are revealed, the more of a benefit I am to all beings. I was as self-centered as humanly possible, and today I am not. Not because of me, but because of all those who came before and laid down the ground work and teachings so I could learn from them, and possibly change. I have to do the investigation, but the answers are there. Not a day goes by where I am not eternally grateful for this.

This journey is never ending, which is fine. It is not a search to find anything. I would not say that one person can ever be more spiritual than another, but some people do have more awareness than others. This is the only difference. Science tells us that the whole world consists of the same energy: from the earthworms and bugs, to mud, rocks and water there is nothing that separates our deepest essence, but the separateness created in our mind. When you get quiet enough you understand this from your heart, from love. What separates the different races, but our mind? If there was only love, would there be separateness?

The miracle is life itself. From the day your existence begins you are dying; it is just a matter of when. Some people live long lives, and some not so long — but our death is inevitable. To know in your heart that every day is a gift allows you to live in freedom. When your energy is channeled in this cooperative direction you will feel peace, as opposed to creating your own reality and living like you are going to live forever. When your energy is channeled to live from a self-centered perspective, life is a constant struggle. It has to be. You become the focus of your energy. When you channel your energy towards hate then hate is what you become. When you channel it towards love, then you become that love. When it is channeled to peace you become that peace. People recognize this in others. You will always reap what you sow is another spiritual law; often called the Law of Attraction.

There is such a difference between living from the inside-out as opposed to looking to the outside to fill an inner need. When you live life from the inside-out nothing is needed for you to be happy. When you live to satisfy the inner thirst with outside activity, there is never enough to fill that thirst. So we become thrill seekers, or we complain we are bored or we say life is the "same old, same old." These are the Mind Patterns that make life mundane. When these Mind Patterns are active they don't allow us to experience the excitement of each moment. Even being a thrill seeker never satisfies us: as soon as the rush of the thrill is over, it's onto the next thrill. If you can't be at peace with being just the way you are, you will never be at peace.

Peace can be found with the awareness of the thoughts that come into your mind. What is the quality of your daily thoughts? Thoughts are part of your conditioning. It is only a thought that tells you that you are not at peace. You are at peace, you just don't know it. If you decide you don't need anything to be at peace and all you need to do is just be, then you will be at peace. It is up to you what you do with your thoughts; you either attach to them or not. Find out what happens when there is no attachment.

Labeling and Attachment

History is important because the longer our Condition Mind Patterns have been around, the more they are engrained in our psyche. That means the more history we have with something, the more power it has over us. Look at your Mother and Father; there is so much history involved it would take a nuclear explosion to dislodge the Mind Patterns associated with them. In reality, what are they, but two human beings, like any other humans, who happened to perform a deed that brought you into existence? Look at your level of attachment to them, the level of conditioning around your association to them. This association is deeply rooted because of your history, but one day you will have to let it all go. When you die, nothing is taken with you.

What you become attached to you depends on your labeling of it. Watch, as you go through your day, how things are instantly labeled. The labeling is derived from an association you assign to a thought. What if you see a person every day, but don't know their name; they stay relatively unknown with no association, until you attach a name or a label to them. The thought of a thing does not make it the thing; you attach your association to the thought. The thought is just a thought. The attachment or association (the labeling) gives the thing its life. The association you attach to the thing makes it a part of your reality. If you don't label it then it doesn't become a part of your reality. The less things are labeled, the less attachments there are in your life, and the more things are seen with an open mind and an open heart.

The labeling process is separated into three categories, like, dislike, and neutral. You pass hundreds of people everyday, either walking or driving. Why are you attracted to some and not to others? It is the same way with food, objects, aromas, music — basically, whatever our senses encounter. The world brings experiences, our senses tune into our conditioning and this is what activates our responses, and the labels we give them. This is when the labeling process begins. Then all the feelings and emotions associated with the attachment arise. At this point it is labeled like, dislike, or neutral. All these labels are thoughts from your past Mind Patterns, they are not real. They may seem real to you, but they are not. This is not easy to comprehend because your mind tries to solidify everything. Your reality is only your conditioning.

We label everything and think it is truth. We can't see this truth through this labeling process. That is where our delusions start. All this labeling creates the delusion and this is what we live by. Things we like give us pleasure; we want more of them. Things we don't like upset and distress us; we don't want them in our lives. Things we are neutral about we couldn't care less if they were there or not. All this is just what we perceive; our mind-generated delusions are not truth. The bottle is neither half-full nor half-empty, there is just liquid in it; that is the *truth*.

This is how our mind operates. It senses, it labels, which causes the attachment, it categorizes, and then it reacts, all in a millisecond. That's why it can't be stopped. You can only create space between the sensing something and the reaction by practicing quieting your mind. If you don't practice, the space needed to be aware of this will not be created.

Where does all this labeling originate? As we've seen, from the past. So much of our past controls our life today. Our preconceived ideas, our concepts, beliefs all derived from our Conditioned Thinking, which became conditioned through our mind always trying to arrange our life to be comfortable. Look at food and the history there. Most diets don't work because there is such a strong association with food and pleasure. It is almost impossible to break that hold.

Look how long the association with food and pleasure has been engrained in our psyche. From the time we were infants, we cried because we were hungry and the food brought us pleasure by satisfying our hunger. It's no wonder that there is a weight problem in this country. The more our mind associates something with pleasure, the harder it is to change the conditioning. This is the delusion the mind creates, it makes you believe the object is going to bring you the pleasure you need for your well-being. But actually, the object is empty. There is no real substance in the pleasure this object will bring you, that is created in your mind only. When you become aware of the object as an object and not as a source of pleasure, you will be free of its hold on you.

This is what you will need to come to terms with, the empty promise of pleasure that is created by the Conditioned Mind Patterns. Become aware of how the developed Conditioned Mind Patterns prevent you from being totally free. There is only freedom when there is a choice. Without choice is to be without freedom. Most people think they are free to choose, but if you look very closely you will understand how your life was shaped for you by your parent's and other outside influences. How you were conditioned to believe certain things, such as, success will bring happiness, religion will bring you a sense of purpose, helping people or being nice to people will bring you fulfillment. This is intellect living. That's what the mind wants you to do, live from there, not from your heart. The heart is the only place of true happiness. You can never be disappointed from there. Learning to live from this place does not mean everything will be the way you want it or that everyone will like you. What it does means is you will learn to be with what is actually occurring and you will love everyone regardless of how they feel about you. It's through that love that you will find your freedom, and not have any hate or disdain in your life; wouldn't that be different?

Learning to live this way does not conform to society's conventional approach. If you really look and see the social structure that has been provided for us, you will understand how the structure is flawed. It tends to keep us captive to our desires. It can be said, we live in an addiction-based society. As long as we desire to feel different, there will be some product on the market that will accommodate that desire. Advertisement tells you to buy this product and it will make you feel better. What is it that makes you not like the way you feel? Why does anything have to be different in order for you to feel good about yourself? I'm not saying don't improve things, but you don't have to derive your sense of well-being from the improvements. You don't have to make life about changing who you are; in hopes that the future will make you feel better.

Look at sports. If your team wins you are happy. If it doesn't win you are sad. Look at the suffering this causes you and all the teams that don't win. There are a lot more teams that don't win, there is only one winner. Even if your team wins, the happiness is fleeting, it doesn't last. The mind will make it part of your conditioning so you can relive it in thought as much as possible. You can pull that thought from your psyche whenever needed. You use it to bring you happiness, but it doesn't really change anything, it's just part of the delusion the mind creates. A false sense of security and well-being; we do this over and over with everything.

We use our memory to try and live from a place in the past to bring us pleasure and alter the way we feel. This was my entire life dilemma. I was always trying to alter the way I felt and I would use anything to accomplish that: Work, sex, drinking, drugs, gambling, etc. Today there isn't a need to alter my state of being. An old acquaintance of mine told me a long time ago to keep my head where my feet are. It took a long time, but today I understand what he meant.

CHAPTER 10

Freedom

I have been on this journey of self discovery for two and a half years. I knew what I was going through was real and it wasn't going to end. I understood what was happening and knew it wasn't an emotional ride I was experiencing. I wasn't "just coping" with life anymore. Situations were occurring in my life and I wasn't reacting the way I previously had. I was really learning to be in harmony with each day and how to respond to life instead of reacting to it. To me the most beautiful part of this was I had a huge part in what was happening. It wasn't some kind magic trick or fairy tale. The quieter my mind became the freer I was from my I Self.

Our psyche has a strong hold on our emotions. I was learning how to bring awareness into my daily life, so I could identify those emotions as they arose and not allow them to control me. I was allowing for spiritual completion, in my own life and in the lives that I touched. This, unlike anything else I had done, was working. I wasn't reading as much during this time because there comes a time when you must put down the books and practice, with diligence, how to discipline an undisciplined mind.

My mind had been undisciplined for so long. It said "jump" and I jumped. I didn't even question how high, I just jumped, so there was a need for discipline. Through this discipline I started understanding how my mind would try to attach to something and create a story. By becoming aware of this through daily practice, I developed the ability to stop the thought process in its tracks and return to my place of peace; by using my breath, or keeping my head where my feet were, or using I AM. Any of these portals stopped the story in my head from going on and on, and this created freedom. This is a 24/7 practice so you will *truly* get out of it, what you put into it. No more, no less.

Our Mind Is a Tool; Learn to Use It Skillfully

Our mind, like any other tool, has a correct way to use it. You can use a wrench to get a nail into a piece of wood and it will get the job done, but it is much easier to get a nail in wood with the proper tool, a hammer. That is what we need to do with our mind: Teach it to do things that cultivate love. Become aware of what brings us our joy, our peace, our place of freedom, and teach the mind to be in harmony with such thoughts and purposes.

Find out how our self-centeredness is at the root of our difficulties, and learn what it will take to pull those roots so all that we are left with is love. What entices us to repeat the same things over and over, are the stubborn roots of our Conditioned Mind Patterns. Investigate what benefits your life and remove the things that don't. Learn to use these tools properly, following the examples of those who went before you. If you have the right tool, but use it incorrectly, what good is it? Learn what truth these tools have to offer and you will learn what it takes to be free. If you are not free maybe you are using your tools incorrectly?

Since I have been living this way I no longer feel isolated. I have a connection with life and with humankind that was never there before. From the beginning of this journey I started writing these daily texts messages and sending them to people who wanted them. They are (as I am still writing and sending them) derived from my direct experience at a particular point of my day. Since I have come to understand this practice of quieting my mind as the only way that has ever allowed me to be in harmony with life, there is usually something in the message that others can identify with. They are not written to make anyone believe anything or understand things as I do, they really don't have a specific purpose. Although people tell me they like them, the important thing, as I have been told, is that the messages make people think. The moment there is a hesitation in our thinking that maybe we don't have all the answers, that there is a possibility of another way, in that moment we have a chance of knowing truth.

I can't attach to the messages, like I can't attach to writing this book. Cooperate with life and it will cooperate with you. There is nothing any of us can do to manufacture a true sense of well-being. This book will not complete me. There is already completeness, whatever happens to it. That completeness occurs when our mind is quiet enough not to reach for things outside ourselves to fill a need. I actually use those text messages as a kind of journal. I read them all the time. They help me. People tell me they help them too. But I know if I didn't write them, life would go on. Remember, everything is impermanent. Attach to nothing and you will never be disappointed. This allows you to be with the truth of what is here.

At times some people have asked me to remove them from the list, which is neither here nor there. Non-attachment is the key to freedom. Everyone has his or her own journey and needs to find the right path. If I can be a part of it so be it, if not that is okay too. I can just share what has happened to me. I don't totally understand what that is so I try and always talk about what I have experienced. A belief can be argued; an experience cannot.

Nothing New Here – Just Another Person Witnessing

I have found a way of living that's has helped me alleviate some of the false ideas that caused me so much suffering. It has showed me how my distorted thinking was at the core of those false ideas. I am more than happy to help anyone who wants it. Knowing I am just an ordinary person trying to be happy is where my connection to others occurs. After all, isn't that what 99.9% of us want, to be happy? Even someone who is locked into a certain life-style that does not conform to society's so-called standards, if they were offered a real way out, if they were honest and not driven by the fear of the unknown, they would take that way out without hesitation, no questions asked. Deep down inside, all anyone truly wants is to *love and be loved.*

If not for our Conditioned Mind Patterns, our innate goodness that is in all of us would be the default setting of all our minds. The struggle we have with life is between the innate goodness that is in all of us, and our Conditioned Mind Patterns. Take away the Conditioned Mind Patterns and find out what is left. The understanding of our mind leads to the opening of our heart. Not only have I learned to understand me, but I have learned to understand others. No longer are people this or that, they just don't know their own mind. How can I find fault in others when I was exactly like them? Not that I am different now; I just have a better understanding of why I did the things that I did, and I found that there is a way to change.

The daily text messages I send to people provided my inspiration for this book. They are my understanding of my journey. The more people I talked to about the content of the text messages and the changes that occurred in the way I viewed life, the more people wanted me to send the messages to them. I'm not even sure how many people get them, but I know they expect them and I enjoy writing them. They arise from the quietness as has this book. It really doesn't matter where they originate from, it just nice to be a channel for something other than my self-centered energy and the negativity I use to emit.

This is where my journey has taken me. Although I didn't feel this way at the beginning of it, I now understand how what I went through can be a help to others. I don't put the label on this as "it was supposed to happen," but I use it because that's what's there. I know I was not helping too many people before. This is not something I can keep to myself, even if I wanted to, for when the heart is open what naturally emerges is love and compassion. This is what makes me want to share with others what happened to me. People are suffering needlessly, whether they know it or not. I feel an obligation, not a purpose, to share what I went through. But only to those who want it. I guard against becoming self-righteous, or a know-it-all. I know my truth, and you will have to discover your own. If I can help in this discovery, it would be an honor bestowed upon me.

What I have learned is not new nor is it difficult to understand, but until I became aware there was another way to view life, my outlook was controlled by my Conditioned Mind Patterns. When I do share my experience with someone, most people understand it. But because it was never pointed out to them and because of their own Conditioned Mind Patterns people would say *"they never looked at it like that."* It isn't a lack of intelligence that blocks us; it is just our lack of understanding of why we are the way we are. Importantly, this new awareness gives us a choice that was never there before. Not a choice because something is wrong, but a choice because by not having a choice we only have one way to view life. This puts us in a very limited box of space and time. When we are not locked into our conditioning we are allowed another view. This other view provides us with our choice. With this choice we can then become aware of what we might do to enhance our life so we can live it to the fullest extent possible.

Living in Harmony: A Choice

Some of the questions I like to ask people, especially when they are going through some self-created drama is; is what you are doing in your life working for you? Is the drama that you are creating benefiting your life and the life of others? If they're honest, most people will understand how there isn't much benefit to living a life based in self-centeredness and most drama is created from there. If you are aware of how you were drawn into the drama from your Conditioned Mind, you can respond to the conditioning and change it. Hence you change Mind Patterns that were firmly entrenched in you. This can save you years of chaos. That's what you can learn from the awareness of the Mind Patterns, how to change them so they stop blocking your happiness and I mean real happiness; experienced like never before. A happiness that is not dependent on anything or anybody. It just arises from the innate wisdom that has always been there, but is now becoming unblocked to manifest itself in your life in the form of love.

This is not something that just a few people can experience; this can be experienced by everyone. All that is needed is a willingness to investigate this for yourself.

I have found life is full of paradoxes. If all truths are knowable, then all truths must in fact be known. Once the unknown is known it cannot be the unknown anymore. In seeking happiness, one does not find happiness. Should one tolerate intolerance; if intolerance would destroy the possibility of tolerance? When one pursues happiness itself, one is miserable; but when one stops pursuing, one achieves happiness. You start to really understand these as your Conditioned Mind Patterns lose their hold on you. When life isn't about stuff, striving to become something, or always wanting things to be different, there is clarity of mind that was never there. The never-ending battle the mind creates in trying to arrange everything the way you like it and believing that is what is going to make you happy, ceases. Although this battle goes on constantly, when quietness becomes the center of your being, you have a sense all is well. The more centered you are, the quieter your mind becomes. The quieter your mind becomes the more centered you are; another paradox.

All that has happened and is happening to me was not planned. I just knew in my heart that something wasn't right. I didn't know what it was, nor did I aspire to consciously do something about it. All this happened to me just from admitting that something in me wasn't right. I don't understand, nor do I need to know exactly why it happened, but I do know it resonated from some inner longing that I am not alone in having. Now as I practice this way of living which puts me in cooperation with life, I have met many others who are open to listening to my experiences, because of their own longing; a longing that is at the root of our freedom. Without this longing it is very difficult to understand the need to change. We will only change something if we understand it isn't working properly. When we understand this, we will have a choice. This choice can't be realized without an option being made available to you. Once life presents the option to live another way you can then choose to do what is necessary to take advantage of the option. Your own inner longing is what creates the option. Without it, you will not be aware of the need to change and because of this; you will remain unaware that you have a choice. You need to be aware of your options so you can have and make a choice. If not, life will be lived unconsciously through the mind based sense of our I Self; not wrong or right, just unconscious.

By now I really understood what was happening to me in this process. As my mind was getting quieter, some of what I read previously made more sense to me. My reading provided me the knowledge for me to understand what was happening. I was learning how to live in cooperation with life. This was the result of my practice. And because of this, knowledge was becoming wisdom. This wisdom or truth is what creates our shift of consciousness; our ability to understand what was previously misunderstood.

As stated earlier everyone must find her or his own path. You can't totally understand what another person goes through until you have gone through it for yourself. This is not a search as much as it is a discovery. This is our own discovery, our own understanding, of our true self; it begins once it is understood that our life has no specific meaning and that it is not about anything in particular. We understand we don't have to do anything or accomplish anything specific; it is then that we will be free to live in full cooperation with life and be in harmony each every day.

CHAPTER 11

The Discovery

Discovering the true cause of our feelings of isolation and separateness is priceless. I have always been divided between what my heart was saying and what my head was doing; between my self, who was always there, and my I Self, the conditioned self. Which one am I? I can't be both. My I Self, what isolates me from my fellow men and women, is the doer. When I use the words I and myself in the same sentence, one is the doer (my I Self) and one is the self who has always been there; the steady self to whom life happens; the self that the doing is being done to.

When you say a sentence like "I want to bring pleasure to myself," who performs the act that creates the pleasure and to whom does the pleasure occur? If the act for pleasure is not performed, the self is still there. It does not shrivel up and die because it didn't get the pleasure. The I Self gets angry when it doesn't get what it wants, but the self that is always there just goes on existing. Throughout my entire life, that self has always been there. So it is my I Self that is the cause of all that is done to my self. Go back in reflection and see how this is true.

An Existence Based on One Letter

When you are born or start your existence in the human form, whatever terminology you prefer, you are free of attachment. What was the first thought you ever had, and what letter do you think it started with? I know it isn't really possible to recall this, but I think for me it probably had something to do with the letter "I." I was hungry or I wanted to be held, or some other thought of I. The point is, look how that one letter controls our life. Our entire existence is based on that one letter.

In the beginning of life we are not consumed with our I. There are no Mind Patterns that are controlling us, yet. As we grow we gain our sense of identity through our concept of I. This is where our problems with life develop because our I comes to control our self. As long as we are alive there is a self that is our true nature, but when the default setting of our mind is "I," it blocks out our connection to life. We live strictly from our egoic side, and that bias creates suffering. Our spiritual nature can't shine through our "I." Although we are all spiritual beings by nature, our I blocks and subdues us from this nature. Look back to when you were a child, look at the memories that start with the word I: "I was fat, I wasn't smart, I was good in sports or I wasn't good in sports," and so on. Like the other list, this one is endless also. The older we get the more our "I" becomes the dominant mode of living.

This is the real culprit of our problems. It doesn't matter whether you are the President of the United States, if you're a homeless person, if you are a billionaire, or if you barely make ends meet: When the driving force behind your existence is your "I," you will be driven by Conditioned Mind Patterns and you will suffer and cause suffering to others.

Under the operating mode of self-centeredness, you can't be in harmony with life, so you will never be in harmony with others, never. There can't be any harmony because the self that allows this is blocked out by your conditioned I. Without this harmony, love can't flow into the world. This is the love that Jesus talked of; the love of your neighbor as yourself. If you can be honest, you will understand this and allow your true self to arise.

You will become aware of how your I has caused, and is causing every problem in your life. Observe how it affects all those around you. Where does your anger come from? Even if someone slaps your face, as soon as it happens it's the past, so the past energies are causing your present moment anger. How does the energy from this anger affect those around you, directly or indirectly? You can turn the other cheek — or not — but understand this; if you don't, you are the one who will suffer, and thus you will cause the suffering of others.

I saw this firsthand when I attended my son's freshman orientation. Each teacher took his or her turn on stage in the high school auditorium, and said a few words; averaging about two minutes each. One teacher was going on and on, longer than the others, maybe five or six minutes. It was amazing the way the energy in the room was transformed. The energy in the auditorium became one of anger. The energy was neutral up to that point, but the more this teacher talked the more anger became the room's energy. It was real and you could feel it. After a couple of more minutes, the teacher finally sat down, but the feelings of anger didn't diminish just because she stopped talking. People held onto the energy and were talking about the long speech after the orientation ended, in the hall way. You could still sense the anger in people's voices. It was an amazing observation for me because I saw how real this energy was and how it affects so many people; whether they know it or not.

This is why negative energy has so much power; the energy that is transformed just feeds off itself. The more people involved the more pull the energy has. If you are not aware of this you get pulled in before you even realize what has happened. Where does this energy come from? What is its cause? Does it come from the thing, or the thought of the thing? Where does the thought come from; your mind-based I. Think about it. The self is just there, it isn't angry, it isn't un-angry; it is just there. Our I is the only thing that has anger, without it, anger would not exist. You become angry because your I tells you to become angry.

How about frustration, that occurs because things aren't the way we want them to be. There is no other cause of our frustration, but that. If you didn't want something to be different, the situation would be the same, except your self would be experiencing it instead of your I Self. If I didn't want the situation to be different, what would be the cause of my frustration? There is no frustration, if I am not my I.

Stopping the Fight

A burden of a lifetime will be lifted from you when you understand this. It is only your I that makes you carry the weight of the world on your shoulders. It has to, because that is where you are deriving your identity. Without this identity there is no burden because there is no I. Without the I, you will no longer have to have things a certain way in order to get your sense of well-being. You no longer need anything. You will no longer have to carry the burden.

Think of all the wasted energy in the default setting of "I." Our Conditioned Mind Patterns constantly try and arrange life to suit this I. Our self doesn't need anything to survive, it is pure love, self-sustaining. Only our I needs, and it isn't even a true need, it is a need made up through thought only. The need is all part of our I-created delusion. If the I-thought is not there, the delusion would not be there, but our true self would be. Our fight is with our I not with anything else. Stop your "I" from controlling your life, stop your fight.

This is why I was always in discord: All my energy was directed to the very things that caused my problems, my discord. My problems were bombarded with this energy. There were very brief moments of harmony, but they only occurred when outside circumstance went the way I wanted them to. So the harmony never really lasted because I was doing things that were mostly destructive, not constructive. I never understood the hold my "I" had on me. Prior to the last five years, it was impossible to change. As long as the energy kept feeding my I Self, my behavior, which was controlled by my Conditioned Mind Patterns, kept getting more self-absorbed.

Although my life has been changing since the day my existence began, it didn't change for the betterment of my self or others. It is not an accident that what is happening to me now is occurring because I'm choosing and taking actions to be in harmony with life. I know in the past I didn't change because my I was always looking to be fed, no matter what it needed to do to find the self-centered fuel to give it energy.

The self that doesn't need anything external is not derived from "I". This can only be understood from a place of quietness. If you want to be happy, joyous, and free, start learning how to quiet your I. Notice how your Conditioned Mind Patterns start to lose their hold on you. See how you can live from a place of freedom, not one of bondage? When you start a sentence with the word "I" at the beginning of it, stop and think about what you are going to say. Ask yourself if it will truly benefit your life, and will it be a benefit to others? Be honest.

It Takes Work, But the Rewards Are Great

There is the real possibility to always be at peace, to be in harmony with life. But it will not happen without your help. Faith without works isn't dead; faith without works is just wishful thinking. What most of us do is hope for life to take care of us instead of putting ourselves in the best possible position to allow the goodness of life to work for us — which is what cooperating with life will do for anyone.

This cooperation has nothing to do with the material plane. We can be greedy, yet still be rich. We can hate, yet still have people who love us. We can be miserable and still live to be a hundred. But there is one thing we will never have when life is lived from the plane of our I Self and that one thing is a connection to Divine Love. Not God's love for us; that's there regardless of what we do, but our love for God. Our love for God is what happens when our heart stays open. The more the heart remains in its natural state of openness, the more love there will be for God and for life itself. Real joy of living is not based in anything outside us; it can only materialize when there is cooperation with life. This can only be done by continual learning what will keep our hearts opened so Universal Love can become our mind's default setting. Universal Love conquers our negative Conditioned Mind Patterns, one day at a time.

What has happened to me is not something special. It is available to anyone who is inclined to believe there is more to life than what meets the eye. If you are willing to search within and learn how to identify and stop the noise in your head from constantly drawing from your Conditioned Mind Patterns, you will have a chance to be in cooperation with the Creative Intelligence of the Universe for a *truly* miraculous change to occur in your life. As the song *Amazing Grace* states: *"I once was lost, but now I'm found; was blind, but now I see."*

CHAPTER 12

Twelve Steps to Freedom: An Interpretation

1. We admitted we were controlled by our Conditioned Mind Patterns and became aware of how they caused our behavior and reactions to be self-centered.
2. Came to understand that cooperation with Universal Energy will allow us to be in harmony with life.
3. Made a decision to practice aligning our will and our lives to be in harmony with the Divine Purpose, so our heart remains opened and our behavior is of Universal Love instead of self-centeredness.
4. Made a searching inventory of the self-centered behavior that kept us in bondage and isolated from our own innate goodness.
5. Identified the exact nature of our wrongs and the associated behavior that held us in our self-created bondage and blocked us from reaching the full potential of our Creative Energy.

6. Were entirely ready to cooperate with Universal Energy so our behavior becomes conducive to what is necessary to be in harmony with life.

7. Humbly learn to cooperate with Universal Energy so our reactions to what happens in life are derived from love instead of a self-centered perspective.

8. Made a list of all persons we had harmed due to our self-centered behavior and became willing to make amends to them all and be an example of Universal Love.

9. Made direct amends to such people wherever possible, but only with the intention that it would benefit them and not serve our own satisfactions.

10. Continued to learn and deepen our spiritual insight by being mindful of each moment and how we react to situations as they occur in our life.

11. Sought through prayer and meditation to improve our consciousness of Universal Love, so knowledge becomes wisdom and our actions make us an example of this love in our relationships with all beings.

12. Having had a spiritual awakening as a result of these steps, we learned to respond to life from love instead of reacting to it from our I Self. In this process we become a benefit to all beings by expressing Universal Love in everything we do.

This interpretation is not an attempt to change the original Twelve Steps of Alcoholics Anonymous. These steps are just an interpretation developed to help anyone who sees a need to change the way he or she has been living. These are a tool to be used to help identify why you do the things you do and a step-by-step model of what can be done, if you want to change. It is all contingent on the willingness of the individual to want to change. The steps are not magical.

Notice how little control you have over things that occur in life; what you can learn to control is the way you respond to what happens to you. Most of us were never given a guide to help us understand this process, nor were we ever taught how to do this.

If you become addicted to a substance or behavior, then you can attend a twelve-step program. But what if you don't necessarily have a clear-cut addiction, but are looking to enhance and understand your life? Maybe you are looking to fill a void or be more at peace. There are many different tools a person can use to foster change, and you may find these steps useful. They can be used to investigate your perspective of life, and if you choose, you can do the things necessary to become aware of your Conditioned Mind Patterns and change that perspective.

As I grew up I didn't have control over many things that happened to me, but I could have reacted differently had I properly learned how to process my reactions and emotions. Instead, I became conditioned. By going along unconsciously I was at the mercy of any number of outside influences and inner repercussions. Unconsciously, I become attached to external things and controlled by them. Reaction don't just happen by themselves, something provokes them. By understanding and utilizing these steps, you can become increasingly aware of your unconsciousness and learn how to be in control of your life — instead of allowing things to control you.

1. **We admitted we were controlled by our Conditioned Mind Patterns and became aware of how they caused our behavior and reactions to be self-centered.**

What is the main reason we behave and react to life the way we do? What is the real culprit to our Conditioned Mind Patterns? Who can we blame why our life is the way it is? Is it our fault? Is it God's fault? Can we change things or is change only for people chosen by God? What did this God have to do with any of this anyway, and what's our part in this? How much of it do we have control over? These are just some of the essential questions you will need to ask yourself if you want to find out the causes of your inner conflict and how to quiet those conflicts. If you don't ask the right questions, you will not get the right answers.

What does it mean to be controlled by a Conditioned Mind Pattern? It means to unconsciously react to things out of habit and ignorance. When we become conscious of what we are doing, we no longer merely react to life, but we start responding to it. That is what happens when our mind becomes quiet; we start to become aware of truth that was blocked out by our Conditioned Mind Patterns. Once we become aware of this, the transformation from ignorance to truth is revealed. Once truth is revealed, we start to understand our mind and we cease to be controlled by it.

Did it really matter what our mind had selected and used as our tantalizing substance of choice? It was all used for the same reason, to bring us the desperately needed satisfaction we sought. So many different things were used to try to quiet this yearning inside of us. It didn't really matter what it was. They were all part of our conditioning. Becoming aware of the reasons why we had to use anything at all is where these steps will lead us.

Of course, the addictive substances or behaviors must be removed, or none of the awareness of our Conditioned Mind Patterns will come about. Still, the substance itself is immaterial. Things don't cause us pain; our Conditioned Mind Patterns derived from our self-centered view cause our pain. This is what is controlling us. This is what we are unaware of. Until we identify the control these Mind Patterns have over us, we can't become free of our conditioned responses. As we learn to stop living from our I Self, we stop looking for anything outside ourselves to fulfill our inner yearning. Until we become aware of this cycle we remain controlled by our Conditioned Mind Patterns and their ways of trying to bring us satisfaction.

The desire to stop living destructively comes from the basic instinct to survive. Just admitting we are being controlled by something will not properly address the true nature of our Conditioned Mind. That admittance alone does not bring relief, because we will just use something different or go back to the substance or thing that was used in the past. We as a society do it all the time, we search out anything that will make us feel good and we have no control to stop it until we become fully aware of what is happening. Once we become fully aware of our Conditioned Mind Patterns, then we can do what is necessary to gain control of them. We start to gain control only by first admitting we were controlled by our Conditioned Mind.

The substance used is only a mask, a substitute. Substitution is a key tool of our ego. If one substance is removed it will just cling to something else. That happens to people all the time. Substitution causes us to remain ignorant to the true nature of our malady. If we are ever going to overcome the I Self cravings, we are going to have to address the underlying cause of our issues: our self-centeredness. When this is discovered, you are no longer controlled or unaware, and you are no longer ignorant.

So it is our self-centered behavior that we are controlled by and unaware of. Operating from this mode is what makes us react to life the way we do. This is the process that causes our life to be the way it is. If it wasn't for the unawareness of our self-centeredness we would have never developed our Conditioned Mind Patterns in the first place. Without the Conditioned Mind Patterns, love would have been the operating energy in our life.

If that isn't true, why don't we experience spiritual bliss when a particular substance is removed? What causes us to still seek outside relief, through some other form? It is not the substance; that has been removed. The self-centered thinking, due to our conditioning, is what makes us think that something outside of us will bring the desired pleasure and relief. The substance has no power unless it is given power. What gives it power, but a Conditioned Mind Pattern. A thought has no substance; it is just a thought, nothing else. There is nothing concrete in a thought. It is just energy that arises and then gets directed. The direction of your energy determines what happens in your life.

Until you become aware of this you will go through many years of unnecessary pain and suffering (clinging to the things that do not cultivate love). Due to the distorted understanding of how this process works we stay marred in our self-absorption. By understanding how all our actions and reactions to life were caused by our Conditioned Mind Patterns and that they do not occur randomly, this will give us the opportunity to start changing the way we view life. When our view is changed, our life is changed.

Being controlled and unaware is not a weakness; it actually becomes our greatest asset because it is the stepping-stone that allows us to become aware of the error in our thinking. We become aware that we react the way we do because of the way we have been influenced and because of the way we attach to what arises. Going from unawareness to awareness is necessary in order for the ego to take a back seat and relinquish its control over us. As long as the ego runs the show, our cooperation and harmony with life will be fleeting, at best. So the more we realize just how controlled we are by our Conditioned Mind, to that extent will we become aware and thus free.

To admit that something is not quite right in our lives is the first step to opening our hearts. This opening gives us the ability to start investigating and to become aware of how our self-centeredness lies at the core of our issues. This admission allows us to transform from living through our intellect to living through our hearts. Mind you, this is just a beginning, but it is all we need to allow our heart to open. This barest of beginnings does not make everything all better at once, but it is a start. Adherence to this way of living goes directly against the way we have been conditioned, but that doesn't mean it can't be changed. If the way we had been conditioned had been right, then why aren't we happy every moment of every day?

For most of us this beginning will probably be the first truly honest desire to live in cooperation with life since childhood. Our cooperation will manifest in the love we have for ourselves and others. And if we had lived our lives from that perspective from the beginning, our life and this entire planet would be much different. It is never too late to change. We just have to understand it will take time, patience and perseverance to build the necessary practices that will change our perspectives from ignorance to truth. That is exactly where the remaining steps come into play. They will help you understand the truth of existence by learning to quiet your mind. The less the default setting of your mind is self-centered, the quieter your mind will become. The quieter your mind becomes the more truth (Love) is revealed.

2. Came to understand that cooperation with Universal Energy will allow us to be in harmony with life.

Truly understanding how our self-centered behavior had been the cause of all our problems, it gives us something tangible to work with. We have something real to identify with. The Conditioned Mind Patterns which manifest in the form of behavior are something we can see, something that was developed over time and can be changed. We look at this behavior and know these are the blocks to our cooperation with Universal Energy (God). With this knowledge we know in our hearts that we are finally on a path to freedom and happiness. No longer are we ignorant of how our lives have been controlled.

Through recognizing our self-centeredness and taking responsibility for it, we learn new aspects of our mind. We learn how our behavior alone can take us out of harmony with life. We no longer look up above (outside ourselves) for our answers. We start to look within because we know this is where we will find them.

We understand that our mind caused our problems by trying to constantly satisfy our ego. We become aware of how disharmony with life arose from our discontented mind; a mind that was always looking for something. This is what kept us in disarray. Nothing else, no Devil, no God, no person, place or thing ever causes our discontentment. It's always a mind conditioned to think and react to things in a certain way. It is an undisciplined mind that takes us along for the ride; a mind that doesn't allow cooperation with life because of its egoic nature.

At this point in our journey we will start to experience just what it means to know we are opening a new chapter in our life. We are not expanding on the old way of thinking; we are starting to understand things as we never have before. This understanding aligns us with the Creative Intelligence of the Universe. Whatever you choose to call this Intelligence, this Universal Energy, is up to you. But know that it is there, and it is pure love. Learn the necessary training to put yourself in alignment with this energy; this is what makes our transformation possible. This transformation occurs by knowing truth, not your truth, but the Creative Intelligence truth;

truth that only becomes known by cooperating with life, by quieting your mind. You do not have to do anything to know this truth, it occurs when love is in your heart.

This Universal Energy is where all creation began. This is the eternal life that Jesus talked about. To me, when Buddha talked about reincarnation, that's what he was talking about; energy being transformed. Energy is energy, it is always there; never bad, never good, it is just energy. Understand you alone are in control of how this energy controls your life. Where it is directed determines how you live and react to situations. How you are conditioned determines where this energy is directed. When you are self-centered this energy will be allowed to control you and create your so-called problems. This energy is directly related to your heart. This I Self energy dictates a closed heart. Universal Energy (Love) dictates an open heart.

Creative Energy is very difficult to align with because of our Conditioned Mind Patterns. If you really want to change, it will take every ounce of will that you have — not because there are outside forces that are trying to hold you back, but because you have so many years of conditioning and your habits have been so deeply engrained in you subconscious. Your own ego will constantly work against you so it can be in control. The ego does not go away quietly and will try anything to survive. This is what causes our struggle with life; the heart tells you to serve others, and the ego tells you to serve yourself.

Since energy can only be transformed, our conditioning is vital to the energy of any situation. Will distress or anger close our heart, or will these emotions be allowed to pass through, allowing our heart to remain open? When we rightly relate ourselves to this Universal Energy, amazing things start to happen. Years of reacting to things in a certain way stop. The things that have attracted us in the past do not have the same hold. They are still there, but with practice their hold is lessened. We cease reaching for our happiness from an outside source. Our internal agitation, our inner sense of lack, diminishes. We stop trying to always arrange life to be a certain way. We become more aware of these occurrences because we understand where the real causes of our problems are derived from.

You will learn that trying to attain harmony by behaving a certain way does not allow it to happen. You don't need to go to church for it to happen. You don't need to do anything for it to happen; matter of fact, anything you do will just hinder your harmony. Learn to be still and let Universal Energy work for you. It is always in stillness that you will be in cooperation with Universal Energy and thus you allow yourself to be in harmony with life.

In essence what we are trying to do is change the solutions that we have developed to cope with life situations. Our previous solutions were based in our selfish pursuit of trying to have things the way we thought was best suited for us and us alone; created by our Conditioned Mind Patterns. We are now on the path to change those solutions, so they are based in love, and we can benefit others. If this change is not given our full attention, we will continue to be controlled by the solutions of the past. So when we learn to cooperate with Universal Energy, we learn to respond from a new place, and the solutions of the past, which were based in self-centeredness, give way to our solutions of the present, which are based in love.

3. **Made a decision to practice aligning our will and our lives to be in harmony with the Divine Purpose, so our heart remains opened and our behavior is of Universal Love instead of self-centeredness.**

Having started the process of identifying our Conditioned Mind Patterns and having our hearts opened so we truly understand Steps One and Two, it is now time to make a commitment to bring more truth, more love, into our daily lives and allow our hearts to remain open as much as possible. This decision is the beginning of a lifelong practice of self-investigation and discovery; harmonizing our lives with Universal Energy is a 24/7 practice. It is not a doing or an attainment of anything; it is a quieting of our mind, which automatically opens our heart.

The lack of love in our lives is what caused our problems. Quieting our mind allows us to understand how this lack of love overtook us in the first place. The core of our commitment is discovering what occasioned our lack, which in turn kept us from cooperating with life. We now decide to adhere to the rest of the steps and remove these blocks. Understand that this decision will be one that we need to affirm over and over, everyday, so we can come to understand what closes our heart and takes us out of harmony with life.

The most important part of our decision is aligning our will with the Divine Purpose. Change does not occur by itself, so developing a steady, regular practice is how this will happen. Our decision entails a practice to develop an awareness of what will bring quietness into our life by learning to live in the present moment. This is the place, being present to what's here, where the quietness begins, and where life as-you-know-it ends. Right now the only place the mind lives is in the past or the future, as our mind has been conditioned to think our past or our future is better than our present. That is what creates the noise in the head and the closing of our heart. Our whole practice is to learn to be present, so our innate goodness is allowed to arise.

Upon arising in the morning, take the necessary time to re-set your mind's default setting away from the self-centeredness and ego grasping that has been developed over the years. Focus on making the mind's default setting one of love and compassion. Otherwise, it will be very difficult to find your place of peace when the busyness of life takes over. If you have to get up early, then that is what you do. This is an individual journey so you need to find a way to practice that will bring you the most benefit, so you can be a benefit to others. Remember this whole practice is for you to find what you need to do, so you can be in cooperation with life and live in harmony with all beings.

When our day is started from a place of quietness, we are in alignment with Universal Energy and it works for us. Our whole being aligns with this energy. This is the exact opposite of what happens when we live from our self-centered Mind Patterns that are based in our I Self. There is often no cooperation, no harmony. So making a decision to investigate and change our view of life is a key if we are to have love as our mind's default setting.

Once the day is started from quietness many tools can help us sustain this state. This is what our practice allows, discovering what is needed to remain in harmony with Universal Energy. In the beginning Conditioned Mind Patterns will constantly pull at you to take you from your state of quietness and try to close your heart, because that is all you know. Change takes time and you have to give it the time needed to allow it. Develop a way to bring yourself back into the quietness, to keep your heart open when some Conditioned Mind Patterns grabs you and tilts your view of life to self-centeredness.

Understand that we are either in harmony with Universal Energy or driven by self-centered energy. Remember that energy can't be created or destroyed, only transformed, so the energy will be there is one form or another. Being aware of this energy and where it tends to bring us, will help us understand that life is random and unpredictable, but that our reactions don't have to be. Remember that various influences have molded our character to believe this is "just the way we are." But it is only the way we have been conditioned to be, and if we want to, we don't have to remain this way.

The Third Step decision will enable you to understand how it is your responsibility to change the way you live, if that is what you *truly* desire. So through a yearning to live differently and dissolve whatever blocks your harmony with Universal Energy, you will be making a commitment to practice the rest of the Steps. This commitment will give you the willingness that is needed, to help you understand your Conditioned Mind Patterns and how they control you. Also how when you are rid of these Mind Patterns, your innate goodness (Love) arises, so you are in harmony with life more often than not.

Having admitted that your Conditioned Mind Patterns are in control of the way you've been living, and understanding that it doesn't have to remain this way, is the foundation of real and profound change. Making a decision to do what is necessary to make this change is the key to what you will discover about yourself, and what you are willing to do about it. You can stay locked into your Conditioned Thinking, and have your heart fluctuate between being opened and closed, as you experience the ups and downs of life. Or you can learn what you need to do to keep your heart open; making your life one of equanimity and love, so you can be a benefit to all beings.

4. Made a searching inventory of the self-centered behavior that kept us in bondage and isolated from our own innate goodness.

Making a searching inventory of the self-centered behavior that kept us is bondage and isolated from our own innate goodness is an everyday practice. It is by far one of the most important decisions that will ever be made in our life. It puts the whole responsibility of our life in our hands. No longer do we have to be unconscious of how we react to life, and we do not have to wait for a miracle to change us. But it will take an endless commitment for us to become a benefit to all beings, and that includes ourselves. The willingness of our commitment will determine the degree of our change. The change begins by taking an inventory of the things that block this commitment from being fulfilled.

Prior to this step we have reflected upon the errors of our past and what has kept our heart from opening. This reflection is a beginning, but it is not enough to become an awakened being, free from the bondage of our I Self. That will take a true understanding of what is inside of you that caused you to become the way you are. That didn't just happen by accident. There were causes and effects, and Step Four will reveal the Conditioned Mind Patterns of those causes . . . and effects.

The first three steps allow the mind to start the process of learning how to become quiet. This step teaches you what caused the mind to become noisy in the first place. You didn't begin your existence with noise; it was developed. What is it that makes us develop this noise? Everyone is born in stillness, so what takes our mind out of this stillness? Noise comes from the development of a separate identity from our true self to our I Self; created by our ego.

We do need to pay some attention to ourselves in order to survive. We need loving contact, food, sleep, oxygen. We do need names in order to live socially. There is nothing unloving about those needs. It is our fixations on outside solutions and the identity we associate to them that gives rise to self-centered and addictive behavior. What exactly does this mean? When you begin your existence on earth you are pure, innocent, and free. You are connected to everything. There is nothing but love in your heart. Your heart is as open as it will ever be. There is nothing to close it. As you grow older, depending on the love that is around you, your attachment to outside things becomes more and more, and this is what closes your heart. The less love that is around you the more you will look outside yourself for some form of fulfillment. Your development in life then becomes one of a self-centered nature, and this does not allow what is necessary for the development of your human manifestation to be conducive to allowing your heart to remain open and for your mind's default setting to be of love.

As you are identified with a name for society's purpose, this is the first step to the attachment to the I Self. With this identity in place it is used by the ego to further engrain its development into the subconscious. An example of this is when you have pure water and it becomes polluted. The true nature of water is always pure, regardless of how polluted it gets. The more pollutants that are added to the water, the more its true nature is hidden, but it is still pure. Nothing needs to be added to the water to return it to a state of purity. Its true nature can never be changed. We need only to remove the pollutants that made it impure. So it is with us, our true nature will always be there, and it will always be based in love, but our pollutants must be removed for us to be the love that we are.

Here is an analogy they may help you understand the contrast between the I Self (ego) and your true self. An opened hand is your *true self.* Now make a fist, this is your I Self. It is real to the point that it's a fist, but it is the closing of the fingers that makes it a fist. So the condition of the fingers closing is where the fist comes from. It only exists because of this condition. When you open the fingers, the fist goes away. It existed yes, but it doesn't always exist, it is contingent on conditions. Although the fist is dependent on the hand, the hand is not dependent on the fist. The hand always exists, whether there is a fist or not. This is how your Conditioned Mind works in conjunction with the ego, to control your life. Certain conditions arise that activate a Conditioned Mind Pattern, and your ego, your "I", assumes control of your life. So the ego activation is contingent on certain conditions arising. Understand, you do not need your "I" to exist, but your "I" needs you to exist. That is why the ego creates Conditioned Mind Patterns, which manifest as wants and desires, so the delusion of "I" holds you in bondage to your I Self.

That is how we are: our attachments, our "I" never become us. Your mind may tell you that is who you are, but the pure being can't change. It is independent of anything. It is energy. It never changes. That pure being is there throughout your entire existence. This is what causes the struggle within. It is not a struggle with things on the outside, it is a struggle with the mind that's been conditioned to make us think we need and are our attachments; this is our delusion.

As we develop and adhere to society's conditioning we learn to seek fulfillment from an outside source. Society holds us captive to things, and to the money system that symbolizes things. This is where evolution has brought us. We have used our scientific, technological intelligence to create enough outside distractions that very few people are in touch with what is needed to be truly happy; to be in unity with themselves and the flow of life. Even when someone comes along who is in touch with this and tries to convey this message to others, he or she is labeled a freak, or something else. Sometimes they are even crucified.

This is exactly what is happening in our world today: the more self-centered we become, the more distracted we are. And the less we understand our true self; the less I understand me, the less I understand you. This creates a world of individuals on one planet who live in their own world, with their own agenda. Maybe the agenda entails getting to heaven or becoming a success, raising a family, driving a luxury car or even becoming President, but without being in touch with your true self there will always be something missing. No matter what is attained no thing will ever be enough. Without a real connection to people you will always be empty. The I Self has evolved to destroy our connection and unity with others. If it's all about "me getting mine," then how can I be concerned with what's happening to you?

What this step will reveal is how our real struggle is between the energy of love and the energy of ego satisfaction; the energy of keeping our heart opened or closed. This is our struggle. So when our energy is channeled to strictly satisfy our I Self there has to be a struggle. This is a Universal Law. You can't break any law and not experience consequences. You can't hide from yourself. The energy that is put out is what is returned. Love out equals love in. It's not love on an individual bases, but love on the Universal level. Why does a child dying in Africa have less affect on you then say if your own child dies? It is only because you are attached more to your own child. This is difficult to understand, but when your heart opens to Universal Love, you become the love that you are; this is unconditional love from the heart not from the Conditioned Mind.

There are no degrees to this love because there are no attachments. You love all humanity equally. Only a quiet mind will grasp this spiritual law at the heart level. Intellectually it sounds insane to love someone you don't know as much as someone you know, but that is the intellect being controlled by a Conditioned Mind. When there is quietness, there is only love, unconditionally.

Here is what happens when a law, whatever it is, is not adhered to. When a speed limit is set, and you adhere to it you are in harmony with the law. Once you go over the speed limit you are breaking the law, and many different things can happen. You do not have to get caught to be breaking the law. Getting caught will only punish you by society's standards, but how about the spiritual standards? What price will you pay for breaking the law? No one can stop you from exerting your will and breaking any law. Only you can do that, but you will pay a price if you don't do it. The price paid will be in the direction of your energy, and that direction determines your life. Breaking any law will close your heart because you are not in cooperation with what is. When you are not in cooperation with what is, you are operating from a self-centered perspective, and with that being the direction of your energy your heart will close. The direction of your energy will either be to love or it will be to satisfy your I Self. This is your choice.

Making an inventory of the self-centered behavior that causes your heart to close is of the utmost importance if you are to ever be in harmony with life. Every time you do something that closes your heart it causes you and those around you to suffer. Ask yourself why you aren't happy all the time? What causes you to fluctuate between happiness and unhappiness? When you are not happy what effect does it have on those around you? Are outside circumstances causing you to be unhappy or is it the self-centered perspective that causes your unhappiness?

There are many forms our self-centered behavior takes on. Whether it's based in greed, hate or delusion, regardless of the manifestation, the root of the behavior is self-centeredness. Look at the root cause of all your problems; you would never have a problem if what you thought about wasn't derived from a self-centered perspective. Even if someone wrongs you, if you are not aware of your reaction, thinking ill of them, you will not have the energy to allow your heart to remain open. When this happens, love ceases to be the operative energy of your life, and you suffer along with those around you.

When you really look at your behavior and start to become aware of how the bases of most of your actions are self-centered, it won't matter what form the behavior takes on. If its greed, lust, envy, sloth, anger, pride, jealousy, envy, fear, it is all self-centered based. Our distortions of this truth are brought on by our degree of excess. Desires for food, warmth, shelter, love, community are not 'self-centered,' but realistic, even loving. Greed, lust, envy, etc. are not necessary, but are grounded in self-centeredness to fulfill our excessive wants and desires. See the difference?

You don't need to make an endless list of the things you did in the past to become aware how your past decisions were based in self-centeredness. You need only to identify the past Conditioned Mind Patterns behaviors that caused you to react to life in a self-centered manner. Look at the things that closed your heart: What situations made you defensive? When life presented a certain situation, why did you act in a manner that made your heart close — which in turn caused suffering, to yourself and to others? Whether it was sex, anger, greed, jealously, or whatever the manifestation, what caused the reaction that closed your heart? This inventory helps you find what situations closed your heart and caused the default setting of your mind to become self-centered.

Once you identify these Conditioned Mind Patterns you will start to understand why you made certain choices, why you behaved as you did. Remember that Mind Patterns will continue to control you if you don't identify them. Do not focus on any one particular behavior, but on the self-centeredness. The manifestation could be addiction to drugs, alcohol, gambling, sex, shopping, eating, success, power, prestige, money, and so on. Underlying all these behaviors is the mind-based sense of the I Self.

How does the I Self affect relationships? In a self-centered relationship, sex often becomes the pivot. This type of relationship will not last because once the ego gets what it wants it has to move on. Eventually the sex will not be enough to sustain the relationship. Even if the people stay together they probably will not be happy because the ego — of one or both people — wants to be somewhere else. There may be a level of tolerance, due to a social belief in the value of staying together. But true love is not experienced because the ego blocks it out. So you stay together, but you are not happy, or you get divorced, and this also causes suffering. Here is the kicker; both scenarios are created by the same mind, and both create suffering.

Think about this: What are you really looking for in a relationship? Any real, working relationship is based in love. I don't mean just romantic and physical relationships; I mean any relationship. The only thing that blocks you from unity with another person is the ego; when egos clash this creates a problem. No ego — no problem. The problem is it is all a created delusion made up by your own mind, created by your ego. Maybe one day we will stop allowing our egos to control us and stop looking at our differences and know ourselves in truth; as one species, on one planet. Maybe one day we'll understand how much we really have in common, how similar we really are.

The ego is insatiable. Once it has had its fill, it looks for something else. Not necessarily something better, just something different. That's why we are always striving to become something, or seeking something, because the ego is always looking for the next satisfaction. It never stays satisfied for long. Even if life were exactly the way you wanted it, you still wouldn't be happy all the time. There will always be something else the ego would make you think you needed, that would make life better, make it perfect. Even if it was perfect, would you remain in a state of happiness forever? Remember, the ego never stays satisfied for long so I would think not. Understanding this about the ego, and by using these steps as a guide to help you identify the things that keeps your energy from operating from a place of love, you will be able to break the hold that your I Self has on you, and hence your heart will remain open, for your own innate goodness to arise.

When you take an inventory and identify how your Conditioned Mind Patterns come from your self-centeredness and that these Mind Patterns control the way you live, you will then be ready to proceed to the next step in becoming more aware and getting rid of the blockage to your own innate goodness. You will understand this innate goodness as the only place you will ever want to live your life from because you will understand there is no other place that will allow you to be *truly* at peace with yourself. In this place there is nothing you have to do to, nothing you have to be. You just accept what is and stay with it, not wanting anything to be any different. When your innate goodness is the default setting of your mind there will never be a need to reach outside yourself to fulfill an inner yearning. There will never be an 'inner yearning.' An inner yearning is created when there is a sense of lack. When you know the cause of that supposed lack, the lack disappears.

Awareness dissolves the manifestation of negative energy and 'lacking.' Knowing transforms a sense of deficiency to the energy of Love. This is why Jesus said, "Know the truth." He didn't say hope for the truth or wish for the truth; He said, "Know the truth." When you know the truth there is no room for the energy that closes your heart. Knowing allows your heart to remain opened. Since all we truly are is energy and that energy has to be channeled somewhere, knowing how to channel it to make love the base of your life, will allow for love to become your truth.

The remaining eight steps will continue to make you more aware of what blocks your innate goodness from arising. By learning what blocks that goodness, you will allow it to come forward, rather than being blocked and controlled by your Conditioned Mind Patterns.

5. Identified the exact nature of our wrongs and the associated behavior that held us in our self-created bondage and blocked us from reaching the full potential of our Creative Energy.

Understanding how our behavior was derived from self-centeredness is invaluable to the freedom that will be experienced, when we realize although we are accountable for all our behavior, we acted in ways which we didn't truly understand how the ramification of this behavior were going to affect of lives. When we consciously or sub-consciously make a decision to do a certain thing if we are not aware of the way our mind has been conditioned, the behavior most likely will be derived from a self-centered perspective; the decision made will be made to only satisfy our I Self.

An example of this would be if you made a decision to drive a car while intoxicated. Because the decision was based in self-centeredness, the consequences of your decision are never considered. And if you get away with it, next time it will be much easier to do. This unawareness is how the unconscious mind justifies what it does. When you realize this is the way you have been making many of your decisions throughout your life, there is a powerful shift in being (the change in your view of life) that changes you forever. You will never again be able to view life as you previously had. The veil of ignorance is removed.

Understanding our self-centeredness is eye–opening; a revelation that leads us to really understanding the exact nature of our wrongs and our behavior. This orientation often started in our infancy and continued on through adulthood. What made us look outside to fill the inner need in the first place? The behavior is manifested in many forms; fear is at the root of most if not all of the behavior issues. Some of the forms manifested are greed, lust, envy, anger, sloth, jealousy pride, etc. Understand they are only the manifestation of our self-centeredness, which is the exact nature of our wrongs. Unless you understand this link with the associated behavior there is nothing to identify with. The wrong is only a vehicle to the behavior. Look at the reason for the behavior. There is always a cause to the way we act. That is what we need to identify; the exact nature that causes us to behave in such a manner that it takes us away from our connectedness to our Creative Energy.

What causes a person to hate, to steal, to rape, to murder, to overeat, to gamble, to use drugs, to be so angry that they want to hurt others, to cheat on their mate, to abuse children, to live life from such a miserable existence that they commit suicide? This by far is not the entire list, it goes on and on, but the essential question is the same: Why are we doing this, and how does it affect our life?

It is an immense benefit for us to share our inventory with someone who understands what we are doing. Sharing allows for a connection to others that we may feel for the first time. When we share honestly from our heart there is no self-centered isolation. Rather, there is trust, vulnerability, care, connection, and bonding.

This is what it means to be in cooperation with Universal Energy; doing the things that put us in harmony with life. Sharing helps us identify the exact nature of our behavior by saying it out loud. When we hear ourselves saying it, we are confirming a truth that has long been hidden. This will probably be the first time in a very long time that we are in touch with truth. The truth is what will unveil our Creative Energy that has long been blocked by our self-centeredness. By verbalizing it, we will get a clearer picture of separating the behavior from who we truly are. We will understand how the behavior was just a manifestation of our Conditioned Mind Patterns, which made us do things that blocked us from our Creative Energy. This sharing allows a unity to our Creative Energy and to all beings that has never been experience before.

That is what the exact nature of our wrongs reveals: Truth that allows us to understand how, through a Conditioned Mind, our behavior became self-centered. Most of, if not all of our decisions were based on this self-satisfaction and egoic pursuits. When decisions are made based from our I Self we are not cooperating with Universal Energy, and there is no way we can be in harmony and unity with the Divine Purpose of the Universe. Our Creativity Energy isn't allowed to flow, and we just live our life through the revolving door of our self-centeredness.

This is what throws us out of kilter with the rest of the world. This is the exact nature of our wrongs; why we behaved and reacted to life the way we did. Our lives were the way they were because of our Conditioned Mind Patterns, which fed the delusion of ego satisfaction. They were based in a false I Self. We didn't consciously set out to become this way, but through ignorance we gave into our Conditioned Mind and let it run the show. This led to folly, dysfunction, to suffering. We can't grow emotionally or spiritually if the default setting of our mind is our I Self.

Consider the Law of Attraction. What you put out is what you will receive in return. If energy isn't derived from love, then we will not be in harmony with life. That is the way the Law of Attraction manifests itself. It will attract what is emitted by the quality of energy. When the view is one of selfish self-centeredness, what do you think will be attracted to you?

When the cause of our wrongs becomes clear and we become aware of the source of our issues, we will be left to look at one individual only — and that is ourselves. No longer will we be able to blame anything that has happened to us on anyone else. We do not even blame ourselves; but we understand our compliance with our Conditioned Mind Patterns. Once we realize this we can begin to control our own destiny. This freeing experience allows us to face the only enemy we've ever had, and that is our ego.

As we identify the source and exact nature of our wrongs, we will understand how our mind created a world of emptiness that made us constantly look outside ourselves for an answer. This emptiness made us create a world of make-believe, based on the "if only" mind, the would've, should've, could've mind, or the "wishful thinking" mind. The wrong created by our mind is the fallacy of constantly trying to make everything fit into our self-created world, by making us think that it needs to be a certain way for us to be happy. The whole structure of our belief system is distorted, and this distortion not only hurts us, but it hurts others as well.

We put so much into what we believe without having any evidence of its veracity. This is not faith; this is a self-created world we use to justify our existence. We need to create this, so we have something to hold onto, to make us think we actually have a purpose in life. We want to believe there is a God up in heaven that really cares. There is a God, but our own self-centeredness makes it invisible to our heart. So much nonsense goes on in our mind once our viewpoint has been distorted. God (Universal Energy) is always there. God is the Universe, and that is the energy that we are all a part of. But with a distorted view there is no way to know this.

Most of our problems arise because we have never gotten quiet enough to become aware of the right view. With a mind that is constantly thinking, we are prevented from being aware of it. The right view — one that understands truth and puts us in harmony with life — is not one of faith, but one of knowing. Knowing is developed by learning what is real, and what is not. It is not about believing or not believing that is a fantasy made up in our mind. A suicide bomber has faith, they believe in what they are doing, but do they know what truth is? Not some fictitious truth made up in their head, but the real truth of the Divine Purpose of the Universe; a truth that is based in love.

We can't justify our anger if we are to understand our wrongs. To know truth to is to know love. The self-centered mind constantly looks to the future or the past, never the Here and Now. The Here and Now is the only place where truth exists, it is the only place from where the exact nature of our wrongs can be eradicated. This is because it is the only place that exists. Any place other than the Here and Now is just a construct in our mind; it is a figment of our imagination.

Never take the word of someone else about truth. Find out where your problems come from. How much of what you think, do, say, or feel is done in the Here and Now? Why do you constantly try to change the past or arrange the future to the way you think it will better suit you instead of accepting what is actually here?

The exact nature of our wrongs is a created self-centered view that makes us believe we will find our answer in something outside of us that lives in the delusion of time. That is the delusion created. It doesn't matter what is used on the outside; it will never last. Looking outside to fix an internal problem, no matter the outside diversion, will not last if it doesn't come from love. There will always be a need for something else to feel a sense of completeness. When we find that anything we use to try and make us complete is not lasting, we will be ready to go deeper to reach the potential of our Creative Energy.

We may have started this journey to better our lives or to possibly stop hurting. Whatever the reason was that made us start questioning things in the first place, there has to be point when we shift into naturally wanting this practice to be done, for the sole purpose of being a benefit to all beings. We come to a point where we are doing this because we know it is the only way to live.

When we learn to be aware that our wrongs come straight from our thoughts, not directly from the first thought, but by the way our ego attaches to the first thought, we get an understanding of why we behaved the way we did throughout our life. It is all done so our ego can create a story; a story (energy) that it needs because that is the fuel that it uses to survive. That wrong is being unaware that this is being done. Not a conscious wrong, but a wrong nonetheless.

When we are aware of how we invest in those thoughts, we can understand the hold they have on us and learn to let go of them. It is not the past that burdens us; it is our thoughts about the past that burden us. It is not the future that burdens us; it is our thoughts that make us anticipate the future as a burden. When we learn to be in the Here and Now it will be impossible for life to ever be a burden.

When we identify and understand the exact nature of our wrongs they will stop being the controlling energy of our life. It is then that our Creative Energy is allowed to be the controlling energy of our life and since it is based in love the possibilities of what can happen to our life are beyond our wildest dreams. Who knows, we may even write a book. ☺

6. Were entirely ready to cooperate with Universal Energy so our behavior becomes conducive to what is necessary to be in harmony with life.

To get to a state in which we are entirely ready to lay aside years of Conditioned Thinking is probably the largest obstacle we will have to overcome. The psyche's hold on us seems permanent. But with persistence, patience, and practice it will slowly lose its grip. The degree the psyche loses its grip depends on our readiness to cooperate with Universal Energy. To be entirely ready allows the cooperation necessary for our heart to remain open and to maximize our spiritual potential.

Just understanding our Conditioned Mind as the major flaw in the way we lived produces a profound change. If you have gotten to this point in the process of consciousness you are well on your way from the freedom of your I Self that very few people understand. This is what it takes to become entirely ready. It is not a belief in anything or an understanding of some deep secret that will allow you to become entirely ready, it is the ability to understand how the Conditioned Mind Patterns were so deeply engrained in your sub-conscious mind that they made you react to life in ways that were not conducive to being in harmony with it.

When we reach the point where we are entirely ready to do this step, we will not want to change the way we view life out of necessity, we will do so because we understand that it really is our only way to a truly happy, joyous, and free life. This is not holding onto some parts of the way we lived and changing other parts; it is a complete transformation of our heart. Unfortunately there is no other way, but to be entirely ready. We can want to change a little, but by wanting to change only a little then you will experience only a little change.

Years and years of old habits, old ideas, concepts that have been engrained in our psyche since the beginning of our existence, have to fall by the wayside for the transformation to really happen. If you don't have an awareness of how your programmed nature keeps you in bondage, then how will you ever experience being at one with the Creative Intelligence and understanding what it means to live by spiritual principles?

Our behavior can change only when our views, our aspirations and desires change. This is not to say that once we're entirely ready to cooperate with Universal Energy that our behavior becomes conducive to what is necessary to be in harmony with life and we just automatically transform. The transformation means becoming entirely ready. That, in and of itself, is the miracle. The change occurs as we become more aware of what it is that needs changing. If we are not aware that something needs changing, how can we be entirely ready to change it?

What happens to us when a transformation of our Spirit occurs is our heart opens and the Universal Energy (God's Love) takes hold of our being. It is impossible for this state to be induced by us or ignored by us. When we experience this opening of our heart, life as we once experienced it is no more. We began the change with Step One, and continue to evolve with the remainder of the steps. As our insight deepens and truth becomes known, we start to learn the differences in our behavior when our heart is closed, and when our heart is opened. We experience situations through our Conditioned Mind Patterns that close our heart and we do not enjoy the way we react. We learn that these reactions do not put us in cooperation with life. In fact, they produce the exact opposite. We might respond from lust, anger, greed, etc., but the point is that we're now aware that our heart has closed and we are behaving from a mode of self-centeredness. The real point of this awareness is that we do not like the way we are acting and we now have something real to look at so we can change it.

Our closed heart behavior is as different from open-hearted behavior as night is from day. An open heart produces love and a closed heart produces negativity. We stop being "just along for the ride" as we become more aware of the closing or opening of our heart. When our heart closes we can pause for a moment, take a deep breath and refocus our energy into the Here and Now. If we focus consciously on our behavior, we then call upon the transforming power of our energy. In the awareness of the Here and Now we are perfect; we are in total harmony with Universal Love. What takes us out of that harmony is our self-centeredness. So we need to be entirely ready to be rid of the behaviors that take us out of harmony. This is a moment-to-moment practice. It can't be done any other way. Perfection can be experienced in the quietness of the present moment. But once we *think* we are perfect, our perfection is lost.

As we live life, conditions arise that make us react in certain ways. Only our willingness to keep our heart open will make us aware when our heart is closing. At that point what we have practiced comes into effect. It will determine if our heart closes all the way or if we remain aware of it closing and use our practice to keep it open. This is what determines the direction of our Universal Energy, the direction our life goes. It determines who and what is attracted to us, and what our future will become.

The willingness to constantly look at our behavior to understand if it is conducive to harmony lies strictly in the discipline of awareness. The Conditioned Mind that built the walls of our psyche and created our defense mechanisms will try and close our heart. That closing takes on many forms and is very subtle. Meditation will be a vital tool if we are to be entirely ready to change. Without the necessary quieting of our mind, we will not gain the awareness to understand the behavior that closes our heart.

Our varying degree of awareness is what causes fluctuations in the way we feel. When we react from self-centeredness, our heart closes and we usually don't feel good about our behavior. We are probably not aware of this; we just know we don't feel connected to life. We can't pinpoint why we are feeling out of step, but for whatever reason we just don't feel right. This is because we think there is something we have to do to bring us a desired result, but the nature of all desires is impermanence and emptiness.

When our heart closes down, the energy created by a situation is not allowed to pass through us. The blocked energy becomes a Conditioned Mind Pattern, engrained in the psyche for future use. This is what happens when the energy is not allowed to pass through, it gets stored in our psyche to arise another time when conditions activate it. How it arises is in the form of some behavior, some form of a self-centered action.

There are other times when we feel good and have a sense of being connected to life. But we are not sure why and it usually doesn't last very long because we are still controlled by our Conditioned Minds. So the key to minimizing, or not having, these fluctuations is to locate the thought behavior continuum that blocks cooperation with life, and be entirely ready to make our life conducive to be in harmony with Universal Energy.

Our main block from peace is our unawareness of what causes our emotional fluctuations and our not being entirely ready to keep our heart open all the time. If we practice being in a state of readiness, we will learn to be in a constant state of harmony and happiness. This will make our lives much more balanced, and not so polarized by fluctuation.

7. Humbly learn to cooperate with Universal Energy so our reactions to what happens in life are derived from love instead of a self-centered perspective.

No quality is more necessary than humility, for the development of awareness needed to understand how the Conditioned Mind Patterns won't allow us to remain in harmony with Universal Energy. Without the ego deflation, which is necessary for any kind of awakening to transpire, it is impossible. The ego is the driving force behind our entire life and it will have to be understood so you know exactly what you are up against.

If there is any form of evil in this world, the ego is at its core because it blocks out the humility that allows us to do the things necessary that puts us in cooperation with life. But it is an evil that is of our own doing, not one that is caused by something from the outside. These are harsh words, but when our behavior has been thoroughly investigated as it has been in the previous steps, we honestly see that it is the development of our ego from childhood to adulthood that has molded us into the person that we have become; with the lack of humility at it base. It is this lack of humility that allows our ego to create our delusions, it causes us to live by these delusions and that is what we base our life on.

It is the ego that starts the process of building our walls to keep us in our self-created prison. It is our ego that is never satisfied? Our ego is the culprit that is always trying to arrange life the way it thinks it should be and when it doesn't work out, it will do anything to try and make it so. It will defend itself to the bitter end if necessary using whatever resources it deems applicable. It is the cause of so many problems yet it makes us believe that it is needed if we are to live happily. As we've discussed, our ego causes our suffering by constantly making us look outside ourselves for answers, solutions, and quick fleeting fixes. Since the satisfaction doesn't last the ego creates more craving, more wanting which in turn creates more suffering. This is what the ego does. This is why the ego must be deflated. When we say, "I have met the enemy and he is me," we mean the ego; that is our enemy. Unfortunately, most of us blame our misfortune on outside entities, including God.

Let us take a long hard look at how this has come about. First, so much of the way we are has been developed through the evolution of our egos. Through this evolutionary process, our energy has made us into the species we are. Look and see the basic structure of the people living in the world and how our egos have evolved to make us try to control our own destiny. By living dependent on fitting into this basic structure, humility is non-existent.

What is at the core of this structure is how our view has become one ruled by our intellect (our ego) instead of our hearts. The more we operate from this intellect the less humility is involved in our decisions. This intellect instantly separates our being from our spiritual nature and aligns us totally with our human nature. It is from our human nature that all suffering suffices. It has to, because the ego is based in the material world and the material world produces nothing but emptiness. When you become aware of this, you cannot help but to be humble.

This is a simple yet profound Universal Truth. When we die, what portion of the material world will we take with us? Since we will take none of it with us when our body ceases to function, then why is it that we try to hold onto things like it is an end to a means? This is just due to our ego's evolutionary process that this has occurred; this has nothing to do with the influences in our life; influences that also mold us and make us form and hold onto beliefs and ideals, which become the way we live our life. In the process because of our lack of humility, these beliefs and ideals become more engrained in our psyche as our egos make us believe in their solidity.

Just look at the things we put value in and the people who are idolized in this world. The irony of all this is, we attain most of the things we put value in, but they are strictly attained to satisfy our ego and do not really fill a need. The things that are attained are used as a diversion, so we don't have to look at ourselves. It is also ironic most of the people we idolize have nothing to do with us. And most of what they do doesn't have any *real* significance to anybody except themselves and that's only because they are being controlled by their ego. This is due to the mind not being quiet enough to understand the truth, and so in turn some people get their identity in either owning some material thing or thinking accomplishing some feat makes them different from everybody else. Where is the humility in that?

Why do we idolize people because they have a talent that not everyone possesses? Someone can sing beautifully and their ego makes them believe they are special and we validate their specialness. Or someone can act, hit a baseball, throw a football, or are born into a family of wealth, and the energy we emit to them gives their ego the energy it needs to make them think they are different than everyone else; special. They already have their own ego issues, and we just feed them with more energy, which just engrains their psyche and ours with this energy that separates us from each other instead of having us live in unity. Humility has a very difficult time surviving in our society.

What does it really mean if someone sells ten million CDs, gets three thousand hits, or throws five hundred touchdown passes? It is only of importance to those who feel a lack. The energy of the lack creates the importance. Whether we make them special or their own egos make them special, it is all derived from the sense of lack created by the ego. We feed their egos with our egos and we make them special. We give them all kinds of money and other accolades and tell them they are different than we are. Why do we give this lack the energy it needs to live, and in the process take away from our own innate goodness energy; because it has never been taught to us how not to.

This lack-created energy feeds the ego which tells us we need the thing or by doing something not many people can do, it makes us or others think they are special. This also makes people think they are better than others. It is the ego that makes us focus on our differences, not on what we have in common. This is caused by the total lack of humility that is at the ego's core. If we lived a humble existence we would notice our similarities, not our differences.

The driving energy behind any ego is this lack of humility; it needs energy to live — its own and the energy of others. What happens is the ego creates this lack inside which makes a person think they need something or that they have to be special or different from everyone else. This lack of humility directs this self-centered energy, which in turn has to constantly be fed in order to be satisfied. So in order for this lack to be satisfied this energy has to create the belief that something is needed, or it is special and different from everyone else. To be humble is to not need and when you don't need anything there can't be any lack.

Because our egos always need to be fed it creates a world of delusion for its feeding. The energy in a world of delusion isn't based in truth; it is based in a world of make-believe. The world of delusion can be anything the ego needs it to be. To be humble is to know truth and truth starves the ego. That is why there is so much resistance to truth. Because we live in a world of delusion and when everyone is projecting this energy, truth is easily blocked out and this is why our delusions seem like they're real. What the ego puts value in doesn't really mean too much in the grand scheme of things, except to the ego. When you become humble enough to allow the mind to settle, you will begin to understand this ego-based energy that creates our lack of humility.

Another way the ego doesn't allow us to be humble — so we are blocked from learning to cooperate with Universal Love and stay absorbed in our self-centered perspective — stems from our childhood, when someone or something hurt us and we vowed to never let that happen again. Where does that vow originate from? From our "I", our ego; it tries to protect us from ever being hurt again, but winds up causing more hurt than what was originally experienced. This happens because the egos fuel becomes stored energy, which does not allow the processing of truth, which in turn creates our lack of humility. It is impossible for our ego and humility to co-exist in the same moment. When we lack humility as an operative force in our life we constantly try creating a world that is based in relative reality (it is only real to us) instead of a reality based in that truth. We create a world of coping instead of really living.

This is a coping mechanism that is developed by our egos to deal with what happens to us in life. This is how the ego survives and keeps any semblance of humility from our lives. This is how our ego has evolved. It does this automatically. It does not need much influence to be this way. In one form or another it is like this for everyone. This is allowed because of our ignorance. We do not even know this is occurring. It is our ego that wants to keep us in ignorance and keep us from learning to be humble; it will do anything to keep us from knowing truth.

When we notice people who seem to have that special gleam in their eye, it is not because they are special; we are all created by the same Creative Intelligence of the Universe. It is because they have learned the truth of existence and they understand it has nothing to do with anything that they do: "*Of myself I am nothing, the father doeth the work.*" They have learned to let go of their human attachments and are free to be at one with the Creative Intelligence of the Universe. It doesn't mean they are not human; even if they become enlightened they are still of human form. That is the manifestation of our existence, our issues arise when we start believing we are human beings instead of spiritual beings, and that belief is caused by our ego. When we learn to discipline our mind and not give into every earthy desire that arises, it is then that we will not be controlled by our ego.

That is the major problem of our existence; we keep trying to fill our spiritual lack with a material solution. It will never work. When you are craving sweets, if you eat a salad the craving will not be satisfied — and even if you ate something sweet, the satisfaction would not last. Whatever the underlying nature of the lack, it can only be filled by the proper solution. Our ego constantly keeps our energy from finding the proper solution, because when the proper solution is found the ego loses the energy it needs to rule our lives. Surrendering the crown hurts. This is what's known as ego deflation.

With humility not being in the forefront of the development of our character, it is very easy for our ego to use different routes to keep us in its grip. Our inner and outside influences are two of these. It is not so much that we have to understand whether we have certain character traits or not, the important thing is our awareness of how our ego developed our

Conditioned Mind Patterns, and how they block our ability for any true humility and thus love to be the default setting of our mind. This keeps us attached to our self-centered perspective. When we look back and are aware of how the Mind Patterns were formed, we understand the problems our egos cause and what we need to do to change it. We desire humility out of necessity.

If we are not aware of our inner and outside influences, the energy from those influences will feed right into the way our ego has evolved. When that energy creates a closed heart it creates a Conditioned Mind Pattern that controls the way we react. Love is energy as is egoic energy. By not being aware of the transformation that occurs with energy, our influences when derived from a self-centered perspective cause us problems by fueling our delusions. We put importance on things that are really of no importance. We search outside ourselves for our answers. We strive to accomplish and achieve instead of being guided by Universal Energy.

Up until now we have been investigating the ego and how it blocks the humility necessary to understand what causes our reactions. Now let's see how humility will be the quality that will transform the ego energy to love. So how exactly is this going to be done? This will take every ounce of willingness we have, so we can become more aware of when our heart is closing (when the reaction is from our ego) and transform the heart closing energy to energy that will keep it open.

When you notice how something arises and what form its energy takes, it is at this point the energy can be identified for what it truly is. We can then use what we have learned in our practice, so the ego energy dissipates instead of being fed. Energy cannot be destroyed, so when the ego energy dissipates with our conscious awareness, it transforms to love. This is how we re-program our mind's default setting. Through meditation and the previous steps, our mind should be quieting enough to understand the power of Universal Energy and how that energy works for us when we cooperate with it. We should have an awareness of the differences between when the ego is in charge and when love is at our center. We know that this awareness has not occurred by intellectual forcing, or by any agenda being fulfilled, and that all our power comes from Universal Energy flowing freely through us. This energy is what and who we *truly* are. When it is realized that there is no I Self, no ego and that we are living a delusional existence solely to satisfy our self, it puts us in another dimension where all there is, is humility.

Ego is contradictory to humility. So ego deflation is at the core of our freedom. Humbly learning to cooperate with Universal Energy, so our reactions to what happens in life are derived from love instead of self-centeredness is exactly what Step Seven is about. Without the ego — based energy, our mind's default setting is love. The more aware we become of this energy the less of our I Self there is. This allows us to be a solution to a world that is full of problems. We are now ready to move onto Step Eight and start the process of being in unity with all beings.

8. Made a list of all persons we had harmed due to our self-centered behavior and became willing to make amends to them all and be an example of Universal Love.

This step entails another inventory. To continue on our journey we need to make a list and become willing to look at the relationships that had been affected by our self-centered behavior. We will need humility to do this honestly. This willingness is similar to becoming. And we'll need to draw upon our will power to be entirely ready as we did in Step Six. Essential to our peace of mind is a willingness to put to rest any animosity or hostility we feel about anyone that were brought on by Conditioned Mind Patterns. This list is to include everyone, for the mind will never become quiet enough and we will never be an example of Universal Love if are not willing to set right all relationships, intimate and casual.

Remember that everyone has his and her own path, and it is not for us to judge where anyone else is at. We must simply be willing to do what is necessary to keep our heart open. When we understand what we have done in our past as a state of unconsciousness we will then understand others. Jesus said, *"Forgive them for they know not what they do."* When we understand we didn't know what we were doing, we will understand that neither do other people understand their own unconsciousness. We will attain compassion to forgive others and not want to repeat our past behavior again. We may repeat it until the practice allows our heart to remain open, but the willingness to not want to repeat it is what's important.

We can't afford to allow anything that has happened in our past or present relationships to control us if we are to continue discovering the truth about ourselves. If Universal Love is to be the default setting of our mind all the time, we can't have one ounce of hate or discord towards anyone or anything, regardless of what has been done to us, or what has been done to those that are closest to us. It matters little who is right or wrong. What matters is what it will take to keep our heart open and be an example of Universal Love. This is a tall order, not to judge when we or those closest to us, are wronged. But at this juncture in our journey we need only to make a list and become willing to make amends to all people.

This list allows us to see on paper and take responsibility for the people we have harmed. Although it is only a list, when it is written down and we can actually see it, it gives us the ability to understand how our self-centeredness controlled our relationships. This is just part of the process of going deeper and getting in touch with what blocked our ability to love unconditionally. We have tangible evidence of these things, which allows the level of our willingness to directly affect our results. So the result of making this list and being willing to handle our relationships from love instead of our ego allows our heart to remain opened as much as possible. This will allow the operative energy in our lives to be based more and more on love. By using the steps as our guide to live our lives from Universal Love instead of a self-centered perspective, we are discovering the things in our life that block our ability to have an open heart all the time.

When we sustain an open heart, we are cooperating with Universal Energy at such a deep level that the transformation is astonishing. All the energy that we put into our list and the degree of willingness we have, puts us in harmony in with Universal Energy (with God) and with our fellow human beings, and all of life. Unity with all beings is such of large part of our journey because when we are at one with others, we are at one with Universal Love. To truly want to look at how we harmed others and be willing to conduct every relationship from love brings so many benefits to ourselves and to all those around us.

Look at a relationship, for example, of a parent and a child. Let's say the parent learned to react to certain situations by yelling. The entire family is affected by this energy. Self-centeredness causes the yelling. If a situation is handled lovingly instead of from our I Self, the heart would remain open and there would be no yelling. The yelling is caused by wanting the situation to be different from what it is; this is what causes most, if not all of our discord. The energy that closes our heart is derived from our wanting things to be different; wanting things to be different is derived from our self-centeredness. The moment we want something to be different, we are no longer in cooperation with life, and our heart closes. In this situation because we want things to be different, the transformation of energy from an open heart to a closed one manifests itself as yelling.

This is how our Conditioned Mind Patterns affect all our relationships. The manifestation takes on many forms. When the base of any relationship, whether intimate or casual, is derived from self-centeredness there are going to be conflicts. It has to happen: No situation, or nobody, will be exactly the way we want them to be all the time. Matter of fact, most things will hardly ever be the way we want them. So how do we deal with things when they are not the way we want them? That depends on our Conditioned Mind Patterns and how they control our heart.

A closed heart develops feelings of isolation from each other. When someone doesn't act the way we want and we get agitated there is instant separation, because we are no longer in harmony with Universal Love. This is what causes us to look at our differences and forget that we are all created by the same Creative Intelligence, that we inhabit the same planet and are composed of the same energy. People who think they are in charge of others, who want things a certain way and attack when they are not, create conflict. If the other person is conscious enough to realize what is happening, the energy of the conflict will be one-sided and it will dissipate a lot quicker; usually though both sides are unconscious and the conflict must run its course.

Our Conditioned Mind Patterns decree that when one ego does the attacking, the other ego will do the defending. The issue at stake is usually petty, even made up in the person's mind. Of course it doesn't feel petty to them; to them it is very real and important. So what occurs is separation of unity because it is coming from the ego. But as the perception tends to come from the ego, it also tends to create the separateness that leads to isolation. When our little world (that is made up in our mind through our conditioning) is messed with and things or people are not in line with the way we want them to be, all kinds of problems occur. Through this unconscious acting out, blame and strife, unity is gone and we become isolated from each other. The heart closes and the ego makes a mountain out of a molehill so it can feel satisfied. 'Being right,' feeling righteous is one of the greatest and most subtle addictions of all.

Until we realize that our ego alone is bruised, we will remain in conflict. We think we are in conflict with a person because they are not doing what we think they should be doing, but the reality is, the only conflict we are having is with our I Self, our ego. We will always be in conflict with something or somebody until we learn to quiet our own inner conflicts,

Our journey is not about having life the way we want it. It is more about learning what to do when it isn't the way we want it, which is most of the time, and understanding how we must stay vigilant if we are to be in brotherhood with those with whom we share this planet. Not many of us really understand how to love unconditionally. We are so controlled by our self-centered Conditioned Mind Patterns that we put many stipulations on our relationships. When those stipulations are not adhered to our heart closes. So we need to learn to stop living in a world of delusion created by our egos, and learn to love ourselves by doing the things that are necessary to keep our heart open and to remain in cooperation with Universal Love. If we don't do this, then how can we expect to love our neighbors as we love ourselves?

This may sound impossible, but it is not. Releasing judgments and preconceived ideas about how a person should act would be a good start. This will go a long way in our willingness to keep our heart open, and not react to past and present relationships from our I Self. This is what is needed, make a list of all persons we have harmed due to our self-centered behavior, become willing to make amends to them all and be an example of Universal Love. Without this willingness we will continue to try and control as much of our life as possible. And when something doesn't go the way we want it to, we will suffer, and if we are suffering through our conditioning we will make sure others suffer along with us.

When we practice living in the Here and Now by learning to quiet the mind, we come to understand what we are really trying to do. We become aware of how the previous steps have gotten us to this point — but there is much more investigating to undergo if we are to experience true freedom and unity with our fellow beings. When something occurs and someone else appears to cause our discontent, we need to find out in ourselves what caused it. We have to be willing to look at our part in what occurred. The others involved are all doing what they have been conditioned to do. They are not bad people, they are not personally attacking us; they are just unconscious. We just happened to be there and certain conditions caused their ego to flare up and react. It had to happen. To a large degree they don't understand what they're doing. Remember, don't take it personal.

When you truly understand this, you will be at a place in your journey where you will want to make your amends. You know this will keep your heart open and with an opened heart you will be cooperating with Universal Energy which puts you in harmony with Universal Love.

9. Made direct amends to such people wherever possible, but only with the intention that it would benefit them and not serve our own satisfactions.

This is a very difficult step in the ego deflation process. But if we want to continue on our path of awakening we must continue purging ourselves of our blockages to love. We will need to make restitution to people and institutions where we were emotionally and financially irresponsible. This can be done only when our intention is to benefit them. If someone does not wish to see us we can't go to them to satisfy ourselves. We need to go into every situation with the energy of love.

The level of our conditioning and the lack of love we had in our life growing up will be the determining factor of how much of our self-centered conditioning is the operating energy in our life. That conditioning will determine how many people may have been affected by our self-centered behavior, and the severity of the harm done. If we were honest in Step Eight, we will have more than a few people on our list. It is not because what we did was intentional; the nature of a self-centered, Conditioned Mind is to get what it wants no matter whom or what gets in the way. At worst self-centered conditioning can lead to criminal and brutal acts, but most do not and are less severe.

Although we are looking at what we have done, we have to realize that many people operate from their self-centered Conditioned Mind Patterns. If we want freedom we will need to let go of any wrongs, imaginary or real, that were done to us. If we let the wrongs done to us fester we will start to create mental scenarios of how our encounters will play out. This is not letting Universal Love be our guide; this is our I Self creating a way for us to show someone how we are right and they are wrong. To be guided by love is our intention, always.

Why are we doing this? We are doing this so love becomes the default setting of our mind, automatically. We want to get to a place where we don't want to have to think about how to act out of love, we want it to be who we are. This can be done if we are vigilant enough, and we constantly practice quieting our mind so our intentions come from our heart more often than not. The only problem we ever have with another person is ego-based, regardless of how the other person behaves.

When we are looking at what we have done to others, we will choose responsibly who on our list to contact. If it is something that still troubles us and keeps our heart closed, we need to come to terms with it, either by going to the person, or practicing loving-kindness by understanding what our intentions are, so as we don't cause any more harm. Loving-kindness should always be practiced with others, but especially when someone does not want to see us, or if we can't get in touch with them. Maybe they are deceased or we just can't find them. This may happen, but our intention should be that if the opportunity ever presents itself we don't hesitate to make our amends. It is better for the amends to be direct because it is so much more liberating, but it just may not be possible. As long as we remain willing to make the amends, our heart will remain opened.

So our intention is to go to those to whom we can make direct amends and pray for those we can't, for whatever reason. We pray for their happiness and well-being. Just a short note here about prayer, which will be discussed further in Step Eleven: I have come to understand prayer as just a simple change in the direction of our energy, from self-centered to energy derived from love, directed to where it is needed. This change in the direction of our energy will help our heart remain open, so we are not stalled in our spiritual journey as we go about making our amends.

If everyone was conscious enough to understand what our best intentions were, they would embrace us with open arms because they would understand the suffering that self-centered behavior causes; ours and theirs. Unfortunately, that is not the case and we can go only to those who allow us and welcome us. We can't clear our guilt to prove a point we have, or for our own benefit without regard to how it will make others feel. We have to be vigilant in this endeavor. We have to be honest with ourselves about our true intentions; we need to clear our side of the street — but not at the expense of others.

If we were honest and humble in Step Eight, we will have quite a list. Why? Because self-centered behavior is the main reason a relationship becomes misguided. When love is absent and the ego takes over, there will be no stopping the harm and havoc until the ego is satisfied. As long as we look at what the other person has done, whether real or not, we will not be in harmony with Universal Energy.

The ego doesn't allow unity; it breeds discord, jealously, anger, slander, prejudice, hate. It separates, never unites. It makes each one of us have our own agenda — and when someone gets in the way of fulfilling that agenda, look out. The behavior this energy causes is so destructive that it has the capability of destroying entire lives. We don't need to go too far to notice this, just look at what goes on in everyday life. Look at all the clashes, personal and global, that go on everyday. Most are derived from someone forcing their will upon another, one ego against another. This force of the will isolates us from each other.

If we were all on this planet without needing to fill our inner deficiencies, we would all have the same agenda of bringing love into the world. We would be in touch with our Universal Creative Energy, which is Universal Love, love for all beings. The only reason there is discord in any relationship is the clashing of two egos. That is what happens. This is the only reason there is even a list in Step Eight. If you didn't feed into someone else's ego and just realized they are just doing what they were conditioned to do and allowed the energy to pass through instead of being stored, it would not matter what they did. You would not take it personally and hence that person would not have made our Step Eight list. But when it becomes personal and it is your ego against theirs, look out; wars have been started this way.

If we had learned at an early age how to let the energy pass through, there would be no list. There would not be a need for any of these steps. But there is a need because our egos have come to control us. And thus we "make it personal," your ego against mine. When this occurs, the isolated energy then gets stored and the clash ensues. This pattern is easy to understand but not easy to transform. Many can intellectualize what goes on, but not many will be able to bring this understanding from their head to their heart. This is the hardest eighteen inches that will ever be traveled.

This critical transformation goes against everything we have been taught. But that is the essence of this process; to selectively unlearn what we were taught that brought suffering into our relationships and to relearn so we can bring love into our relationships. Making direct amends is part of this process. It is needed to identify what are causes to suffering are. By being free of the hold the causes have on us, and by not carrying around their stored energy, we are allowing our being to do what is necessary to cooperate with Universal Energy and thus be in harmony with Universal Love. We learn to understand the harm that was caused by our behavior and choose another direction based on love and respect. That is the benefit of Step Nine: to watch years of a hardened heart become soft. Our heart was hardened by stored energy that never allowed us to connect and be in harmony with anybody but our I Self.

At this stage in our development we have come a long way in identifying the things that will aide us in the transformation of our minds from a self–centered perspective to a perspective based in love. We have identified many life patterns and behaviors that were not derived from truth, but were created from a false sense of I, based in this self-centeredness. This investigation and inventory has allowed us to become aware of the things in us that cause us to suffer and also to understand how we cause others to suffer as well.

Learning these truths about ourselves will go a long way in bringing love into a world that so desperately needs it. But these steps are not a one-shot-deal, to be looked at once and say, "I'm glad that's over with, I'll never have to do that again." These steps are to be cultivated, so they become a part of our subconscious and allow us to view life from a different perspective than we had previously. This is the beginning of a new way of living that becomes a lifelong practice.

Our Conditioned Mind Patterns do not change because we have become aware of them. They change because of our practice and that is what the next three steps teach us, how to continue the development of our inner being, so we are not controlled by the world of outer circumstances. The quieter the mind becomes the more in touch we get with our conditioning that we didn't even know existed.

If you have honestly investigated your life up to this point, you have discovered a large amount of truth about yourself that wasn't previously known. You are well aware of the possibility these steps have to continually enhance your life. You will understand you are on a path to a way of life you never thought possible. You will not be controlled by your past anymore nor will you ignore it. You will use it for reflection purposes only and to help others. The freedom experienced will be everlasting because it will be from within and not from an ego based Mind Pattern, telling you to look for answers outside yourself. You will be in unity with all beings by knowing we are all part of the same Creative Intelligence regardless of what it is called. You will understand the conditioning of others and have deep compassion for them because you will understand the suffering Conditioned Mind Patterns cause. The self-centeredness that caused so much harm to you and to others will be replaced by Universal Love and you will want that love to be the default setting of your mind; you know it is the only way you will ever be free. Instead of striving to become you will be guided by the Creative Intelligence of the Universe and you will be in harmony with life. You will realize you are complete just as you are and nothing added can make you more complete. You will come to know how you limit yourself through your own ego and you will learn how not to be controlled by those limitations. You will be aware when the mind becomes agitated due to some self-created lack, how it is the ego doing the creating and how you can do what is necessary to transform that energy from lack to love. These are just some of the benefits you will reap if have seriously applied these steps to your life and are honest about changing its view. The alternative to this is to ignore the truth of what has been written and continue living life the way you have been conditioned to and not change. That is entirely up to you.

It is now time to move onto the remaining three steps, which can be viewed as the maintenance steps. They will keep this process on going for the rest of your life if you choose to do so.

10. Continued to learn and deepen our spiritual insight by being mindful of each moment and how we react to situations as they occur in our life.

Our process should now be at a point where we have a keen sense of awareness of our self-centered reactions and how each situation is affected by this behavior. We should be able to decipher whether we are being self-centered or God-centered, whether our heart closes or stays open. If we react just because something doesn't go our way, or someone doesn't act the way we want them to and our reaction generates anger, or some other emotion which isolates us from others, we need to keep our heart open and transform our energy to that of Universal Love. Whenever we react to not getting our way and our heart closes it destroys our ability to love. We are of no use to anyone. We may think we are doing this for the good of something or someone, but all we are doing is lying to ourselves to satisfy our ego. If it is not from love, then it is of no use to anyone. This is the way it is, no matter the situation.

Is it really possible to have this awareness all the time? It will take constant practice to get to this stage in our development, but the answer is yes. It truly is possible to be aware of how we are acting and if those actions close or open our heart. To really understand the cause and effect of our reactions is the only way that our spiritual insight will deepen to the point where we will be aware of what closes our heart and what it will take to keep it open. The most important part of the development will be living in the present moment. This is the only place where we can live from the heart. When we live in the present, we are in harmony with the Creative Intelligence; we are living in love.

The past and the future are directly linked to the intellect and our egos. It is impossible to be in harmony with life when we are not living in the present. The foundation of living in the future or the past is from our Conditioned Mind Patterns, which is from our ego. Love will never be our operative energy when we live in the past or the future. Think about it: When someone does something we don't like, what makes us not like it? Is it because we are living in the present moment, or is it because their action is associated with a Mind Pattern from the past that make us think we don't like what was done?

What is occurring is happening in the present moment, but we are drawing our conclusion to that moment with a Conditioned Mind Pattern from the past. So we may physically be in the present moment, but mentally we are somewhere else. It works the same way when we react and wish for something in the future or for something to be different than what it is. Each reaction, though different, creates the same conclusion. We leave the present moment and close our heart. The self-centered Conditioned Mind Pattern flares up and an eruption of our ego starts up again.

Since we already have the energy stored in our psyche (our story) that we don't like this particular thing, it is just waiting to be activated. This is what happens when we do not live in the present moment; certain events activate certain Mind Patterns. Because they are preconceived ideas that have already formed in our psyche, neither our mind nor our heart can remain open. It is impossible to operate from love in this state of being, but this is how most of us live. We physically are always in the present moment, but mentally we are mostly elsewhere. Now and then, during an outdoor activity like fishing or camping, our minds focuses on the task at hand and we don't become distracted by our Conditioned Mind, This focus occurs naturally, we are not aware of it. We may be present because our outside distractions are minimized. But when this is not our normal mode of living our conditioning takes over again once the task or activity is finished. This is a common theme in our daily lives.

Our practice is to not allow outside or mental distractions to infiltrate our present moment awareness. The more we are lost in the past or future the more our life seems like a struggle. The past or future divides our life into segments or tasks. It creates the delusion that life will be different when we get to a different place. That's why we look forward to vacations or retirement. But really, those times are no different than now, when you get there; it will be the same now that it is in the present moment. It is always the present moment. The only place that isn't now is in the construct we have devised in our Conditioned Mind. It is all self-created because our ego can't survive in the now.

If we are to be present, we have to be aware of this tendency. If we are not aware of this we will need to go back to the previous steps and find what is blocking our awareness of this truth. No one is more gifted than anyone else. God's gift to us is life itself. If you are reading this, your manifestation has taken on a human form and it is up to you to make the most of the gift you have been given. We all have different talents. But as far as the gift of life is concerned, if you are alive, you are gifted. It matters little how long our manifestation lasts. What matters is how our gift is used while we are here. Is it used to benefit others or is it used to satisfy an ego — driven sense of self?

With ourselves as the only block to this awareness, the onus is upon us to find our goodness in life. If our innate goodness is not rising to the surface, something was missed. Something isn't allowing our mind to become quiet enough to allow our innate goodness to be our life energy. If relationships are still troublesome, or if life feels like the same struggle it always has always been go back and investigate why. There is a reason. It is not because that's just the way you are.

By now if you are not experiencing a different view of life it is because you are still caught in the grips of your Conditioned Mind Patterns, which don't allow Universal Love to flow through your life. If you think, "life is just suffering and then you die," that is your own fault.

You should find yourself naturally living more and more in the present moment because by now you're aware it is the only real time and place that exist. Life doesn't exist in the past, although that is where you like to live it. It doesn't exist in the future although your ego wants you to think that the future holds your salvation; and when you get there, the future becomes the Here and Now anyway. So where does that leave you to live your life?

Here is a basic outline of what happens and how to keep our heart opened. Everyday living presents many opportunities for practice. When we are attracted to something it becomes the thing that takes our attention away from the present moment to that object. The form that the object takes on, whether it's a car, a person, food, etc. becomes our focal point. The reason we are attracted to the object is because through one of our senses or maybe more than one, we believe the object will bring us pleasure. That pleasure is derived from a Conditioned Mind Pattern created by our ego. It was created for the sole purpose of keeping our ego alive. That is what our ego needs to survive. It stays alive by creating the delusion that successively satisfied cravings equal happiness. Once this perception is stored in the psyche as energy it will be used to feed our ego again and again. This stored energy lays dormant until a certain condition arises that activates it, and then it flares up.

This subtle programming pattern makes change so hard for many people. Fluctuations were discussed in a previous step, and fluctuations keep us bound to an ego-based viewpoint. The reason it is so hard to change is because the ego is not always causing noticeable problems in our life, so it makes us believe we are in control. It is not easy to admit that we are not in control, but look how little control we really have in life. The people who usually overcome these fluctuations come to realize that their problems are derived from their self-centeredness and that unless they overcome this dilemma they will probably never be truly happy.

Without constant chaos, the ego tells us we do not need to change? We generally prefer to keep doing what we know than jump into the unknown even if it causes suffering. This is why a person usually has to hit some kind of emotional bottom before they are willing to change. It's because we have to be convinced that the way we've been living is not benefiting us. We do not need to know what the answer is, but we have to get to a point where we know the way we are living is not the answer. Then we can change. We can start to become aware of and deepen our life's spiritual direction. It is almost impossible for this to happen any other way because all change will be derived from the intellect, which means the ego will still be in charge. It is not impossible for a spiritual awakening to occur in this manner, but it will take a very long time with much suffering in between.

It's unfortunate, but this is the path that many people use to awaken. This is mostly because of the unawareness of the delusions that are caused by our ego and how these self-created delusions block out as much truth as possible to make us justify everything we do. If we thought everything we did was right, why would we need to change? There would be no need, so there would be no change. Our defense mechanisms, which have been developed to protect us, actually keep us in the prison of our own egos which will constantly use whatever they need to justify what we do. This is why our delusions are created. The truth is we can do anything we want, we can be whatever we want, as long as our decisions are base in love.

If our decisions are not base in love and they are driven by a need to compensate for some inner deficiency, regardless of what is used to fill that deficiency, life becomes painful and difficult. If those same decisions were based in love, then the difficulties would not occur. Life was meant to be lived from a base of love, difficulties are self-created. They are not caused by things outside of us; they are caused by our ego. The base of love is always there. The construct in our mind creates difficulties.

Here is an example. You are a Vice President in charge of a department in a corporation. You started at an entry-level position, say the mailroom. You worked very hard to get to your current position. Very few people have accomplished what you have as far as where you started and the position you are in now. You develop a set of standards and beliefs along the way that you think others should abide by. After all, you are highly successful and your standards and beliefs are what allowed you to achieve your level of success. Those standards and beliefs will be incorporated into how you run your department. These beliefs and standards do not take into account that everyone is conditioned differently, so when someone doesn't conform to your standards it activates a Conditioned Mind Pattern that separates you from others.

This separation has nothing to do with the people that work for you because these decisions that are being made by you are from the mind-based sense of self. Other people have nothing to do with them. You believe they do, because through your conditioning you think the people are the cause of what is happening to you. But the stark fact is that your own ego is causing all of this.

No one can make you do anything without your permission. It's all about satisfying an ego that needs things to be a certain way. If someone doesn't conform to that way, for whatever reason, there is no trying to understand the person, there is only strong-arming him or her to conform to your way. After all, you have earned the right to control people's lives because you are highly educated and successful; to your ego. In today's society we call this Bullying. This is being done as adults, so how can we expect our children not to do it?

When you look upon someone as a problem and tell them to do what you want – and they don't – your ego responds the only way it knows. It erupts and all kinds of dysfunctional behaviors ensue. You justify your actions, you blame others. Your Conditioned Mind Patterns want the world to be the way you want it. The way you think it needs it to be and anything or anybody that disrupts your wishes is deemed a problem. The ego tells you get rid of the problem and all will be well.

You tell yourself you're looking at the big picture and need to get rid anything that disrupts this picture. But really, someone is not in alignment with your ego, so you need to either control them or get rid of them. That is the real cause of your discontent; your ego is being challenged. There are dictators all over the world, past and present, which have murdered millions of people for these exact reasons — to satisfy their ego.

We now understand how the heart closes when a Conditioned Mind Pattern is activated, and how dangerous this cycle can become. How can we prevent this from reoccurring over and over? The Conditioned Mind Patterns are just waiting to be activated, it doesn't matter who the employee is or what the situation is, all that matters is your Conditioned Mind Pattern has been activated by something and you need to react in a manner to satisfy your ego, because it is your ego that has become unsatisfied. This demand by the ego for satisfaction and such reactions isolate you from others. They make you act the way a two-year-old-would act when they don't get their way. You think you are right, so you deal with this as you have been conditioned. Unfortunately that conditioning is from your ego and not from love. Understand that your ego has been attacked and not your true self. This understanding will allow space to be created between what happens and your reaction. This space is your energy being transformed from a self-centered base to love. This powerful discipline is what keeps your heart open.

Without this understanding the Conditioned Mind Pattern keeps occurring over and over. Today this person is not conforming, the next day it is someone or something else. This is what happens when a Conditioned Mind Pattern is activated; your heart closes. To become aware of this tendency is the beginning of the end of your ego, and the beginning of the end of your heart closing down. You can actually sense your heart closing when you go from being present into a Conditioned Mind Pattern. At that point, if you are mindful enough, you can make a decision to keep your heart open and alleviate the suffering and negative energy associated with that Conditioned Mind Pattern.

Through awareness, you will be able to continuously watch the things in you that want to close your heart. You can practice allowing the energy that wants to close your heart to pass through and keep your heart open. These occurrences will happen throughout the day. They will be different for each one of us. The amount of time we practice is usually dependent on how aware a person is of his or her conditioning. The more we lack awareness, the more we need to practice. Because we are all conditioned in our own way, we all have our own path. But our differences don't really matter. We are all engaged in the same sacred quest whether we are aware of it or not.

What matters is being aware of what occurs in our life — not anyone else's life but ours — and staying present. By being present and sustaining a constant state of presence, we deepen our awareness and we have to deal with only what arises in each moment. We will not carry the past or future into every moment. With presence, the burden of the past and future doesn't exist.

The energy that you live by is the energy that you bring into the world. If your energy is directed to find satisfaction in the material world, then don't be surprised if you are up all hours of the night and have very little peace in your life. You can't serve two masters. You are a part of this world in the human form, but your heart is of the spirit. The Spirit is only blocked out by the attachment to this world.

One tool to help you let go of these attachments is visualization. When you become aware how something affected you and your reaction was from a self-serving perspective, find a quiet place to sit and visualize how you would have preferred to have responded to the situation. Or you can visualize a situation that expresses a great wish and see if it really changes your inner life. This will help in changing the way you react to situations. Always visualize the response to be from love. Use love as your refuge, your inner place of peace. If you really don't want to act a certain way, you will change, it will just take time and practice.

Be patient, for the ego is a dangerous foe. It will take constant vigilance to overcome these Mind Patterns that have been in place nearly as long as you have been in existence, but it is possible and worth it if you are willing to be persistent enough to keep your heart open. To have an open heart all the time will make Universal Love the energy that will make life more meaningful than any material possession or anything else for that matter. You will not need to accomplish anything to have this sense of well-being. You will treat everyone with Universal Love and thus be in harmony with all beings. Eventually if you keep on practicing, your heart will never close. You will understand what happens when it closes and you will not want that to happen because you know it causes suffering to you and to others. When your body can no longer sustain life and it shuts down, the transforming energy of Universal Love, of who you *truly* are, will be here for all eternity.

11. Sought through prayer and meditation to improve our consciousness of Universal Love, so knowledge becomes wisdom and our actions make us an example of this love in our relationships with all beings.

When we come to understand what will keep our heart open, so that love and compassion can be our normal mode of living, we will put our being in complete cooperation and harmony with Universal Love. By now this should be a conscious choice, but it still will not happen without our assistance. This assistance comes in the form of prayer and meditation. Prayer is anything that is used to keep our heart open. We can kneel, we can chant, we can recite prayers from a particular faith. We can do it in the morning, in the evening, on our lunch break, while driving in our car, it does not matter. What does matter is it comes from love, which will keep our heart open. Our Conditioned Mind Patterns will try and close our heart throughout the day, but if we ever want to tune into our true power and Creative Potential, we must develop a practice that will stop the closing of our heart instantly. The more prayer is used to do this, the more love we will have in our life which will allow our Creative Energy to flow freely.

When there is a situation which activates a Conditioned Mind Pattern either it will run its course or it will be stopped. The only way for it to be stopped is through awareness, and a tool of deactivation. There are many forms of prayer that can be used for this. Taking a deep breath is one; using some scripture that has been memorized and has touched our heart is another. Mantras are a good source to stop the Conditioned Mind. Many books have been written on prayer; find what works for you. Whatever can be used to keep Universal Love as the energy we live our life by is prayer. We need to find what that entails so we are always in harmony with life.

This is extremely difficult to do because we must contend not only with our own egos, but also with the egos of others. Not everyone will understand this book from a wisdom point of view. It will be understood from an intellectual point of view, but unless what is read is felt in the heart, the mind will try and intellectualize it. It will try to make it all fit into a nice little make-believe concept, but it will not be understood at the

194

heart level. The mind has to try and make sense and justify everything, but the spiritual realm can't be understood or explained by our mind. It can only be experienced, but such an experience can't really be put into words that explain it properly.

It will take all the will that is in us to constantly use prayer as a way to keep our heart open, for knowledge to become wisdom; A Lao Tzu quote: "Knowledge studies others, wisdom studies the self." We have to constantly practice quieting our mind to allow truth to enter our being. Knowing about God is not the same as knowing God. Knowing about you is not the same as knowing you. You can learn so much about something, but it does not mean you truly know the thing. It is when our mind is quiet that we allow our created concepts to drop away. This peace allows truth to arise.

Most of us know all about ourselves, but we don't know who we truly are. We don't understand our true nature. We limit ourselves through our thought process. We do not make ourselves breathe, it just happens. We don't make our heart pump blood to our internal organs, it just happens. There are so many unexplained occurrences that happen in our bodies alone every second of every day, but we really don't give them much thought. So we create this make-believe world in our head that causes nothing, but suffering to ourselves and others and we think this is what life is all about.

Most of the time knowledge stays as knowledge until something happens that makes us become aware of our mind-created delusions. When this occurs we start questioning — not that we get answers, but the questioning itself is a form of prayer. The questioning itself is a prayer because it stops the mind from thinking; this keeps our heart from closing. Truth opens the heart; delusion will constantly try and close it. This questioning opens our heart, probably for the first time in our life, and with this opening we experience truth; even though we don't know this is occurring. With an opened heart, truth can not be denied.

Prayer affords us the ability to become aware of the delusions created by our ego and stops us from living the lie it creates. The only way to ever stop living in the land of make-believe is to quiet our mind. Prayer is the start of this. We must learn how not to be drawn into our own or someone else's unconsciousness. This is done by keeping our heart open and having Universal Love as our energy. We can overcome any obstacle, the ones we create and the ones other people present, through prayer.

Then there are life occurrences that have to be dealt with: Accidents, flat tires, leaking roofs, children getting sick, people dying — occurrences that aren't directly brought about by other people, but are circumstantial. How do we keep our heart open when things like this happen? This is very difficult when allowing the Conditioned Mind Patterns to run the show. When we use prayer to quiet our own inner disturbances, we will understand the emptiness in our attachment to these things as they just fall away. Where do they go?

How much of what we think will happen actually does? Practically nothing we think will occur does, and most of what occurs is beyond our control. So what gives anything its life is the story we attach to it. Prayer will stop the story from becoming the epic novel we are so use to creating.

Although prayer is used to allow truth to arise, this truth will not necessarily manifest as wisdom. Truth being; we are going to act in certain ways and instead of allowing the energy to manifest in some negative form, we stop it. When we are aware of stopping the negative form from arising, we realize we do not have to be controlled by our Conditioned Mind Patterns anymore and we understand what we need to do for this not to occur. This is truth. We do not have to rely on some outside deity or hope for this to occur. Our transforming energy of prayer will make this happen. We will attain wisdom when we understand what happens if we don't use prayer as a tool to combat our Conditioned Mind.

There will be hurdles to overcome in our life if we are to continually grow spiritually; they become burdens and stop our spiritual development when we don't deal with them. Hurdles are dealt with in the present moment and we do not get over them unless they are dealt with as they arise. A hurdle becomes a burden when it is not overcome. Our hurdles arise because of our Conditioned Mind Patterns and when dealt with strictly from those Mind Patterns, they trip us up and make us fall. Prayer allows us to overcome our hurdles so they don't become burdens by redirecting their energy. Our life is changed one hurdle at a time. We do not make vows or take oaths, or pledges to never act a certain way again. We don't have to. We only have to deal with what arises in the present moment with prayer, so our heart stays open to Universal Love.

Prayer is a key element in the development of the consciousness of Universal Love in our lives so we can be a benefit to all beings. When we are off the beam, we can use prayer to bring us back to our place of God-centeredness. We are either of God or of our I Self, so as our awareness increases so does our God-centeredness. The real question is this, what will bring about our awareness so we will want truth (Love) to be the operative energy in our life? Through the discipline of meditation we will develop our awareness of the delusional life we have been living. Meditation is the most important tool we have to combat our ego and the ego of others.

A large part of the way we are is due to an undisciplined mind. Impulses control so much of what we do, whether we realize it or not. Just observe this for yourself. Think of something that you're attracted to, and explore where the attraction comes from. Remember, the thing itself, whatever it is, has no power. So what causes the attraction and then the attachment? We need to discipline our mind so we can start controlling the way we respond to situations, instead of being controlled by them.

Developing this discipline will be one of, if not the most difficult thing that we will ever do in our life. There is so much conditioning, so much negative energy engrained in our psyche that it will seem like it can't be done, but that is only part of the conditioning. It can be done. It will just take constant practice.

This is what happens with the practice of meditation. Once you find a place that is quiet and you know you will not be disturbed you can use the breath to quiet your mind. Since the mind can't have two thoughts at the same time, by focusing on the breath you will alleviate some of the noise in your head. Maybe you can follow your breath for twenty seconds before a thought pops in, and then another and another. Then you start thinking about all the things you have to do and how this practice of meditation is really just a waste of time. But then you remember you made a commitment to yourself to do this so you return to following your breath. Maybe this time you get fifteen seconds of following your breath or maybe thirty seconds. The point is that this is all part of disciplining an undisciplined mind.

Believe me, it will take many, many hours of practice before you will probably be able to sit for ten minutes undisturbed, but when it happens it will be the most peaceful ten minutes you will have ever experienced. Meditation can't be ignored if you truly want to live freely and in unity with all beings.

Practice through concentration; use whatever words or methods work for you. Meditation like anything else will take experimentation and practice if you wish to become skilled at it. Practicing allows the mind to settle. It will take many hours of concentration and discipline for this to occur to a level where you can go deeper and deeper, to truly understand who you are. In the beginning you will be lucky if you can sit for ten seconds before the mind starts to wander. But that time will increase the more you sit and practice. The intervals between the wandering and quiet mind will increase as the practice and quieting increases.

Developing concentration gives us something to return to when the mind wanders. You will be sitting and all of a sudden a thought will just pop in your head and before you even realize it you get lost in that thought. It doesn't matter what the thought is; it can be about anything. What matters is the mind is not disciplined enough to stop the attachment to the thought, so it grabs a hold of you and you no longer have a quiet mind. Return to your focal point — like the breath — when you realize you are lost in the thought. Start the practice of concentration from there. Concentration is not something to be attained, it is developed through practice, practice and then more practice. There isn't a right or wrong result in what happens when you are sitting, it is just a development. Whatever happens to you is to be used in your learning process. This is the essence of life: not so much what happens to us, but what we learn from it and how it is used.

Another benefit of meditation is in the practicing itself. Although many times nothing special happens when you sit in quiet, the benefit of sitting occurs when something arises that activates a Conditioned Mind Pattern and lo and behold, you do not react. You watch your anger arise because you always reacted to this type of situation in the past with anger, but because of your practicing – although you are still angry — you do not react. You do not stop yourself from reacting; this resistance seems to have occurred on its own. But it didn't, it occurred from the disciplining of your mind. When you practice meditation, space is created between your Conditioned Mind Patterns and your reactions. The more you practice the more space you create and the better you get at it. This allows for more awareness of the blocks to your own innate goodness, your consciousness to Universal Love.

This is how our conditioning changes, and in the process the way we react to situations changes. What we are doing by meditating and quieting our mind is transforming the energy that was derived from our Conditioned Mind Patterns into energy that is now derived from stillness, from love.

There are many different ways to meditate (to quiet your mind) and it will take a lot of practice to find out which method or methods work best for you. Which ones allow the quietness needed to discover your truth? Which ones will allow knowledge to become wisdom, or knowing about God, to become knowing God. This transformation is what meditation allows; it allows you to discover the things in yourself that block the energy of Universal Love from being the operative force in your life. The more that you practice, the more you will discover about Universal Love and yourself. The more you discover Universal Love, the less you live through your intellect and the more you live from your heart; knowledge (the intellect) becomes wisdom (from your heart).

Investigate what goes on inside of you, your reactions to things and how they close your heart. This is what meditation will reveal. So much truth is blocked out by the noise in our head; it is the cause of all our suffering. When you mind can't get quiet that is when your world of delusion is created. The delusions created are the energy of the noise. The noise is just energy and since love is not a part of the energy of the noise in our head, it creates whatever it needs to cope with situations as they arise; but understand what it creates will never be in the form of our Creative Energy, it can only come from the energy of our ego.

It is solely because of the ego that our delusions are created. This has to occur when we live from a self-centered perspective. Because there is no quietness, there is no choice. The mind just keeps going, creating whatever it needs from the energy of the noise; whether it's the delusion that you will be happy when you attain a certain status, or when you get material possessions, or whatever it is that you believe will bring you happiness. Maybe it will incite a riot or just wreak havoc in your life or the lives of those around you, but understand this: energy of the mental noise generates this; the energy of our ego.

The more settled your mind gets, the less you'll be dominated by the noise in your head. Automatically, through this conscious and disciplined quieting of your mind, Universal Love becomes the operative force in your life. You will become an example of that love to all beings. This is the essence of meditation, to be an example of Universal Love and to be a benefit to all beings.

You can have many different experiences when you begin to meditate. Everyone is different, but the one common thread throughout is Universal Love becomes the base of our being. Don't hold onto an expectation that this or that should be happening; that's all part of the noise. If in one sitting you experience a sense of peace like never before, don't try to reproduce the experience by attempting to recreate the same situation; let each sitting unfold as its own. In each sitting you are developing the discipline to produce a quiet mind; whatever it is that you experience, don't add anything to it.

Suppose you work out in the gym, you do not visually see the benefits of the activities performed to your body while you are working out, but the benefits are being produced nonetheless. You don't produce the benefits, the working out does. All you can do is to be willing to do the necessary activity that produces the benefits. It's the same with meditation. You don't really see the benefits that sitting will have in life situations while you are doing it, but you are developing the discipline which produces quietness. Benefits are being produced, but it isn't you who produces the benefits; it is the sitting that does it. All you can do is have the willingness to sit. So you sit and then you live your life. You watch what arises and you learn to be with it. Because of the sitting you mind is quiet so you don't attach to what arises; it is allowed to pass through you and then just like that you are free to let it go.

Be persistent in your practice. The ego does not like you learning to discipline your mind because it loses its hold on you. Develop this discipline, and you will become aware of a miracle occurring right before your very eyes. You will act in ways you never imagined. You will understand and notice things occurring that very few people understand. If helping someone comes about because of some experience you have had, then so be it. But don't be surprised when nobody really cares about your new-found discoveries. Everyone has his or her own path and they are just in a different place than you. Not better, not worse — just different.

So learn what will benefit your life and benefit others. Learn to quiet your mind so your operative life energy doesn't come from your ego, but from your sense of love for all beings. Through meditation cultivate what will allow Universal Love to be the default setting of your mind, so you can stop reacting to life from your Conditioned Mind and you can be an example of Universal Love to all beings.

This is a lifelong practice, which will allow harmony with the Creative Intelligence of the Universe, which will allow you to experience life as never before. To be at one with all beings is to be at one with God. If God is for you, who can be against you?

12. Having had a spiritual awakening as a result of these steps, we learned to respond to life from love instead of reacting to it from our I Self. In this process we become a benefit to all beings by expressing Universal Love in everything we do.

Lets us summarize what we have done up to this point in our development and see if anything was missed that will prevent Universal Love from being the operative force of our life. In Step One we came to an understanding that Conditioned Mind Patterns have dominated our lives. These patterns were developed by different influences, some from outside of us (like our families and culture) and some from inside of us, from our preferences and bias, from our ego. Regardless of where they come from, the conditioning itself is the focal point of Step One. We understood how that conditioning drove most of our decisions and reactions and how we lived from a self-centered warp. If we are to go any further in our process, this warp must be understood at the heart level. The intellect can understand this, but the warp and the lack of harmony must be felt in our heart if we're to become willing to do everything necessary to be free of the bondage of our Conditioned Mind Patterns.

All progress is based on this understanding because it will be the cornerstone of our remaining journey. Without this understanding we will not have the willingness to change, nor will we think there is anything that needs to be changed. We will continue to look at that world through our senses and be a slave to them. The only way to cut the strings that control us is to become aware that we are attached. This has to come from the heart because it will be at this level of understanding that will allow the start of our process of learning how our heart needs to be open for God's Universal Love to flow.

In Step Two this understanding leads to us becoming aware that our Conditioned Mind was developed, and that this development was derived from our self-centered nature (our ego), which blocked out our ability to cooperate with Universal Energy (God). We know this is what created conflict with life and what kept us going from one thing to the other to try and find inner peace. This is the peace that was there when our existence started, but was slowly pushed into the background as our self-centered identity took more and more control of our life, and our Conditioned Mind Patterns were reinforced. We are aware this was not of our conscious doing, and it happened all without our permission. The development of our Conditioned Mind was learned behavior and can be unlearned and replaced with something (Universal Love) that is more beneficial to us and to others.

Step Three is strictly making a decision to practice doing what needs to be done to live in harmony with the Divine Purpose. Practice looking at the things that are derived from our self-centered nature and be willing to stop doing them so God's Love is allowed to become the energy we live by. Recommitting to this decision constantly as situations arise; becoming more aware of how God's Love is blocked out and what causes those block. With this decision we begin to discover what it means to have a closed heart or an opened heart. We begin to cultivate the type of behavior that is more beneficial to our life. With the ability to make this decision comes a choice we never had before. We were controlled by our conditioning, but are now deciding to fight back, to take control of our lives instead of being controlled by our ego. We will start to understand how our self-centeredness closes our heart and by making a decision to practice aligning our will and life with the Divine Purpose, our heart will stay open and we will be in harmony with that Purpose. This transforming energy of love changes our entire existence. This decision will be made over and over until it is engrained in our psyche — until it becomes the default setting of the direction we live our life.

Step Four is where our practice starts identifying the behavior that kept us entrapped to our Conditioned Mind Patterns; to our ego, to our I Self. Really looking at our behavior is how we become more aware of this behavior and how we will be able to create the necessary changes. Without identifying the behavior and vicious cycles we can't understand that there is even anything that needs to be changed. That is how our ego (our I Self) keeps us in our own bondage, by blocking out truth and sustaining our delusions. It keeps us looking outside to satisfy an internal need.

Without an inventory it is nearly impossible to gain a true assessment of why we do what we do. We need an inventory to search out the traits in ourselves that we need to overcome, so we can stop reacting to life from our self-centered Mind Patterns. What this behavior does is block our own innate goodness from arising. So our inventory helps us understand how our behavior needs to be changed. It doesn't label it as good or bad or right or wrong, but it checks to see whether it's conducive to Universal Love. We will then be aware of what behavior is a benefit to our lives, and what is not.

In Step Five we acquire an understanding of how our behavior was derived from self-centeredness and how this formed the core of our distorted thinking. We experienced freedom when we realized we were not to blame for the way we behaved in our life, though we are held accountable. Our reactions to situations that arose were not of our conscious choice; we were just doing what we had been conditioned to do. By identifying the exact nature of our behavior (our wrongs) a shift occurs in our being that changes us forever. We never again view life as we had previously. When this veil of ignorance is removed it allows us to be at one with the Creative Energy that had been blocked out by our self-centeredness.

When we finally understand what caused us to act the way we did, we realize how it isolated us from others and that it is imperative for us to share our hearts with someone who understands what we are doing. We are aware of how this sharing puts us in harmony with other people and thus puts us in harmony with life. This is when our isolation ends and our connectedness to life begins. The key to becoming aware of something is the understanding of it; one becomes more aware of God's Love when one understands God is Love.

That is what occurs in Step Five; we understand the exact nature of our wrongs and we become more aware of them. By becoming more aware of them, we understand their emptiness and we start behaving in more fulfilling ways. We behave in ways that allow the Creative Intelligence of the Universe to be the guiding energy in our life. This guidance, instead of us trying to force our wants and desire into the way we think things should be, is what allows our Creative Energy to finally emerge.

Going forward in our process Step Six is where we start the actual practice of bringing Universal Love into our daily living. We practice keeping our heart open so we can remain entirely ready to do what is necessary to remain in harmony with life. We watch as situations arise and how our heart tries to close down with our Conditioned Mind Patterns. Because we are aware of this cycle, we do whatever we need to do to keep our heart open. We watch how being entirely ready to do this or not being entirely ready is the difference in understanding truth or living our life based in a self-created delusion. These truths or delusions are manifested in the form of energy, which in turn is what causes us to behave in ways that either puts us in cooperation with life or not. This is the energy that will be allowed to pass through and keep our heart open, or become stored in our psyche to keep our heart closed and create a Conditioned Mind Pattern. So just by remaining entirely ready to cooperate with Universal Energy, our behavior becomes conducive to what is necessary for harmony with life. When we remain entirely ready to keep our hearts open we keep discovering truth and slowly cease succumbing to our self-centered behavior. It is not necessarily something to accomplish or strive to achieve, but it is necessary to just keep practicing to remain entirely ready.

By coming to realize our true nature of existence we can't be in anything but awe of our life. Understanding that life itself is our gift affords us the necessary humility to understand how fragile our life is, and how much trouble our ego has caused us. This should also help us to be more aware of what we will need to do in order to stop being controlled by our ego. Step Seven provides the ego deflation necessary to transforming our energy into Universal Love instead of self-centered cravings. Without this degree of humility, the awareness of the behavior that blocks this love will not expand. Understanding how the ego drove our self-centered behavior is the key to being happy, joyous, and free.

Without this awareness, our Conditioned Mind Patterns will continue to hold us prisoner to our I Self and we will continue to be pulled around by life like we are on a leash. Cultivating awareness of the behaviors that create suffering will entail an exceptional amount of ego deflation. That ego is the only thing that will block our awareness that is why this step is vital for our continuing expansion. The less our ego is in charge the less our reactions are derived from our self-centeredness and the more our responses to what occurs in life is derived from Universal Love.

Thus far we will find ourselves learning to cooperate with life instead of resisting, resenting and attacking it. If we haven't become sufficiently humble by Step Seven, we need to look at why. This will be very difficult because without this level of humility it is not possible to look at our faults, and without looking at our faults it is almost impossible to acquire the humility necessary for deep spiritual growth; quite a dilemma, to say the least. This is what we are up against and this is why humility is so vital. By this time, though, we should be well on our way to understanding what we need to do and how we need to do it.

In Step Eight we begin to correct and resolve our relationships and understand our commonality rather than our differences. We become willing to look at the people who have been harmed by our self-centered behavior and notice how that behavior was at the core of our isolation. The less we mindlessly repeat the behavior that caused harm, the more Universal Love is the energy of our existence. When we Love we are in unity with others, when we act from a self-centered perspective we are implicitly in conflict with them.

Our willingness to practice, to meditate, to take honest inventory is key because that willingness will keep our heart open. Always looking at our side and not putting blame on anything or anyone is the key to freedom that Step Eight avails us. If the willingness is not there to look at ourselves we will need to go back and identify the blocks to our willingness. The degree of our vigilance will determine the degree of our freedom.

At Step Eight we need to constantly explore our conflicts with others and understand the cause of those conflicts. This willingness is what gives us the ability to be responsible for how we create conflict in relationships and not to focus on the other person, no matter how they act. They may be at fault, but that is not our concern. Our behavior is all we can be responsible for, and we can understand how we block Universal Love from *our* relationships. The benefit of our list and the willingness to make amends for our past infractions allows us to cooperate with others instead of perpetuating conflict.

Now it is onto Step Nine, where we take full responsibility for our actions and go to those who have been harmed by our behavior; keeping in mind that the full intention of our amends is to benefit the person who we have harmed. We can't get something off our chest at the expense of someone else's feelings; we need to be prudent about who we contact and why. The understanding of what we will gain by this really helps us align with the human race. Not wanting to hurt anyone allows our heart to stay open. This is what allows us to be the instrument to spread Universal Love throughout the world. Think about it, if we could live a life of not harming anyone or at least not wanting to, how much better this world would be.

Although it is not easy to meet people face-to-face in order to make amends, the value of this outreach helps us learn what it will take to not repeat our harmful behavior. It is at this point that our isolation really ends. By understanding how our Conditioned Mind Patterns drove us, we understand why others acted the way they did towards us. By understanding me, I understand you, and I don't want to harm me so why would I want to harm you? Making amends or being willing to make amends allows the past to remain in the past, which allows the Here and Now to become the dominant place from which to live. Without being bogged down by the burden of the harms we have caused others we are free to live in the present moment with Universal Love.

My understanding of Jesus' saying, "*May he who is without sin cast the first stone*" suggests that when I look at you honestly; I am looking at my reflection. We all do the best we can with what we have been conditioned to do. It is not for us to point out the faults of others. It is for us to show others how God's Love makes our existence so much more gratifying than living by Conditioned Mind Patterns, and to be an example of that Love. In Step Nine we come to understand not much that happens really matters, but everything that really matters, happens. So we go to others to make our amends with our intentions not to cause any more harm, and in the process we drop our stones and go and sin no more.

In Step Ten we understand the present moment as the only place from which to live harmoniously. Not because this is "a philosophy to live by," but because it is the only place where reality exists. We understand the delusions created by our ego. We understand that all our delusions occur in the past or the future, by trying to recapture a point in our life that brought us some form of pleasure. Or we look to the future, for salvation in something that hasn't yet happened, but we hope it does. We understand hope as wanting things to be in some other way, and not being in the reality of the present moment. The reality of what is.

With the previous nine steps incorporated into our daily living, Step Ten is our practice during which we are learning to deepen our spiritual insight by being mindful of each moment. Our awareness of how we react to situations as they occur in our life is the foundation of our whole life. Without the continuous awareness that occurs with the practice of Step Ten, we will not continue to change. Our view of life will remain based in the delusions our ego creates and we will stay entrapped to our Conditioned Mind Patterns; our self-centered thinking. The practice of this step keeps the necessity of enhancing our awareness continuous, so we deepen our insights. Our process is on going, so our practice has to be on going.

With our on going practice we are becoming so much more aware of our inner conflicts, and of how our Conditioned Mind always tries to find an outside solution. We want to be rid of these conflicts because we understand how they add nothing to our life; there is nothing useful in their purpose, nothing to benefit others or ourselves. This awareness allows our mind to get quieter and quieter. With this quietness we are ready to really experience some of the benefits of prayer and meditation, which brings us to Step Eleven.

Step Eleven allows us to deepen our awareness so we are able to bring the necessary assets into our lives that are conducive to our spiritual growth. When we become aware of what is useful and what is not, we will want to do what we deem useful. We utilize some of the tools that others have used and have proven to work. Prayer is one of these tools and when it is used properly we can experience instant results. When our prayers are not selfishly driven they will manifest because our hearts are open. If they are selfish the energy of manifestation will not transpire.

To quiet the mind is to pray. That is the essence of prayer. When we transform our energy from the noise going on in our head, to peace, the quality of our energy transforms from destructive to constructive. This can be done with something as simple as a deep breath. This is the true nature of prayer; anything that can be used to keep our self-centered Conditioned Mind Patterns from controlling our life. The more we learn to use it, the more we will want to use it. *"Praying ceaselessly"* means being aware of your thoughts, understanding which ones are useful and letting go of the ones that are not. It is very simple: we will either do the things that are useful and a benefit to our life or we will not. The key is to know what is useful and beneficial.

Once we learn what is useful we can exert our will to bring that usefulness into our daily living. The more this is done the less control our Conditioned Mind Patterns have over our reactions and decisions. The power that is derived from prayer allows our reactions and decisions to be based in Love instead of selfishness.

This brings us to meditation; this practice will give our mind the discipline and concentration it needs to settle. Through meditation we become quiet enough to get in touch with our true spiritual nature and live in harmony with the Creative Intelligence, or God, if you like.

Our mind should have some degree of quietness by now, to allow us to be more aware of what it will take to allow our mind to settle more. If we remain open in our journey we will come to understand not only what makes us do what we do, but also how to bring more truth into our life.

After all regardless of the words we use to describe our experiences it can all be summarized in one word and that word is *TRUTH.*

Ego creates our delusions; meditation allows us to quiet our mind so we can see truth. By Step Eleven we've undergone the necessary preparation to allow us to sit in quiet. The previous steps are all a preparation to get us to this point. Without the previous steps it will be very hard to sit quietly for any period of time because we'll lack discipline and concentration when the mind becomes agitated. The concentration we need to focus on, the breath, or whatever we use to keep our mind from wandering, will not be there. The delusions created by our Conditioned Mind Patterns will remain, so we will continue to be controlled by our conditioning. We will be controlled by our self-centered mind and we will have limited access to truth because of our limited understanding and quietness. That limited understanding and quietness, limits the understanding we will get of ourselves.

From our quietness we learn so much truth about ourselves: How we are just visitors on this planet and have a very limited amount of time to experience our human manifestation. How everything is gone (except for our thoughts, our memories) the moment it arises; the impermanence of all things including life itself. We understand how the only true enemy any of us really ever had is our own ego and the struggles we experience come from that ego. We will go through many experiences by investigating ourselves; some will be pleasant, some will not. But they will all allow us to learn and become freer from the grip of our ego each time we experience something. We will learn how to keep our heart open to constantly experience Universal Love in our life.

These are just a few of the truths that will be revealed in our practice. But the most important truth, the one that really brings it all together, the one that all our practice points us to, is understanding that the present moment is the only place that truly exists. Without this we can't experience the truth necessary to transform knowledge into wisdom. We will not become aware of the things we need to change so we can be in harmony with life. We won't even realize we aren't in harmony.

We can't become conscious by living in the past or the future. Living our life in either one of those places is the epitome of unconsciousness. Quietness can only occur in the present moment. Truth can only be revealed in the present moment. When we are at this point in our process, the whole practice becomes one of Presence, we understand that reality only exists in the Here and Now, and there is no other place. If we aren't living our life in the Here and Now then where are we living it from?

When we are in the present moment our life is lived from a place of love and compassion. When we live in the past or future, our life is derived from an inner sense of lack which isolates us from life itself. This is why we reach outside ourselves for satisfaction. So with meditation the quietness that we experience, the truth revealed, allows us to become aware of this inner lack and not succumb to it. We remain quiet and settled. In this state of being we allow ourselves to be guided by life instead of trying to control it. This is our state of Presence, our state of oneness with all things that allows us to live a life of love instead of a life driven by our ego.

The transformation that occurs is nothing short of a modern-day miracle. If we have honestly applied the previous steps to the best of our ability, we are a different person because of it. We have not changed us, the process has. We are transformed, never to return to the ignorant self-centered individual who inhabited this planet. Prior to the start of our transformation we didn't know why we did what we did or how we affected others. When we do have momentarily lapses (which will occur), of being controlled by our Conditioned Mind Patterns, we now have the tools to become aware of what's going on and to regain our freedom and open heart. We learn from these lapses and remain willing to keep our heart open because we now know we have tapped into a source of energy, a power greater than ourselves, and have found a far better way to live, and it is real. We come to an understanding that our part in all of this is our willingness, not our doing of anything, but just to remain willing to do what is necessary to allow for our transformation to occur. We are longer ignorant of our Conditioned Mind Patterns.

At Step Twelve we have a spiritual awakening as a result of the previous steps, which teach us to respond to life from love instead of reacting to it from our I Self. We have been transformed into a new being, being one of the Spirit. To be one with the Spirit does not mean we are not human, it means being conscious of our human manifestation moment by moment. Our transformation allows us to not be controlled by our ego anymore. We come to understand our ego and how it works and we cut the ties that have kept us in bondage, the ties to all our suffering. We have freedoms we have never experienced before.

Step Twelve is the essence of life. We become a benefit to all beings by expressing God's Universal Love in everything we do. We learn to stop acting like a self-centered baby who is always looking for internal fulfillment outside ourselves and we cooperate with life by not being controlled by our Conditioned Mind Patterns; by looking inward. As we awaken, we become a benefit to whomever we come in contact with. We no longer struggle with life as we once did. We have an inner peace, which seems to come about almost by itself, but it doesn't happen that way. Actually, we've consciously put ourselves in alignment with the actions and behaviors that are necessary to transform our self-centered energy to the energy of Universal Love. Then our transforming energy of love replaces our negative energy induced by our ego. That is how we become a person transformed.

Our outlook undergoes a profound change and our understanding will continue to expand as long as we remain willing to keep the channel to Universal Love open. Our mind expands when our heart remains open. Nothing else needs to be done. Nothing can block our expansion unless we become unwilling to practice, which will bring us back to our blocks. But by this point in our process we are well aware of those blocks so we recognize them when they occur and say a prayer or use a developed tool to allow them to pass through us. This way, we remain open, in harmony with life and our mind continues to expand.

How exactly are we to express God's Universal Love in everything we do? Our transformation allows us to be liberated from the attachment to our

I Self. Our awareness shows us how our association with our "I" is the major cause of our conflicts, the only true block to our ability to be an expression of Universal Love. Whether we are driving on the road, are on line in the supermarket, at work, at home working on our to-do list, or whatever it is we are doing, if we live from our I Self some kind of dysfunctional behavior will occur in that moment. There is no way around this.

The handling of any situation from our I is a selfish approach. Selfishness is the nature of I. So when we are living with some space from our I, what naturally arises is love. We already did what was necessary to allow this to happen with the previous steps. This is not something that we manufacture; it is something that occurs naturally. All we need to do is constantly be aware of when our actions or reactions are self-centered and be willing through prayer and meditation to not want them to be that way. We change to the degree that we practice. No practice, no change. The changes that occur are as natural as aging. When we live our life in cooperation with Universal Love, then that will be the energy that takes over our life. When we live our life from a base of negativity, then that will be the energy that will take over our life.

This is not to say we are either negative or loving, there is a lot of neutrality in life, a lot of mixture. This is where the majority of our practice takes place. Most of the time there will not be anything going on, but these are the moments we need to practice. Notice how the mind wanders and in what direction it wants to go. When we are in the shower, are we in the shower or is our mind all over the place, possibly planning our whole day or reliving something that happened yesterday? How about driving, or doing yard work or whatever; where does the mind go at these times? These are the moments that practice is so important. When we are practicing in a state of neutrality we develop the quietness needed when our Conditioned Mind Patterns are activated. So our behavior will manifest as love because that is what we are practicing. Or it will manifest in the form of whatever conditioning is in place, if we are not practicing. This is the difference in being a puppet on the string or having those strings cut.

Life happens whether we're here or not, it isn't negative or positive, it just is. It's the direction of our energy that makes our particular life what it is. So doing what's necessary to establish love as the default setting of our mind will allow us to become a benefit to all beings by expressing God's Universal Love in everything we do. We allow our Creative Energy to manifest itself in whatever form it takes. We do not have to force anything to happen, it will happen on its own when we are ready for it to happen. And if something we want doesn't happen that is okay too. Life isn't about doing anything; it is an expression of God's love, whatever form it takes. It is not derived from our I, it is derived from our love.

What I have written is one person's experience. It should not be taken as the ultimate truth. You will need to do your own investigation; to discover your truth that can possibly help you overcome some of the barriers that have been blocking you from a happy, joyous, and free life. And what is it that we become free of, the bondage of our I Self. After all, that is *truly* the only freedom needed.

Daily Spiritual Messages

I previously mentioned my writing and sending daily text messages to people about some of my experiences and insights. A selection of these text messages are presented in this section to be enjoyed. These were written by me, for the sole purpose of benefiting others.

When I say they are written by me I do not mean that in the I Self sense. Many people have inspired me; the writings including in this book are just an extension of those who have paved the way before me. It is really an example of the Creative Energy that I wrote about. I never thought of writing a book or anything else. I lived a self-centered existence until September of 2007. What has happened since then is just what has arisen. It is not anything that I can take credit for. I am eternally grateful to all the people who came before me and helped me to become open to a whole new existence. This existence is open to anyone who is willing to do what is necessary to allow it to occur. Namaste.

Our contribution to our spiritual growth depends on the awareness of what needs to be changed in us to allow our spiritual growth to occur. We can only change what we are aware of.

The facade we create is our prison created. We have to constantly arrange life to keep our created image the way we think it should be. This is our bondage created.

We can pray fervently for change to occur in our life, but if we don't do what's necessary for that change to occur, it will not happen. We don't change just because we want to.

Life is categorized so it can be a certain way. When something changes to change the created category of like, there's suffering. But who creates the category that creates the suffering?

The eyes of Love are the eyes of God. To understand the view that we project out we need only to look at our judgments. The less we judge the more Love we have to give.

The answer to all questions is Love. So the only question that one should ever ask is "How can I bring more Love into the world?"

Nothing inherently happens outside of us. It all begins and ends within. It may feel like it occurs out there somewhere, but if you look closely you will notice that everything comes from the inside.

Our ego is what makes us believe in only things that can be seen. It is very difficult to understand the true nature of our human dilemma viewing life from this view.

Our mind is what tries to put on label on the unknown. It has been conditioned to do so. That's what causes our noise, wanting to always know. When we are still, we know.

We will be remembered in our life for one thing, the people we touch with our hearts. Our Love for others will truly be the only thing we leave behind. This Love conquers all our imperfections.

As the hold of our self-created delusions to what we think we need to bring us the happiness we so desire lessens, we are able to see truth and experience the happiness we so desire.

The filter that is used to view life through will produce either selfishness (what can I get) or Love (what can I give). The filter that is cultivated determines our spiritual maturity.

Our judgments of others will be the exact energy that we will live our own lives by. How can we say we truly Love ourselves when we are so critical of others?

Our reactions don't just happen. Their energy is stored in our psyche waiting for the proper trigger to activate it. Our degree of attachment determines the reactions severity.

The thoughts we attract are from our own subconscious mind. They are given the energy to manifest when they are accepted. The choices of which ones are accepted are up to us.

Love can only teach us when our mind is quiet enough to become aware of our true self. Not some made up role we create for ourselves through a delusionary concept of who we are.

We can't smell, taste, hear, see, or touch God yet we waste so much of our energy trying to define that which is indefinable. Any definition would just limit the unlimited.

There will come a time when you will understand that the reason of existence is a manifestation of God's Love & not much else matters, in terms of being fulfilled.

Our Freedom isn't in letting go of doing. It is in learning how not to get attached to the results of the doing, but still being able to do what the necessary task at hand is.

Taking on the burden of this day is only the ball and chain of our ego making us believe the fallacy that we need to do something for our sense of our self-worth. We only need to be-not do.

Nothing out there causes our happiness or discontentment. Our distorted view creates the perception of what's out there which causes the fluctuations between the two.

The search and desire of each being is to know the fulfillment of God's Love. When our behavior is such that it puts us in harmony with life, the results will be of that Love.

A musical instrument has the potential to produce beautiful sounds. So it is with us, we have the potential to produce Love. Neither will occur without practice.

When we are right with God we are right with ourselves. When God is put first, we are complete. There is only incompleteness when life is lived through the mind-based sense of self.

The more we grasp for answers outside ourselves the more in the grasp of fear we are. When we look outside, its only because we are fearful of what we might find inside.

Awareness to the subtleness of our habitual thinking is vital if we are to experience freedom from the bondage of self. To be aware is to know truth and that is our freedom

Happiness comes from within, by being secure in the knowledge of God's Love for us. We may truly know happiness when we have lost sight of ourselves in the Love for God.

Our preconceived ideas are how we associate with the things in our life. We put a label of like or dislike on something and that determines how we will react. Our labeling makes up our world.

Prayer is our plea for Gods companionship; a realization that without God there is only isolation. In this realization is the PRIVILEGED place of union with God.

When a thought is attached to over and over a habit is formed. From the habit derives an action. Depending if the thought is based in Love or if it is based in selfishness that is what will determine the action.

Our spiritual maturity is measured by the amount of earthly desires we think we need to gain a sense of completeness. With God nothing is needed to be complete.

Learn to be guided by Universal Love and you understand how to be with a peace that is always there. This is not something you will get. It is something you will receive.

Our transformation is complete when it is known that God is everything. Not to understand this is to suffer under the guise of our humanness, to be separated from God.

The understanding that a quiet mind is the gateway to God leads to the understanding that it is the only thing that you will truly ever need to know. It is in quietness that all Love arises.

When we want things to be different than what they are in our life, we block out our ability to see the truth of what is going on right now. It is only in truth that freedom can be experienced.

Forgiving others is not a burden. Judging others creates a burden. Judge not & you shall not be burdened. You are forgiven when you realize you cannot cast the first stone . . . .

When we are so engrossed in our "I" we can't see beyond it. This is the root cause of all suffering. If it was not for our "I" there would not be any suffering. There would not be anyone to take on a created burden.

If we want to continue on our path of awakening, we must continue purging ourselves of the things that block out our ability to Love. The more Love we have in our life the less self there is.

Understanding what our human relation is to the Divine Purpose determines how much we are guided by that purpose or how much of our ego is running the show.

There is a Divine Structure to the Universe that has principles. If adhered to, they will bring the fulfillment that is sought; if not, there will always be seeking.

A sense of incompleteness can only arise when we put our trust in a material world. When we open our hearts to God it will be the Love of God that completes us.

Why many of us don't seem to be truly happy is due to our inability to see past our I's need to constantly be fulfilled. The indwelling God needs nothing for fulfillment.

Viewing life from the outside in, keeps us locked into a self-centered perspective. With the view switched to the inside out our operative energy becomes one of Love.

The thoughts you have of something only become your reality when you attach to it. That gives it the energy it needs to obtain the substance to become a story in your head.

Most of the thoughts we have are about something constructed from our past to fill some preconceived idea we believe will make us happy. Our thoughts become the prison that we live in.

God is the silence between our thoughts, the stillness that a deep breath produces. God is the joy that arises from a baby's innocence. Be in the stillness of life, be with God.

When the very thing that causes all our problems (our I) is the operative energy behind every decision we make, we shouldn't except to have anything but disharmony in our life.

Whether a person is happy or sad, it is the same mind that creates these two states of being by associating with something outside ourselves that our mind uses to justify its choice.

When God seems distant, remember: The silence of God is not the silence of a graveyard, but the silence of a beautiful sunrise on clear summer day.

One day we have solutions that bring us the desired results that we are looking for, but then one day just like that, those same solutions become the very thing that are causing us problems.

The thoughts that pop into your head have no power. When the choice is made to follow the thought, that is what gives it the energy it needs to create a story in your head.

This day would be even if you were not. So don't allow the chaos the world creates to pull you in. Don't lose the majesty of the day by viewing it from a self-centered perspective.

It is very difficult to understand our own mind creates everything we perceive. This mind generated energy creates the noise in our head which creates the world we live in.

Freedom isn't being at peace because everything is the way you think it should be. Freedom is when nothing is the way you think it should be and yet you are at peace.

Our incessant thoughts are of an agitated mind that has never been developed to have the ability not to think. Our mind can only do what it has been taught to do.

Don't limit yourself by what you know. If what is known is perceived as all that there is, then what is perceived becomes all that you know. The unknown can never be known.

Every difficulty we have is brought about by not having our Will in alignment with the Divine Will. This occurs when we live from a "what can I get" instead of a "what can I give" mind.

It is the distorted way we view life that creates our difficulties. A difficulty is created by not knowing truth, which is what is at the core of our distorted view.

Learn to do the things necessary that puts you in harmony with God's Spirit. Aligning your Will with God's Will allows your own innate goodness to arise and fulfill you.

If you can understand the difference between the silence of the graveyard and the silence of a flower growing you will understand the silence needed to be at one with God.

Our relation to what happens to us and how we attach to it, is how we allow what happens in our life to affect us and thus control the emotions associated with the situation.

Our need to reach outside ourselves for fulfillment is created by our own sense of lack that arises from within ourselves. If this lack didn't exist there wouldn't be a need to reach.

With a mind that is allowed to settle, comes an understanding of yourself that cannot be known when the mind is agitated. In quietness all truth is revealed.

The only block to God's Love is our unawareness of how much of our life is made up of a thought from our past. Our past is our limit because it is all that is known.

Trusting God doesn't mean we get all our answers. Trusting God means we stop questioning. God's Love has to be sufficient for us, if we are going to ever be truly free.

We are of human form which is the vehicle that Gods uses to emanate Love. To live for the soul purpose of satisfying that human form blocks out Gods Love from our life.

We live in God. Through God alone we find completeness & perfection. Apart from God we are as trees uprooted from the ground-as waves separate from the ocean.

The more you view life from your I, the less of you there is. When you view life from a base of Love, you become the energy of the Universe-timeless-ageless-boundless.

It is in the questions that you pose to yourself, which arise when the mind is quiet, that you find your answers. Without the quietness you will just be controlled by the noise in your head.

Have you ever looked up at a plane in the sky and wished you were on it, not really caring where it was going as long as it took you away from where you were. Remember, though; wherever you go, there you will still be.

It isn't the results that measure the success of our life. It's our Love of the journey and what seeds we plant as we go about our daily chores throughout the day.

Most of life is a preparation for things to come. And when they do come, how well we are prepared for them determines what realm our reactions are derived from; either from Spirit or from self.

Love is the essence of all existence. Its absence is the root of all evil. To have this understanding go from the head to the heart, will be the longest 18 inches ever traveled.

The only way that life becomes a burden is if we make it so. When we try to control the uncontrollable we put life upon our shoulders and hence the burden ensues.

We respond to life out of impulse when the voice in our head is in control. A power greater than ourselves is always with us, but without quietness it isn't allowed to be our guide.

When the view of what occurs in our life is from the base of I (our ego) we instantly prevent Love from being the objective view of the situation. There is no I in LOVE.

Growing up we become conditioned by our environment, if we want change, the patterns engrained in our subconscious need to be identified. Change occurs when this is understood.

Who among us is perfect that we can judge another? We walk our path with the tools that life has given us. Not to use them to judge other, but to spread the seeds of Love.

The mind uses the labeling process as a means of betrayal. It justifies everything to the way it wants it and tells us to like or dislike it. We are limited by the labels we attach.

Everything arises from quietness. The form taken will be relative to the energy that is given to the moment. Since energy can only be transformed, the energy given to each moment becomes your reality.

Our entire struggle with life is in seeking that which we already know. It is the way our instinctual desires have been developed that creates our void and brings on the way our thinking becomes misconstrued. This thinking becomes our environment.

Trust in the Universe. We are limited by a mind that can't understand what is not known. It constantly seeks a solution that is known even if the solution isn't what is best for us.

If our primordial sense of self isn't understood, it will be very difficult to see the forest from the trees. This base of self creates a faulty view of life which is from our "I".

Until we realize our completeness is not something attained, it is something that is and nothing added will change that, we will seek our completeness which keeps our mind in a constant state of agitation.

Being at ease when things are going the way we think they should is relatively easy. But how do we act when they aren't to our liking? Why do we lose our easiness to agitation so quickly?

What keeps us from truly experiencing inner peace is our ego is using our own mind to make us believe that the past or future is better than what is occurring right now

The draw of the outside view is how we limit ourselves by constantly trying to satisfy a mind that isn't really understood nor does it stay satisfied for long.

The more we try to control our life so it's the way we think it should be, the more discontented we become because we are trying to control something that is beyond our control.

The only way anything, be it a person, place, or thing can gain control over us is if we give the controlling thought the energy it needs so its manifestation can occur.

It is our anticipation about something that allows it to control our emotions. We are giving control to something that isn't even occurring. Learn to be with what's here.

Each day upon arising we have the choice to bring God's vision of Love into the world or we can bring the vision of satisfying our self into the world. It is up to you.

The little world we devise in our head limits us to the little world devised in our head. The ignorance of our own mind keeps us locked to our self-created limits.

It takes a lot of work to produce a beautiful garden. When the garden is in full bloom it is very gratifying. The question is, are you doing the required work to allow your own full bloom?

Look at the beauty of the flowers, the grace of a swan. Now look in the mirror and without labeling the image that appears, see the miracle that God has created.

When we understand how it is our self that holds us in captivity, our heart begins to open and we unlock the door to Love that has been kept closed by our own egoic mind.

As long as we seek our inner contentment, it will elude us. The seeking itself is where the problem lies. We already have all that we seek; we just need to stop looking for it.

To pull out the weeds in our garden we have to learn which plants are the weeds so when we are finished, we have a beautiful garden. So it is with our mind, we have to learn what our weeds are so all we are left with is Love.

To be in touch with our Divine Purpose is so difficult because of all the things that we attach to. We attach to everything, but when we learn to let go, it is then that we are free.

There are two ways to view life. One is through the eyes of Love which is a giving view. The other is through the eyes of selfishness which is taking, a "what can I get view". Our view is our choice.

The spiritual life isn't some theory we make up in our head. The principle of Love for the benefit of <u>ALL</u> beings has to be practiced constantly so it becomes the way we live our life.

Through the world of thought we are limited. We try and define the indefinable with words. Such words as Love and God encompass their own true nature without a needed explanation.

You can never experience lack in your life unless it is accepted. Why would you accept it unless you didn't know the cause of it and how not to accept it? It is only our "I" that lacks.

What makes It "One of those days?" It seems to occur as soon as our eyes are opened. But does it have to be that way? What if we don't make it personal and just accept what is here?

Unity with all beings is our gauge for the Love that is in our heart. If we Love some then we will have some Love. If we Love all then we will have a heart that is all Love.

It is impossible to be anything, but what we are conditioned to be. We use the tools to live our life that we ourselves have honed. If we are to change and that is if we want to, we will need to hone a different set of tools.

The less we judge others the more our hearts open to Love. The more we Love the less we want to judge others. This occurs naturally, but not without our cooperation.

When a want arises regardless of its nature, a reaction is created in our mind that makes the want become a need. When there isn't a want to fulfill, there isn't a need. When there isn't a need, there is Peace.

It is the underlying nature of a thought that determines whether it is a benefit (from Love) or just noise. Most are just noise because they are derived from our "I".

It is the reason behind why we use the past and future that cause problems. We use them to try and find comfort because of the created delusion that right now isn't good enough.

When it is understood that you have thoughts, that they are not who you are, there's a release from the world of thought that hold you captive. The thought of being free is not freedom.

Since energy can only be transformed how our energy is directed to what occurs in our life is in direct relation to what we become, when our energy is directed to Love we become that Love.

All craving is a control mechanism used by the ego. The thing used to satisfy the craving doesn't matter because regardless of what it is the ego (our I) is in control.

We are as free as the next thing that we reach for that we think will bring us what is needed to make us complete. When we keep looking for things on the outside, it prevents us from looking within.

With a wandering mind there are problems because our center of being is lost. With no center, our mind just bounces from one thing to another in search of something to grab a hold of.

No matter what we do, life goes on. So learn how to respond to the things that occur from a place of Love and you will be a benefit to all beings. After all, life goes on anyway.

What is done is done. No matter how hard we try, it can not be undone. Our mental anguish is wasted energy created by a Conditioned Mind that tells us not to accept the things that it tells us to do.

We can only be an instrument of Universal Love when there is guidance. We can only be guided when our mind is settled and there is silence. The more silence the less we are guided by our selfish desires.

Our life really isn't the way it appears. Our mind constantly tries to create a world that makes us happy. When it's that way and it changes, it is the cause of all our suffering.

To understand our own insignificance is to understand our place in the world, and that the part we play in the world is attributed more to circumstance than anything we have done.

Our spiritual journey isn't one of mystical proportion. It is based in being with what occurs in life and not embellishing on it to make it more or less than what it is.

The anticipation the mind creates doesn't usually occur the way it is projected. When we minimize the story, we minimize our anxiety, which allows for more peace in our life.

We can never give more Love than we receive. It is the law of Love. When you give Love, the blessings received are ten fold. Learn to open your heart to God and completeness will be eternal.

Our thoughts are the base of what we think. What we think is the base of what we become. Whether we are based in selfishness or of Love will depend on what we practice.

No one is more gifted than anyone else. We all have different talents. But as far as the gift of life is concerned, if you are alive, you are gifted. This gift is our freedom.

It is very difficult to accept something when it isn't the way we think it should be. But that is our dilemma because wanting it to be in some other way is the cause of discontentment.

Our mind has been conditioned to constantly pull us from the present moment. It makes you believe that the past or future is a better place to live.

The discovery of who and what we truly are leads us to God. The delusion of who and what we think God is through our minds limited view usually leads to confusion.

The realm of the Spirit can not exist when we are living in the past or the future. Those places are derived from thought, and the Spirit exists beyond the thought realm.

You can only be grateful when you are content with what you have, not with what you want or are going to get. Wanting is never from our true self, it always arises from our egoic self.

A sense of lack is the cause of our mind agitations. This lack is only possible in the material realm. The Spirit realm is of Love and isn't capable of producing lack.

If all we do is constantly look for the pot of gold, we will never have the awareness to see the beauty of the rainbow. Life is a journey; it's up to us to enjoy the ride.

When things don't go according to the plan devised in our head, we tend to look to the outside and blame other, but if we turn inward it can be used as something to learn from.

It is our false identification with our thoughts that allows them to control us. We give them the energy needed by attaching "I" to them and making them who we are.

Its unfortunate, but most of our life is wasted looking for our answers outside of us. They have always been as close to us as our heart. We've just never awakened to see this.

We can know truth intellectually, but until we know it from our heart, it is a decision between right and wrong. When it is in our heart, there is no decision; we just do what is right.

When something occurs, try not to attach a label to it. Our labels become our limits. In this limitation there is no space created for our mind to expand our vision.

The influence we have on people is in our actions. It is the subtle reactions that are noticed. The more pleasure in our association to things, the more will be our habitual reactions.

We use so much energy trying to arrange our life to be a certain way, this blocks us from being aware of what is really happening. Wrong effort will never produce beneficial results.

Acknowledgments

I sit here today *truly grateful* for all the people who have been in my life, who have loved me until I learned to love myself. If it were not for their love, I don't think I would be alive today; I definitely would not be the person I am today. First and foremost I want to thank my wife Maureen, for loving me unconditionally. Her love is what kept me going at times. I would also like to thank my daughter Alexa, and my son Steven, for being the most understanding children any parent could have asked for, as I went through my difficult process of discovery.

There are two people who have really helped me with the process of making this book a reality, my editor Naomi Rosenblatt, whose honesty kept me investigating how to convey the message of my book so anyone reading it could understand it, and my friend David Rosen, who was the person who started this process with me, working together on my raw manuscript. He is the one who helped me become the writer I am today by urging me to put more of *me* into my writing. This has become the touchstone of my writings, and is what has allowed me to touch many people.

I know this is a little unorthodox, but I would also like to thank Jesus, the Buddha, The Divine Life Society, which is based in Hinduism, The Infinite Way established by Joel S Goldsmith, and countless others who have traveled this path before me, and left me an array of books and material that has become a blueprint for my own awakening to transpire. For this I will forever be indebted, and I will continue sharing their message until the day I pass on. Namaste

—M.C., August 2012

About the Author

I grew up in Newark, New Jersey, one of six children. I have been married for twenty one years. I own a home and have two children. I have been at the same job for twenty four years. I am the happiest I have ever been, and it is all because of the Love that has always been in my life. I attribute all that has happened to me to this Love. None of what has transpired in the last five years of my life has anything to do with any accomplishments on my part.

There was always a lot of love in our home as I grew up, but for reasons unknown to me at the time I was always in trouble. I was at the top of my brother-in-law's "Who My Sister Shouldn't Marry" list. I drank alcoholically, gambled, abused drugs and painkillers. I bounced from relationship to relationship. Even after I stopped abusing alcohol and drugs in 1987, my so-called outer troubles stopped, but my self-centered behavior never changed. All I did was substitute one compulsion for another. Although my addiction became more respectable — taking the form of material possessions — I was still trapped, migrating restlessly from one obsession to another.

I went to Twelve Step meetings, derived some benefit from them, and then fell away. My loved ones got me into de-tox and rehab programs. But once I was released, the cycle of insatiable craving started all over again. This cycle seemed to work for me . . . until it didn't. And then my life changed — not instantly or magically, but profoundly.

I share this change in *It's Monday Only in Your Mind: You Are Not Your Thoughts.* I discovered that I wasn't dependent upon a substance or activity, but ruled by my ego. My need to reach outside myself for fulfillment was created by a false perception of deficiency. If this sense of lack didn't exist in me, there wouldn't have been a need to reach and grasp.

My credentials for writing this book are simply that I live this change each day. My view of life is so different from the way it used to be. Through the practice outlined in my book, I have learned to quiet my mind enough to allow my heart to open. The quieter my mind becomes, the more Love becomes the default setting of my life. This is truly a modern-day miracle, a miracle that can happen to anyone who has the desire to change.

—M. C.

CPSIA information can be obtained
at www.ICGtesting.com
Printed in the USA
FFOW03n0857160615
14306FF